AF266986

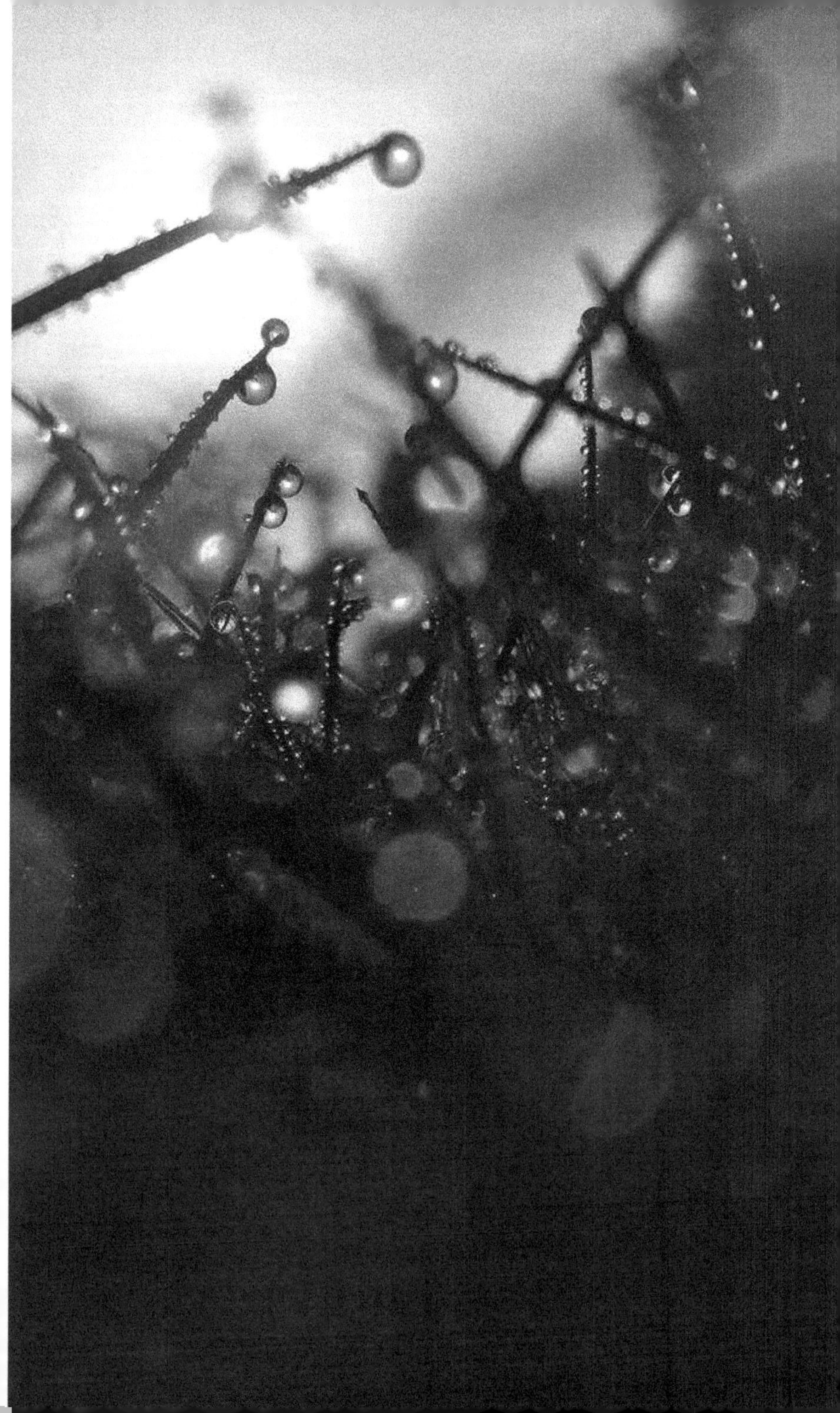

# WA IS WATER

## An Intimate Portrait

Exploring Washington in
Poems, Photos and Facts

Jennifer Preston Chushcoff

*This book is published with the assistance of the Tacoma Artists Initiative Program Grant from the Tacoma Arts Commission.*

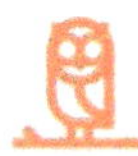

**Autumn's End Press**
JB Properties, Inc
PO Box 999
Tacoma, WA 98401

*Dedicated to my grandmother, Gloria Parish.
She taught me to look closer;
dandelions are beautiful.*

# CONTENTS

# INTRODUCTION

When I first conceived of this book, I had no idea what was in store for me.  I set out to bring together my love of photography and poetry, while enhancing the work with facts, all while traveling each of Washington's four corners.

One of these tasks would have been plenty – a book of poetry; a book of photography; a book of facts; a travelogue. But I pitched it all. I bit off quite a lot!

I began the project stout-hearted, which shortly transitioned into self-doubt and chaos.  There was so much to learn, read, write, photograph, and lots and lots of driving.

One of the most difficult things was whittling down what I had uncovered and wanted to share. Also, without fail, when I got to talking about the project, people would invariably ask if I'd been to this or that waterfall, or beach, or vista, or perhaps tried scuba diving. Everyone had a favorite spot that I just *had* to mention otherwise risk having an incomplete book.

Early poems were bacchanalian celebrations of water, tender, joyous odes! But the more I researched, the more the book's tone shifted. Environmental concerns could not be ignored. The perilous condition of waterways and wildlife had to be addressed.

Add to that the fact that the book was being written during our terrible drought, the Tacoma methanol plant protests and the discovery of lead in the nearby water system. A propitious time, yes?

I dove into newspaper reports about the state of our shellfish harvests, bought books about dams, watched river documentaries and fish hatchery videos. I started up a Facebook page where I shared what I discovered. Sometimes, what I learned broke my heart. Things looked bleak. But, and this is a big but, things were also improving and nature was making a comeback. Dams that were no longer useful, like the Elwha, were removed and delicate ecosystems resurrected.

I strive to be succinct in all things, but the story of water in Washington is complicated. For example, it's easy to condemn those that came before us building dams that brought ecosystems to the brink. Yet, they were providing flood control, electricity and water to their early communities. As in all things, a balance must be struck. I hope that in the future our community planners and leaders will be more sensitive to trade-offs and their long-term effects.

Overall, the research was exciting and I learned a lot. The journey could've take the rest of my life, so it was good that I had a deadline to meet! One of the most powerful experiences of this project was that I did things that I normally wouldn't, like approaching strangers with questions and traveling to places I might have gone my whole life without seeing. I sought out collaborations and made new friends.

Bear in mind, this is not a geology or climatology book, even though I consulted stacks, nor a trail guide or sightseeing manual. This is a glimpse of Washington through my lens. My hope is that between these pages you will find inspiration for your own journey and perhaps a new appreciation for our water. Yes, even for rain.

- Jennifer

When you put your hand in a flowing stream,
you touch the last that has gone before and
the first of what is still to come.

- Leonardo da Vinci

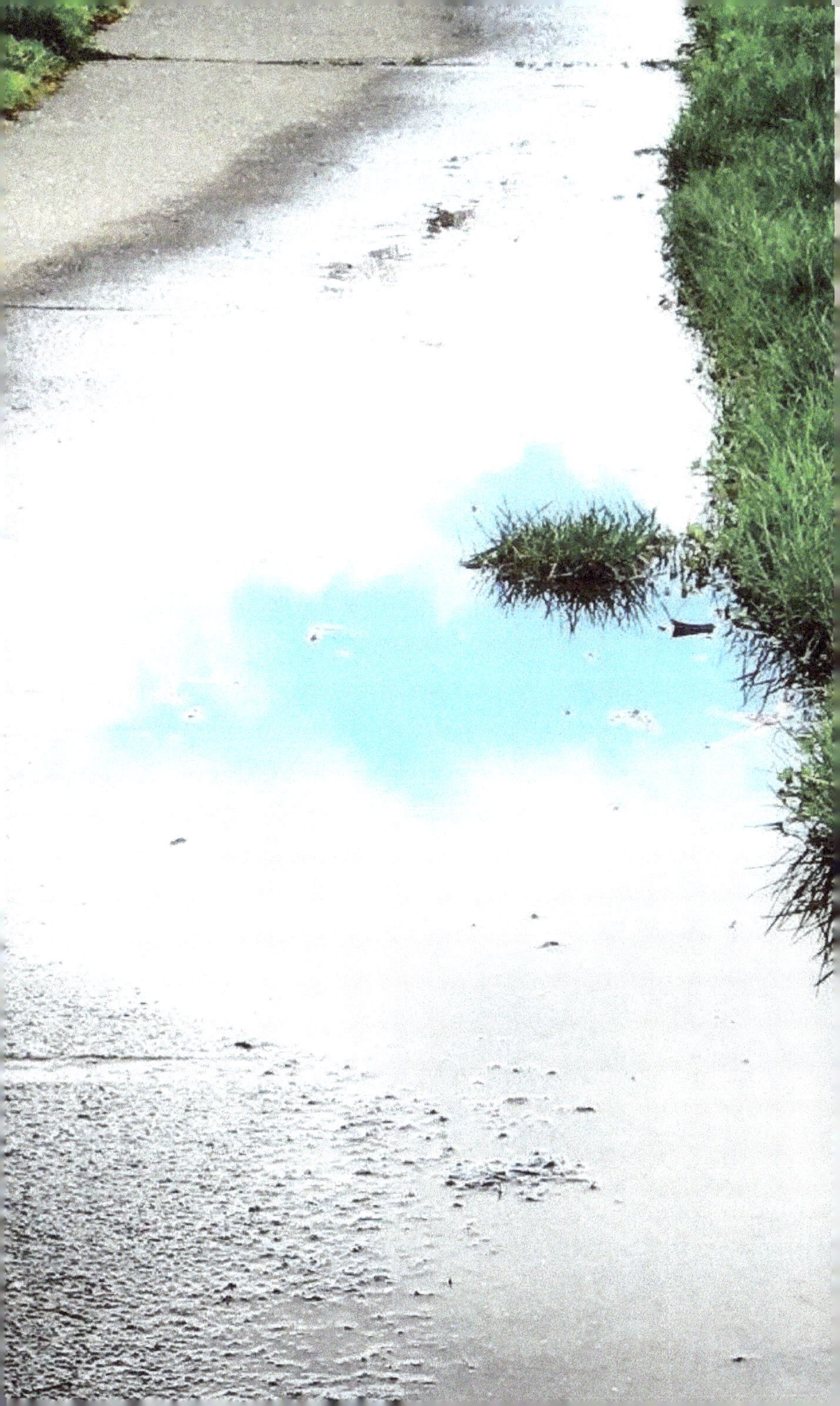

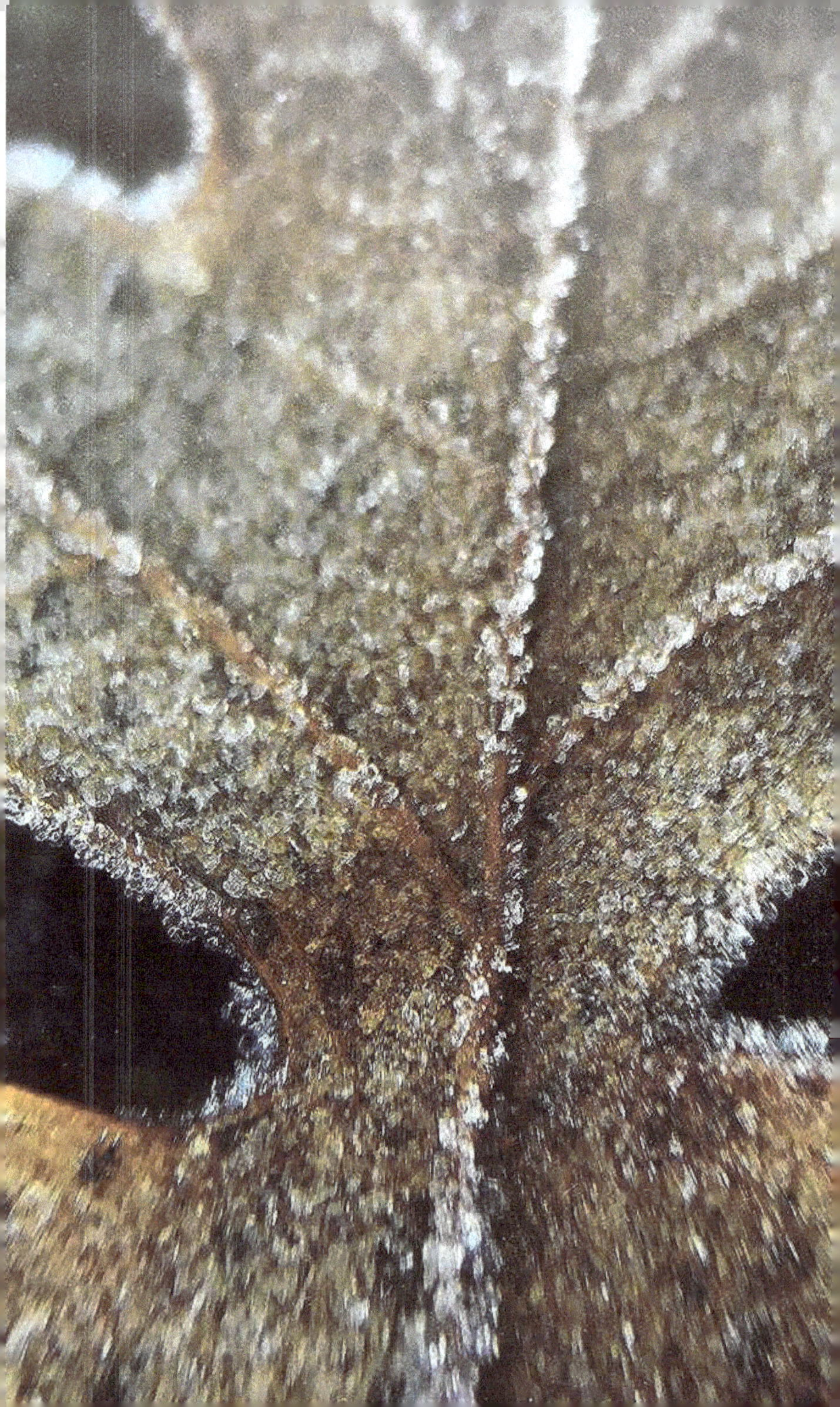

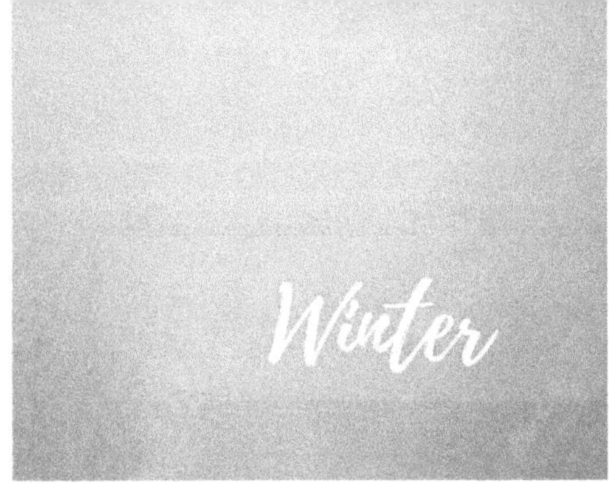


Winter is not the end of the seasons, it is the beginning. Winter flurries ensure summer's crops and promise a bountiful harvest. Without it, we face drought. Of course, snow is also required for popular outdoor sports in Washington, like skiing, snowboarding and snowshoeing.

Thankfully, high up in the Cascade and Olympic mountains, immense reserves of water wait as snow and glaciers. In the spring, they melt into streams and join rivers. Before the melt water joins the Pacific, dams stop it and reservoirs capture it for drinking, irrigation and power.

Nature's water system is simple and elegant, but human intervention has made it complex. Since we require water for survival, our demands shape its storage and disbursement, which has a direct impact on the environment.

We've been inextricably linked to water since the beginning.

GENESIS

People ask, where are you from?
It's always hard to answer.
How far back should I go?
Knit together in my own dark ocean,
my bones were handed down
from the beginning, inscribed
with ancestral marks.
How far back should I go?
When Earth dust mingled
with the stars? When exhalations
built fair snowflakes,
to fall and melt on fingertips,
or when my tears were added
to the sea?
We are more serous than solid
stuff, my friend,
and our red water pulse
is saline.
The story of water, is the story of us.
So let's begin here.

*A single raindrop enters the sea*

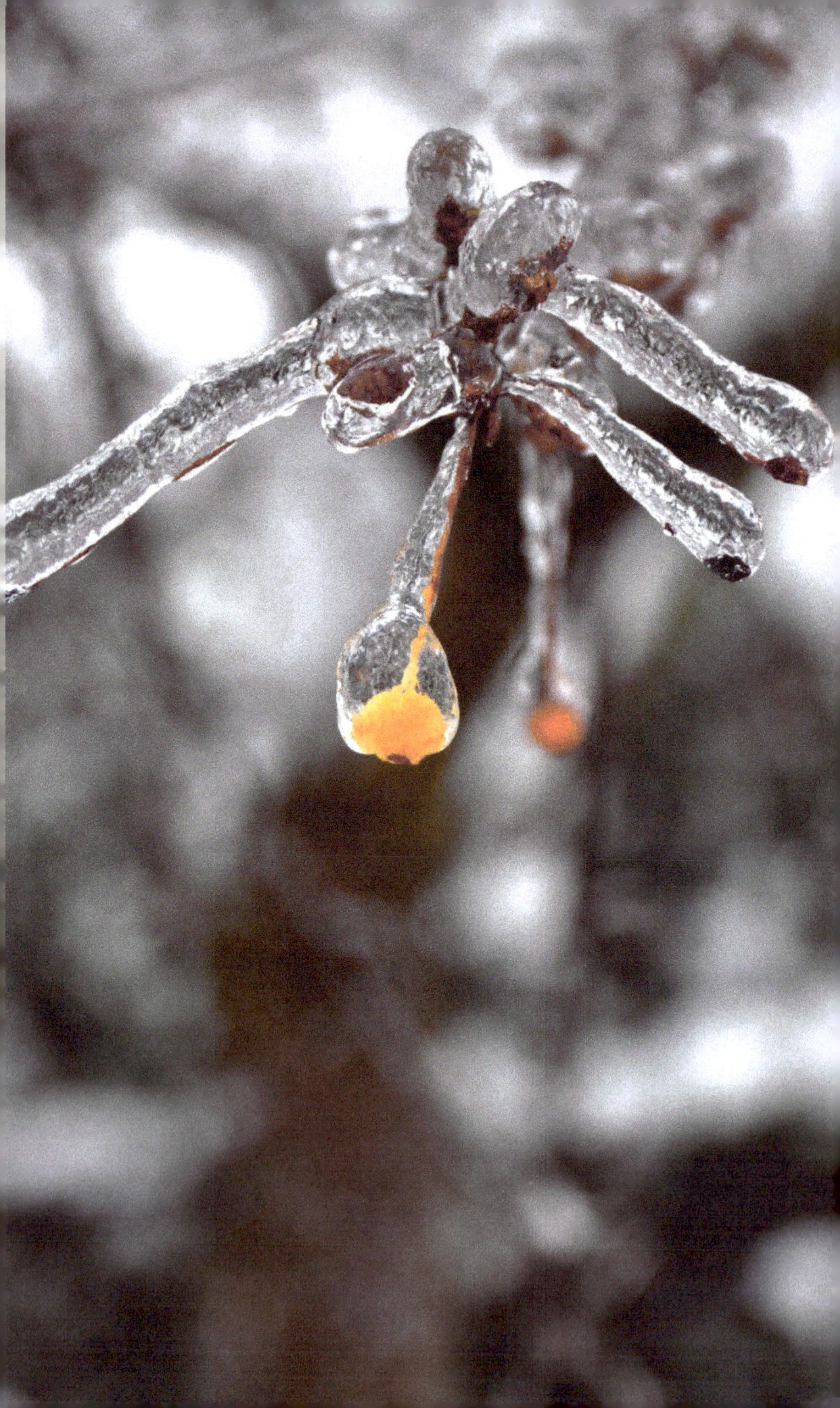

# A CLOSER LOOK
## winter weather

* There are ten ski resorts in Washington.

* Paradise Rainier Ranger Station ranks #1 for snowiest location in the USA with an average annual snowfall of 680 inches.

* Washington has more glaciers than all 47 contiguous states combined.

* Snowflakes are born out of a speck of dust and water vapor, not a rain droplet. They take shape as they move through a cloud and down to us. Since no two will ever travel the exact same path, no two snowflakes will ever be identical.

* The word "facet" is use to describe snow crystals, which means "little face."

* At least 100 of our molecules are in every snowflake.

* Ice will form on branches when two layers of cold air sandwich a layer of warm air, causing the precipitation to melt and refreeze. The ice glaze is beautiful, but extremely dangerous.

*Crabapple encased in ice*

SNOWFLAKES

In these small worlds
a universe
a fragile life
built in their short history.

Slivers of translucent glass
born in cold, dark hours
to vanish at first light.

But, who am I
to speak of time
when the weight of centuries
cannot crush the ageless stars?

A hundred thousand years
of sweeping shadows
chase the moons, while
primal clocks tick tock
like death knell drumbeats
to mark the day-long lifespans.

 *Snowflake with six-fold radial symmetry*

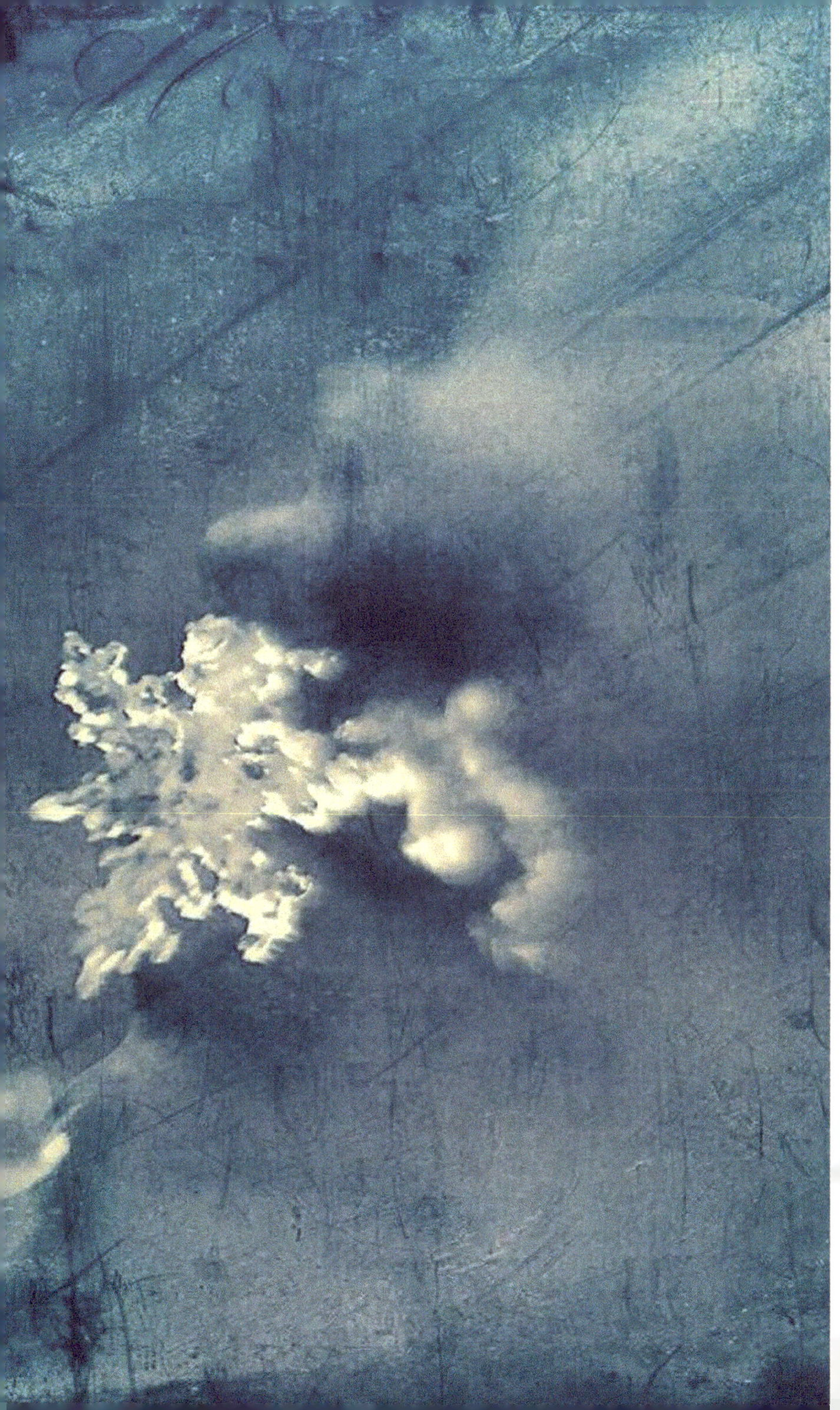

# GRAVITATIONAL FORCES

A sleeping Sisyphus
controls our tides.

We are born addicted
to time
to life
to dreams of
everlasting

when it's enough
to just be born.

*Columnar hoarfrost*
*(Next page: North Head Lighthouse, Ilwaco)*

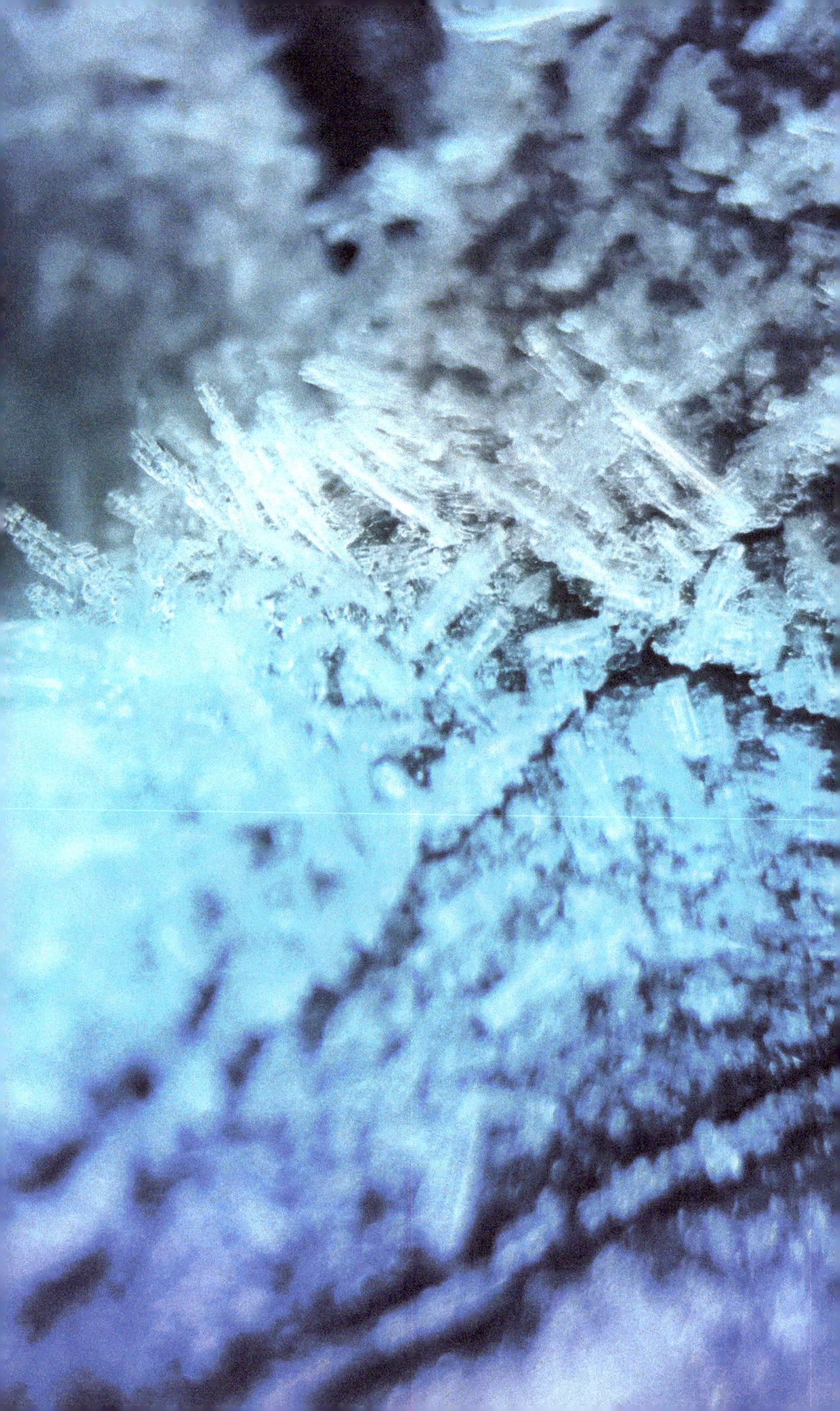

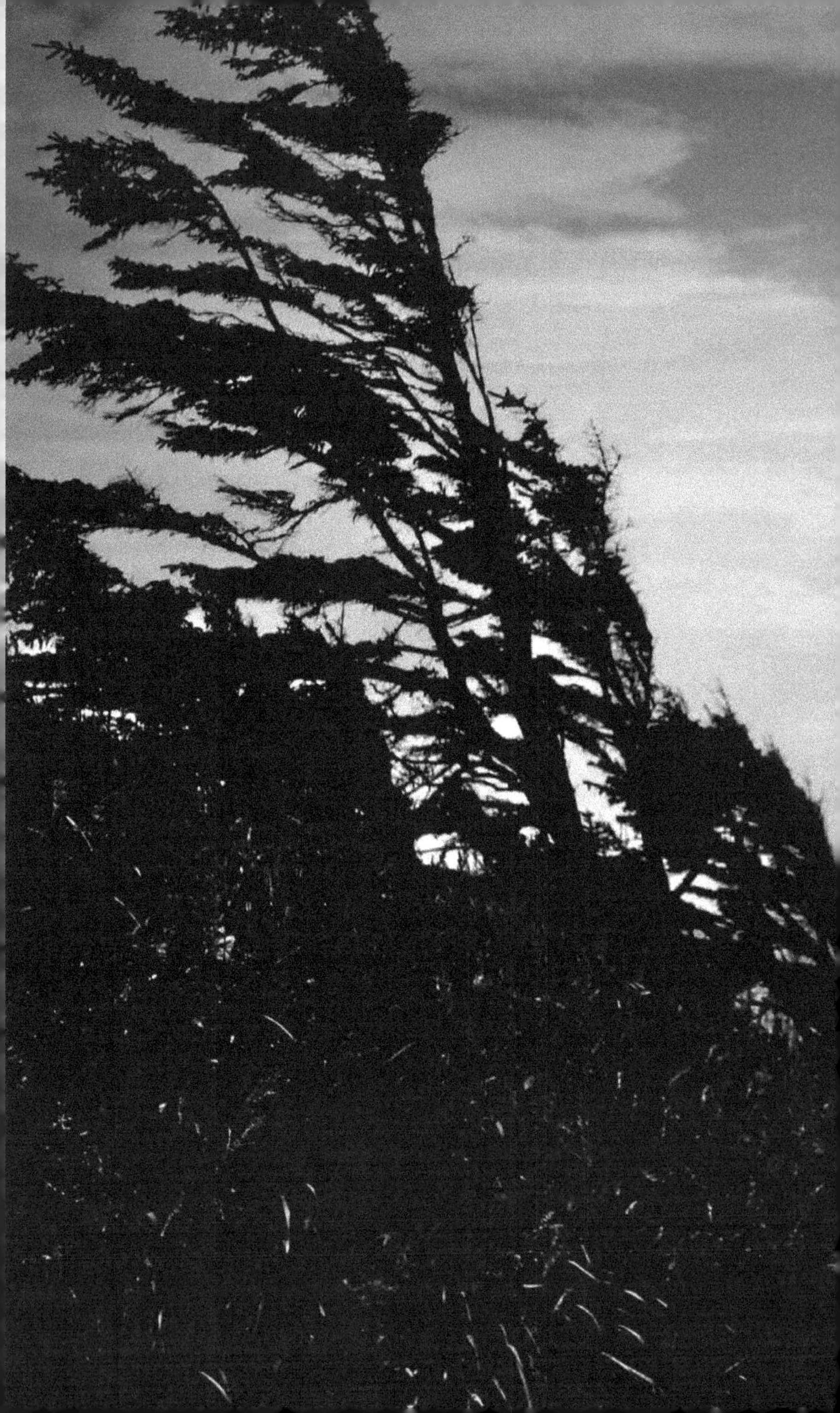

# A CLOSER LOOK

*lighthouses*

* Cape Disappointment, Ilwaco

(oldest operating lighthouse on the West Coast)

* Point Robinson, Vashon Island

* Admiralty Head, Coupeville

* Lime Kiln, Friday Harbor

* Point No Point, Hansville

* New Dungeness, Sequim

* Mukilteo, Mukilteo

* North Head, Ilwaco

* West Point, Seattle

* Alki, Seattle

## SEATTLE
*Written after taking the Seattle Underground Tour*


This city, it floats
on the sea
it floats on the
pioneer's homes
and bones.

Its dark, quiet corners
and underground
caverns rest
away from the sun –
the tumult and blare.

Drip
            drops

of water
echo down
weeping corridors
that move by
shifting shadows
as evening settles
on the glass
skyline.

*Lake Minterwood, Lakebay*
*(Next page: a snow crystal classified*
*as a plate with dendritic extensions.)*

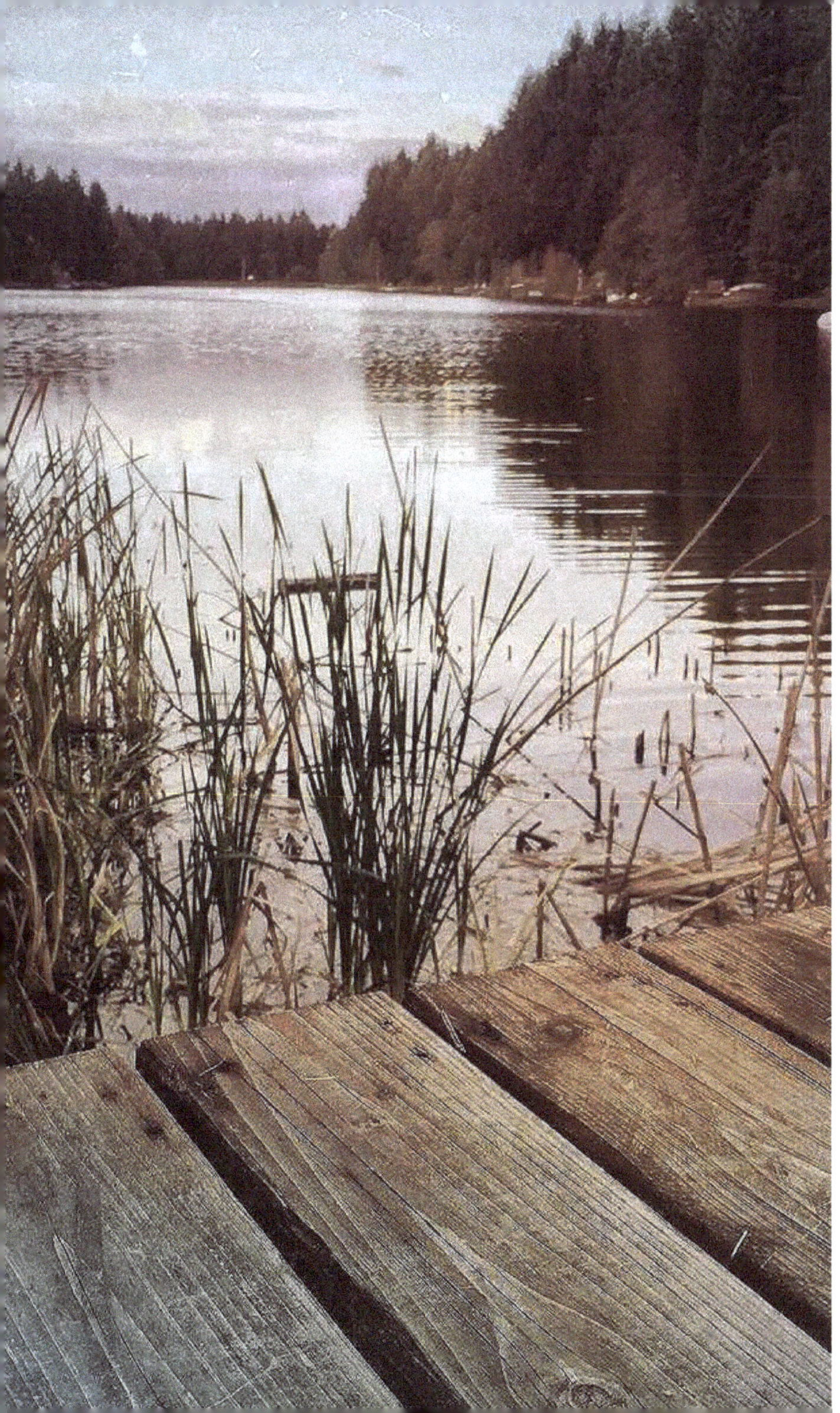

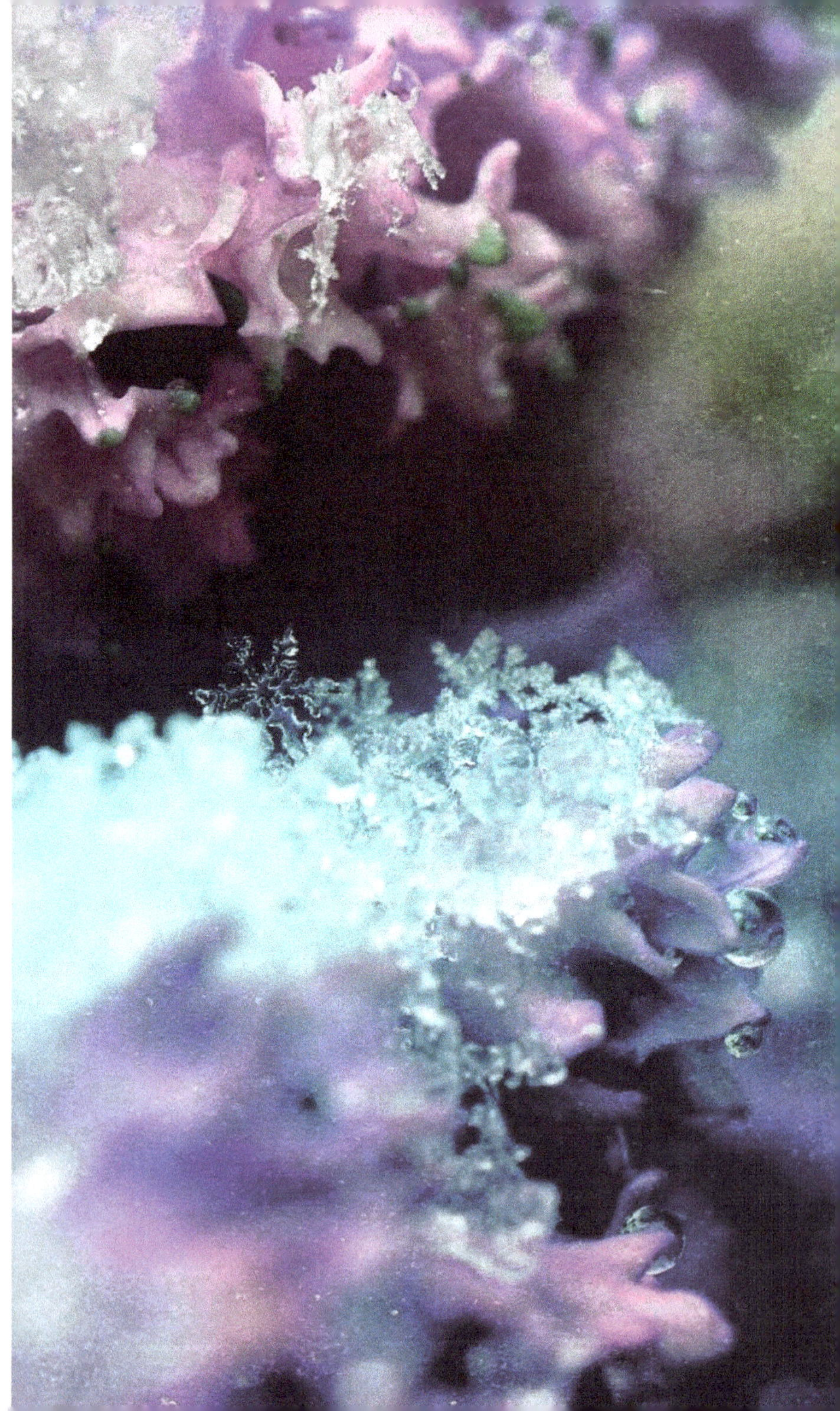

TINY TREASURES

The stillness of the winter sky
surrenders frosty flowers
for making forts and snowmen
snowballs and icy towers.

From specks of dust and water's breath
these crystals form and float,
unique like snowy fingerprints
catch them on your coat!

See the tiny winter stars
with six ferny, feather arms?
Their joyful little faces shine
cut like gems and lacy charms.

Winter clouds are factories
of soft and quiet gears
    that drift

        that drift

            that drift

across our atmosphere.
They're puffing prose and poetry
in semaphores and codes,
which tumble down to yards and lakes,
as weather's ancient odes.

We're in each dainty flake
our breath, its crystal bone
so as it glides to earth,
it's really coming home.

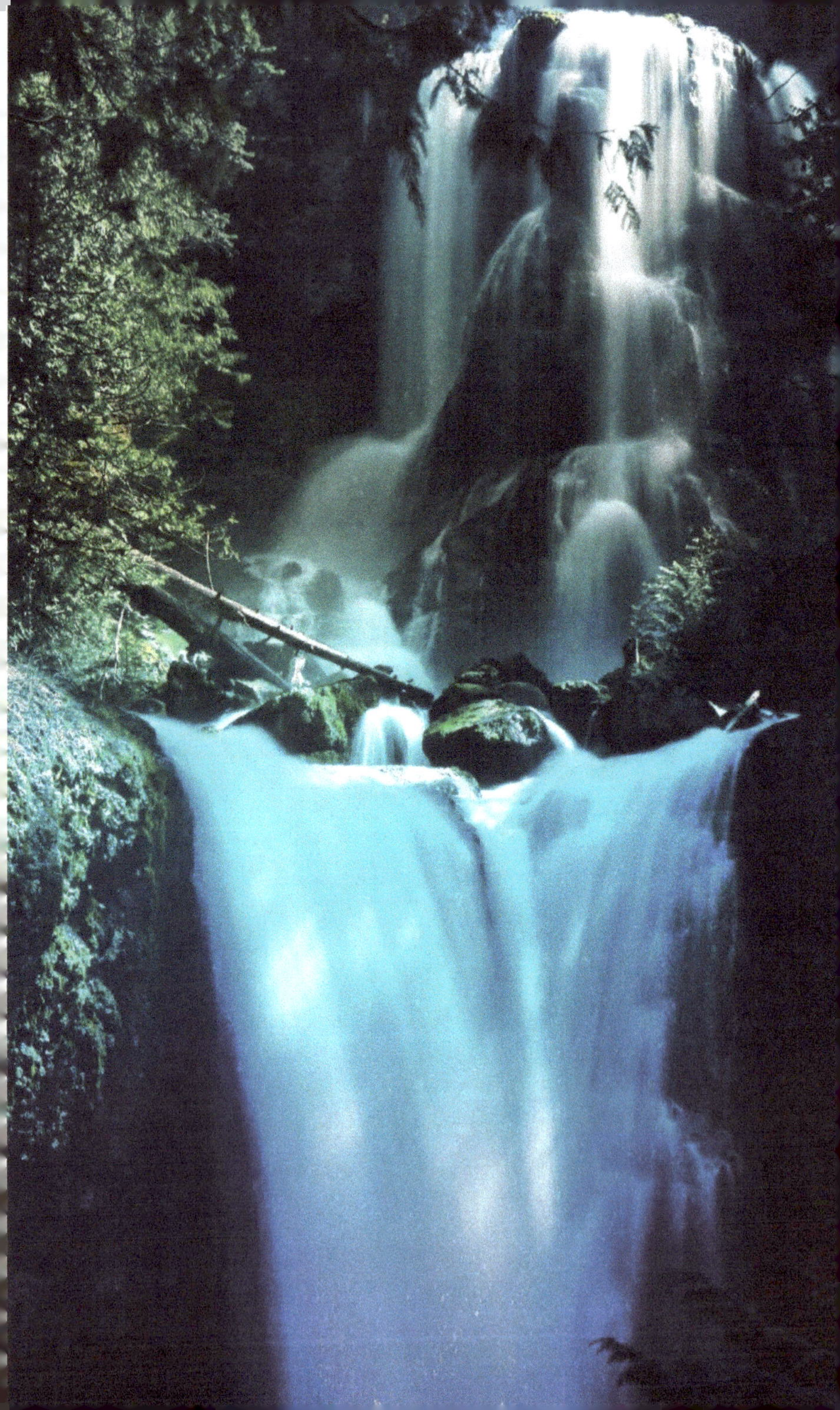

# A CLOSER LOOK
## *waterfalls*

*Washington has over 2,700 waterfalls. They range in size from several feet tall to hundreds. Here are just a few.*

**NORTH CASCADES**
Cedar Falls
Boulder River
Wallace Falls

**CENTRAL CASCADES**
Bridal Veil Falls
Franklin Falls
Snoqualmie Falls
Twin Falls

**OLYMPIC PENINSULA**
Sol Duc Falls
Marymere Falls
Upper Siouxon Horseshoe Falls
Lower Falls Creek

**CENTRAL WA**
Ancient Lake
Dry Falls
Palouse

*Falls Creek Falls, Skammania County*

COLD SNAP

A filigree of
hoarfrost
a beautiful end
for something just beginning,
these too early, tender buds
of sweet, green
garden flesh.

     *Most snowflakes are not symmetrical*

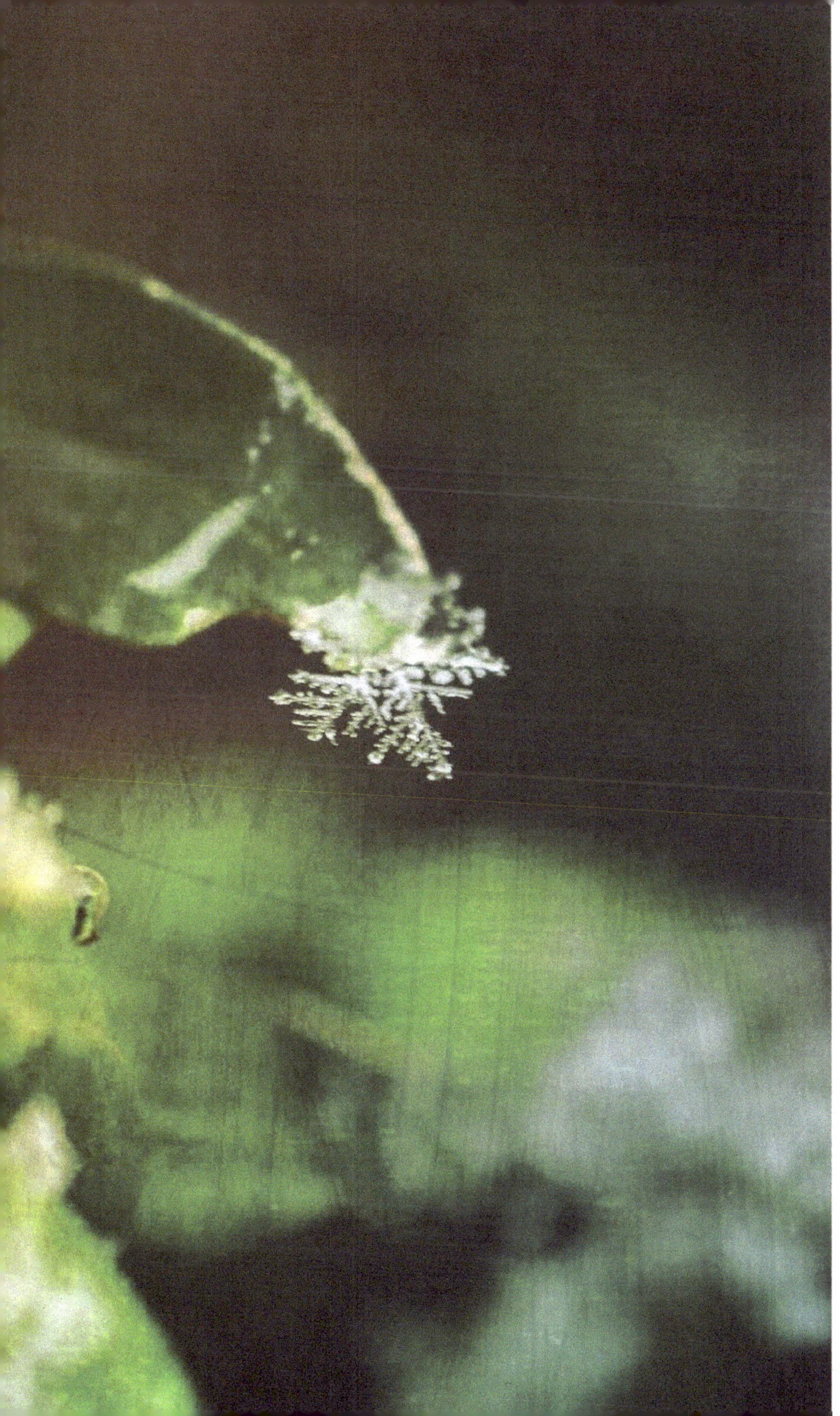

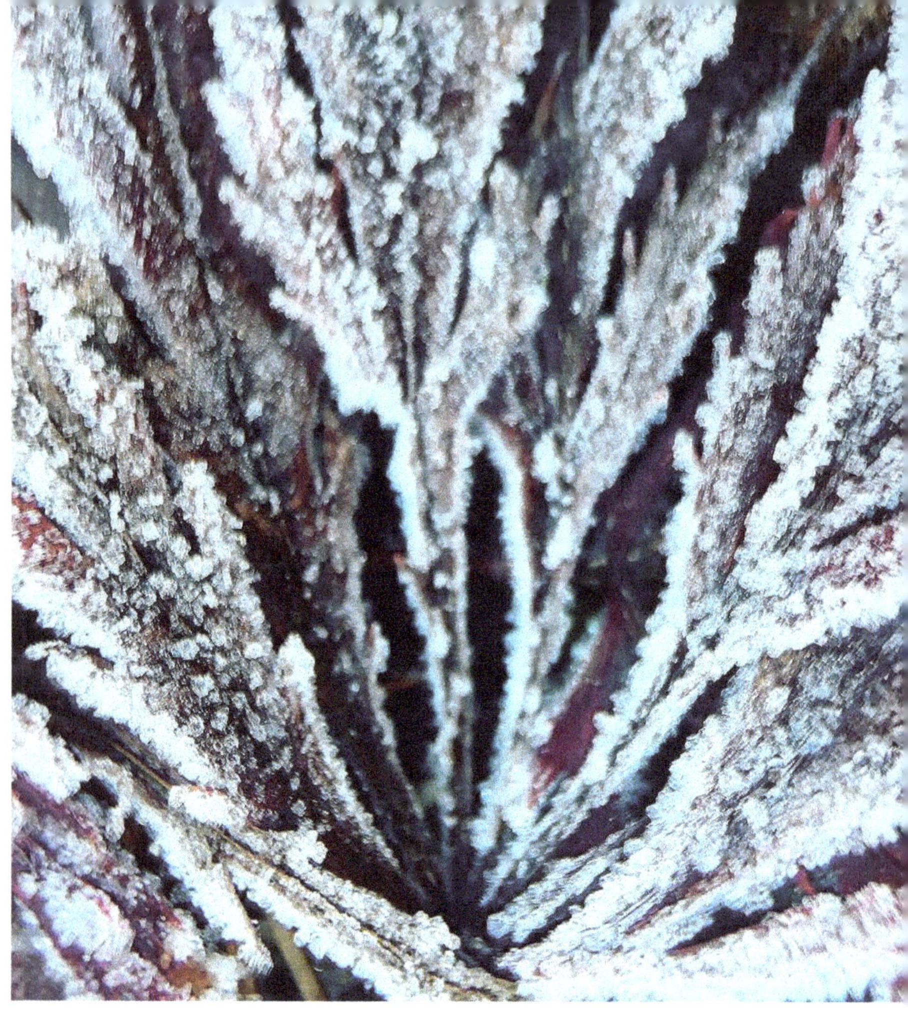

*Advection hoarfrost (wind frost)*

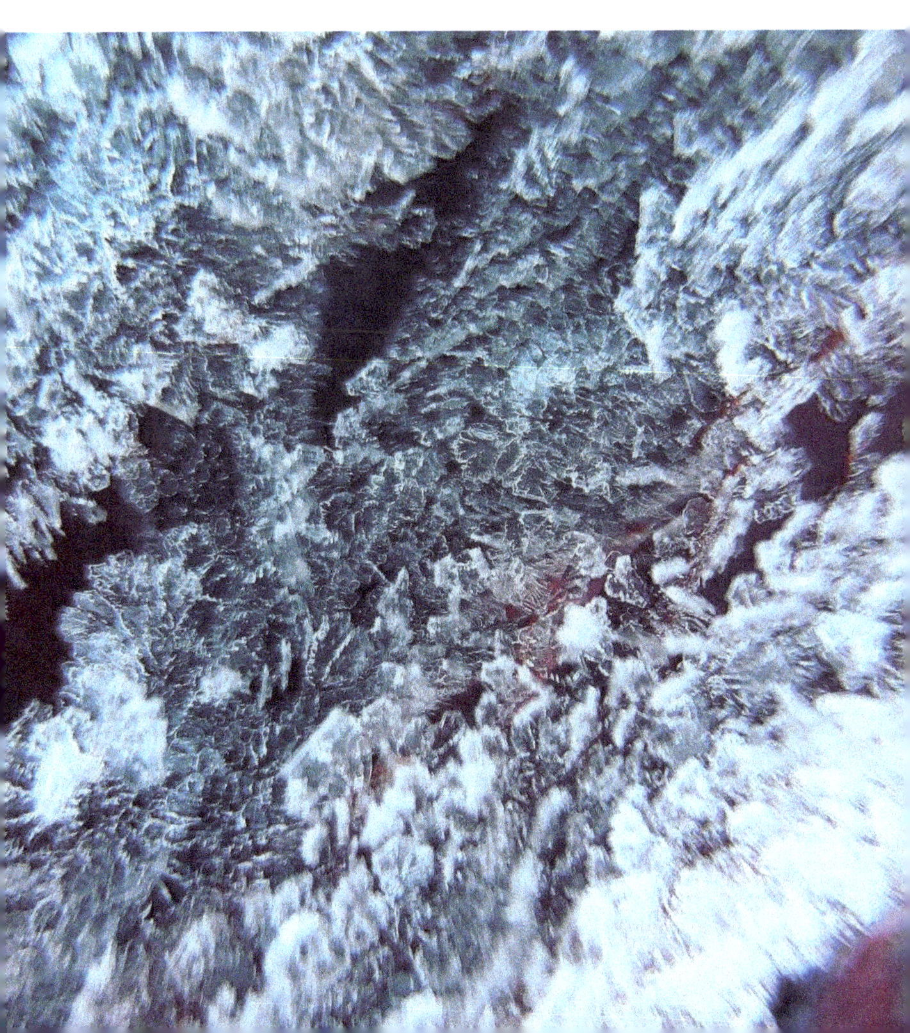

*Tabular hoarfrost*

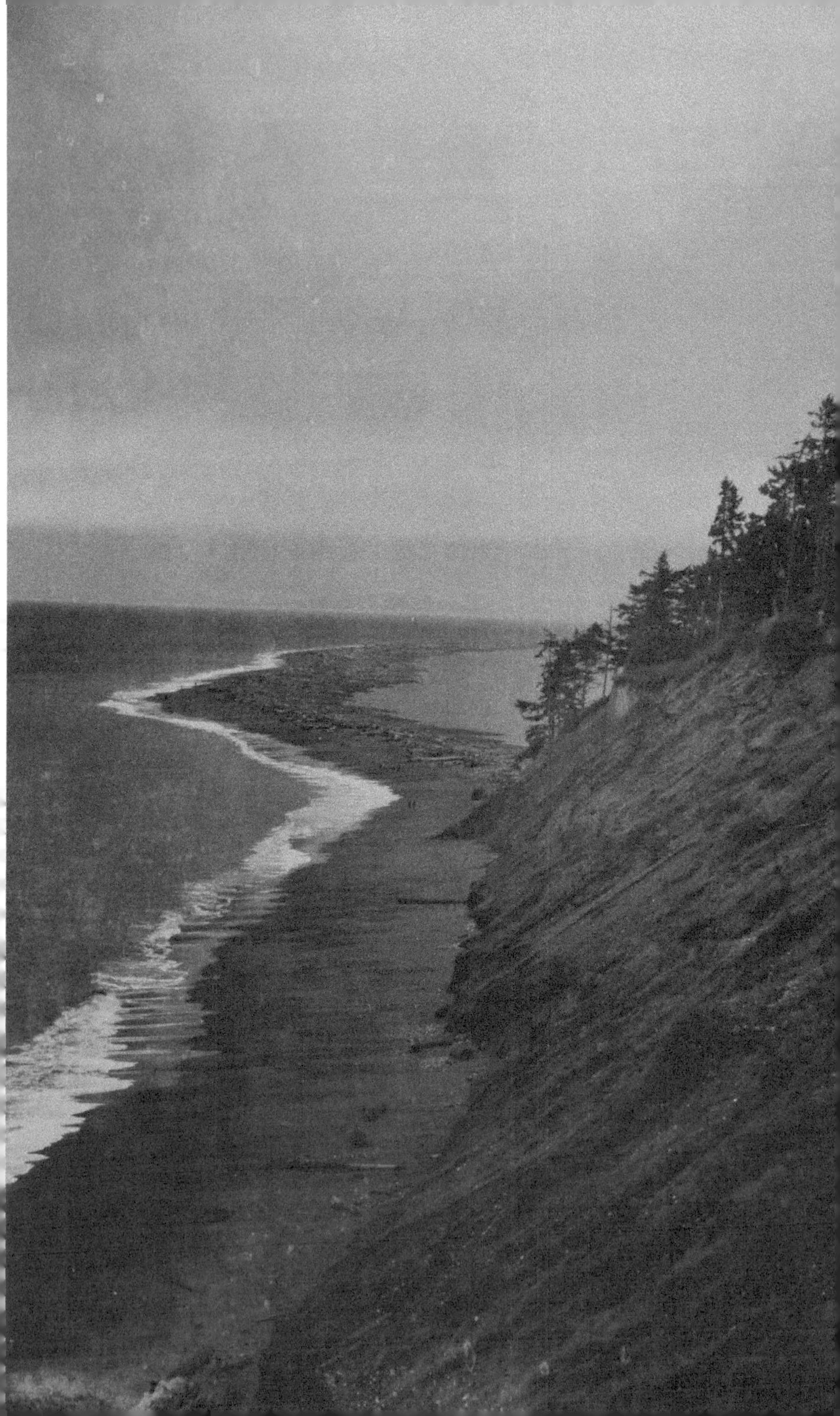

# A CLOSER LOOK
## *dungeness spit*

The Dungeness Spit is 5.5 Miles in length, making it the largest natural sand spit in the world. It reaches out from the Olympic Peninsula into the Strait of Juan de Fuca.

In 1792, the English explorer George Vancouver named it after its resemblance to the British Channel's own Dungeness. In turn, the famous Dungeness crabs are named for it.

The area is also a designated National Wildlife Refuge, providing sanctuary for 250 bird species, 41 land mammal species and 8 water mammal species.

At the end of its long arm is the Dungeness Lighthouse, which was built in 1857. If you plan to hike to it, be sure to leave enough time to get there and back during low tide.

*Dungeness Spit from the Pacific Ocean*

THERE IS ONLY THIS

There is only
this.
The sea never
sleeps.
It stays up
after dark,
rolls in and out
while we dream
under bright
cold constellations,
a constant servant
to the moon.

We are the only ones
who can't see the end
of anything.



*Columbia River Gorge*

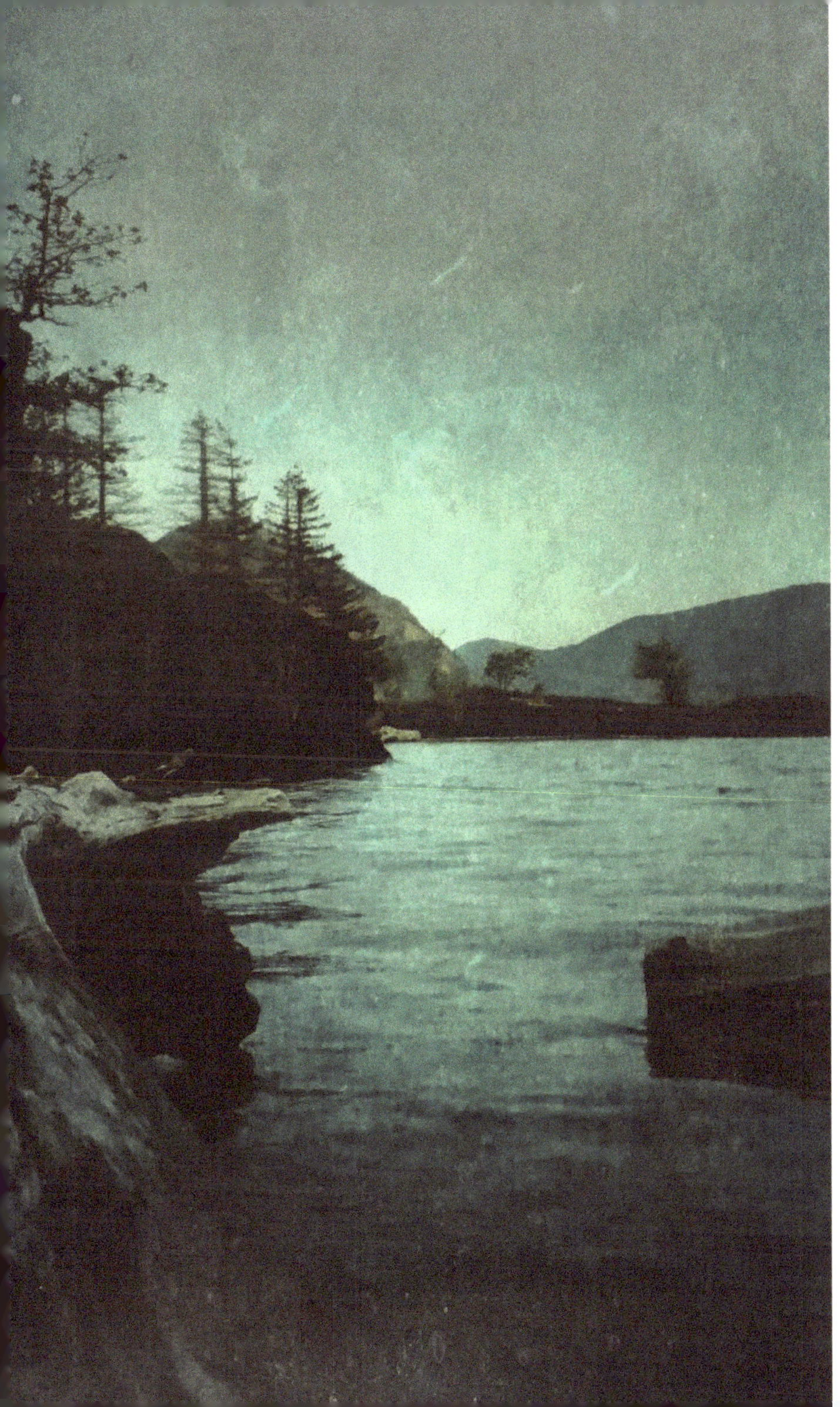

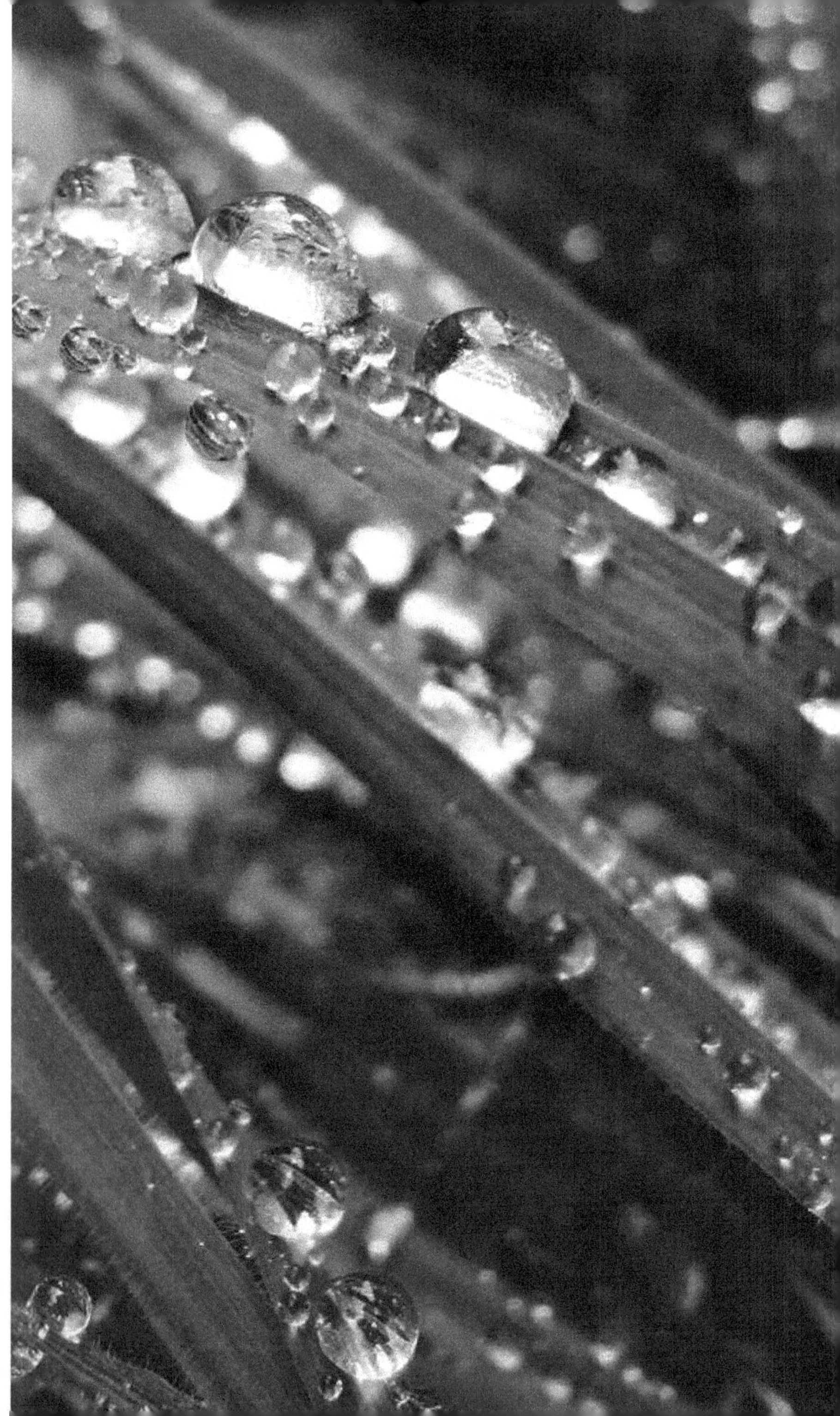

# A CLOSER LOOK
## *rain*

* 67% of Washington rain is considered "light."

* In Western Washington, October is usually the wettest month. September is the driest and best bet for an outdoor wedding. Most don't realize that we have relatively dry summers and must use irrigation to keep non-native plants green.

* The Seattle/Tacoma area doesn't get as much rain compared to several other states (about 38" annually). The area ranks 44th in the nation for average annual rainfall. A few cities that get more rain include: Houston (48"), New Orleans (60"), Mobile (65"), Memphis (52"), and most major cities on the east coast, including New York (43"), Miami (58") and Boston (44").

* Why do we have the reputation for rain? Most likely because those 38" are spread out over more days, giving us almost an additional month of wet weather. We also have a lot of gray days, which give the impression of rain.

*Unlike dew, beads of water called guttation form when moisture is extruded through a plant's leaves because the soil is saturated. (Next page: Ruston)*

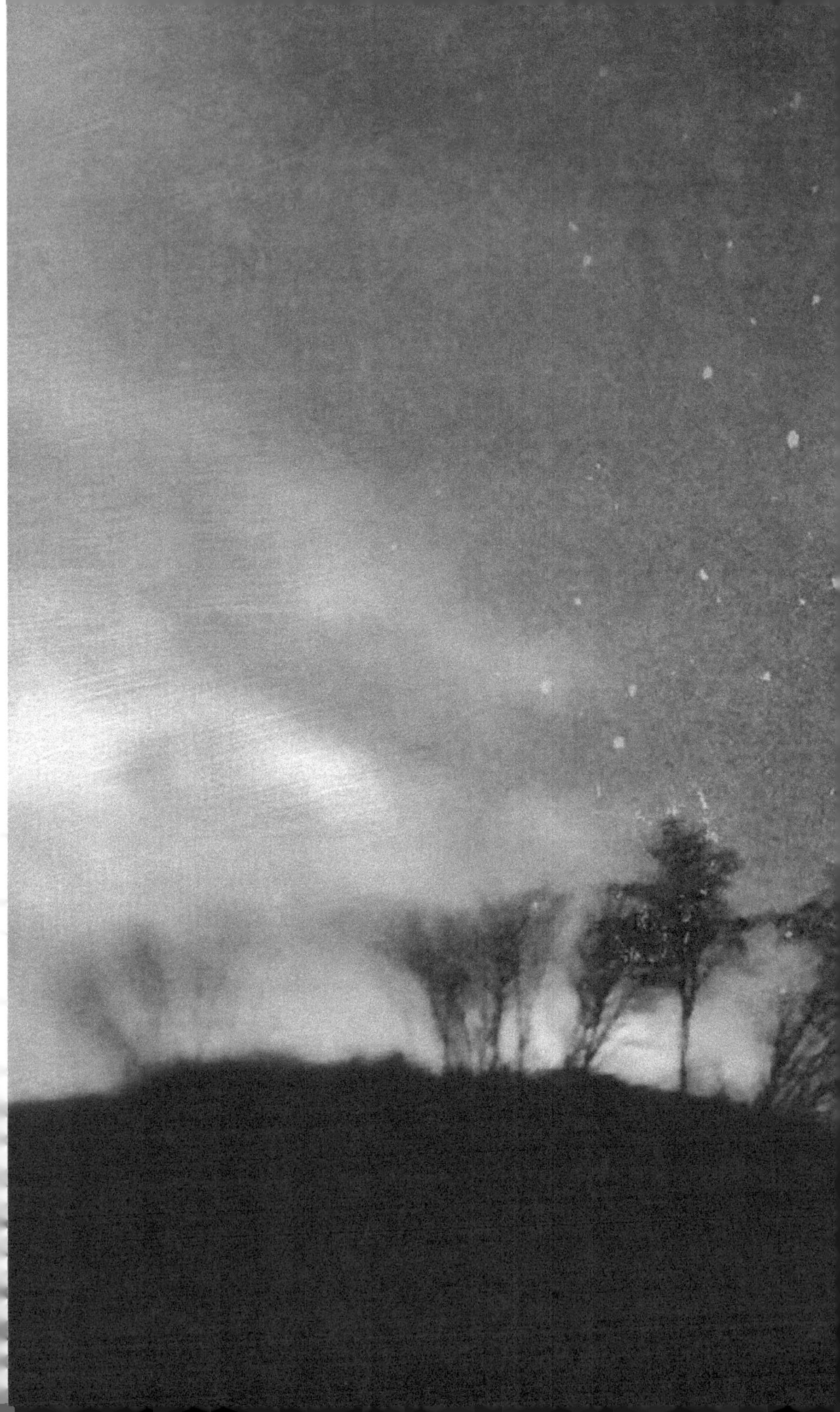

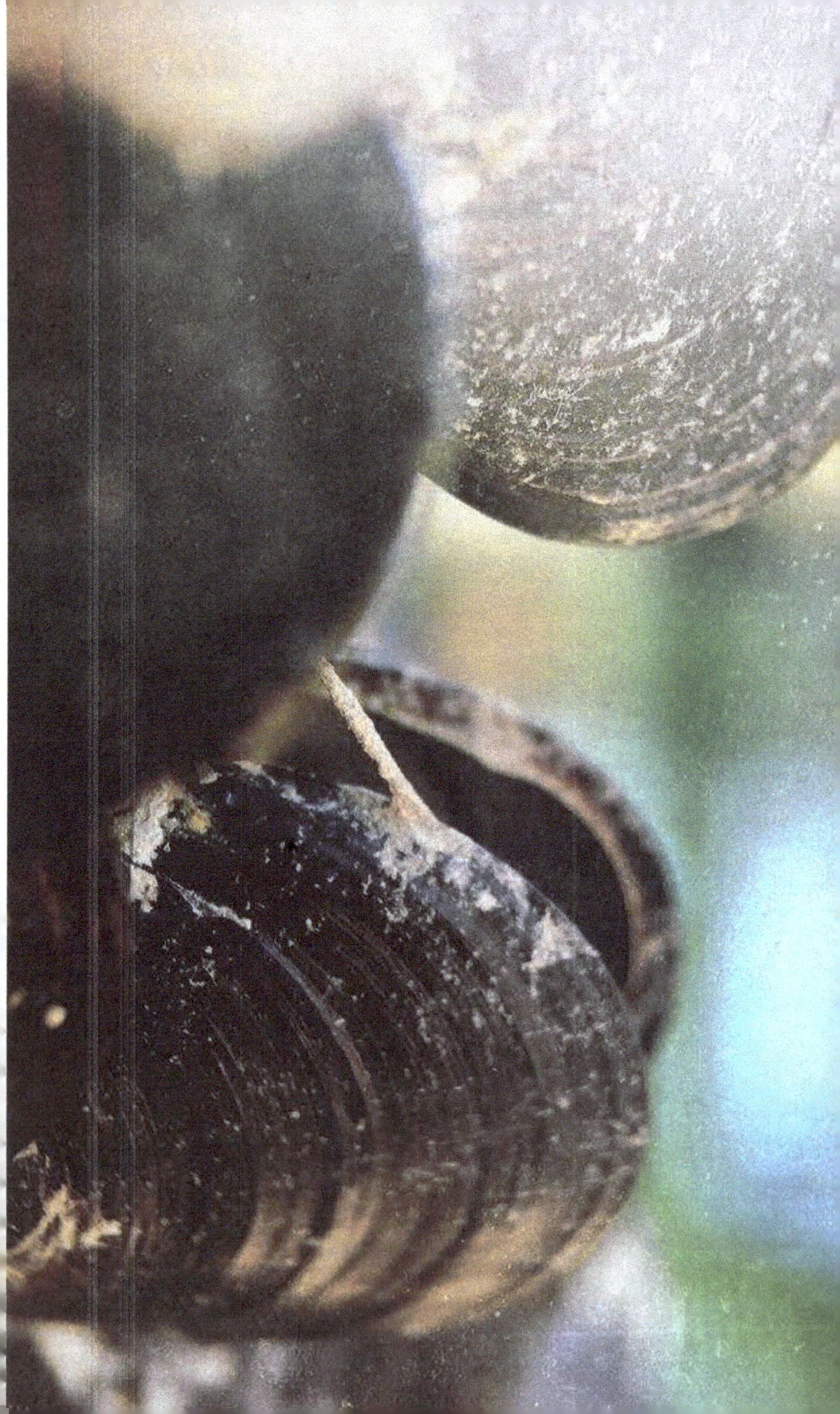

# A CLOSER LOOK

## *commonly harvested sea creatures*

Barnacles: Goose Neck

Clams: Eastern soft shell, Geoduck, Horse, Native

Littleneck, Manila, Razor, Butter, Cockle

Crab: Dungeness, Red Rock

Crayfish: Signal, Rusty

Mussels: Foolish (Bay) and California

Octopus: Giant Pacific

Scallops: Pink, Spiny, Weathervane, Rock

Sea Cucumbers

Sea Urchins: Green, Purple, Red

Seaweed

Shrimp: Spot, Sidestripe, Dock, Humpback,

Humpy, Northern Pink, Ocean Pink

Squid: Pacific

Oysters: Pacific, Olympia

*Whidbey Island is home to Penn Cove Shellfish,*
*the oldest and largest commercial mussel farm in the U.S.*

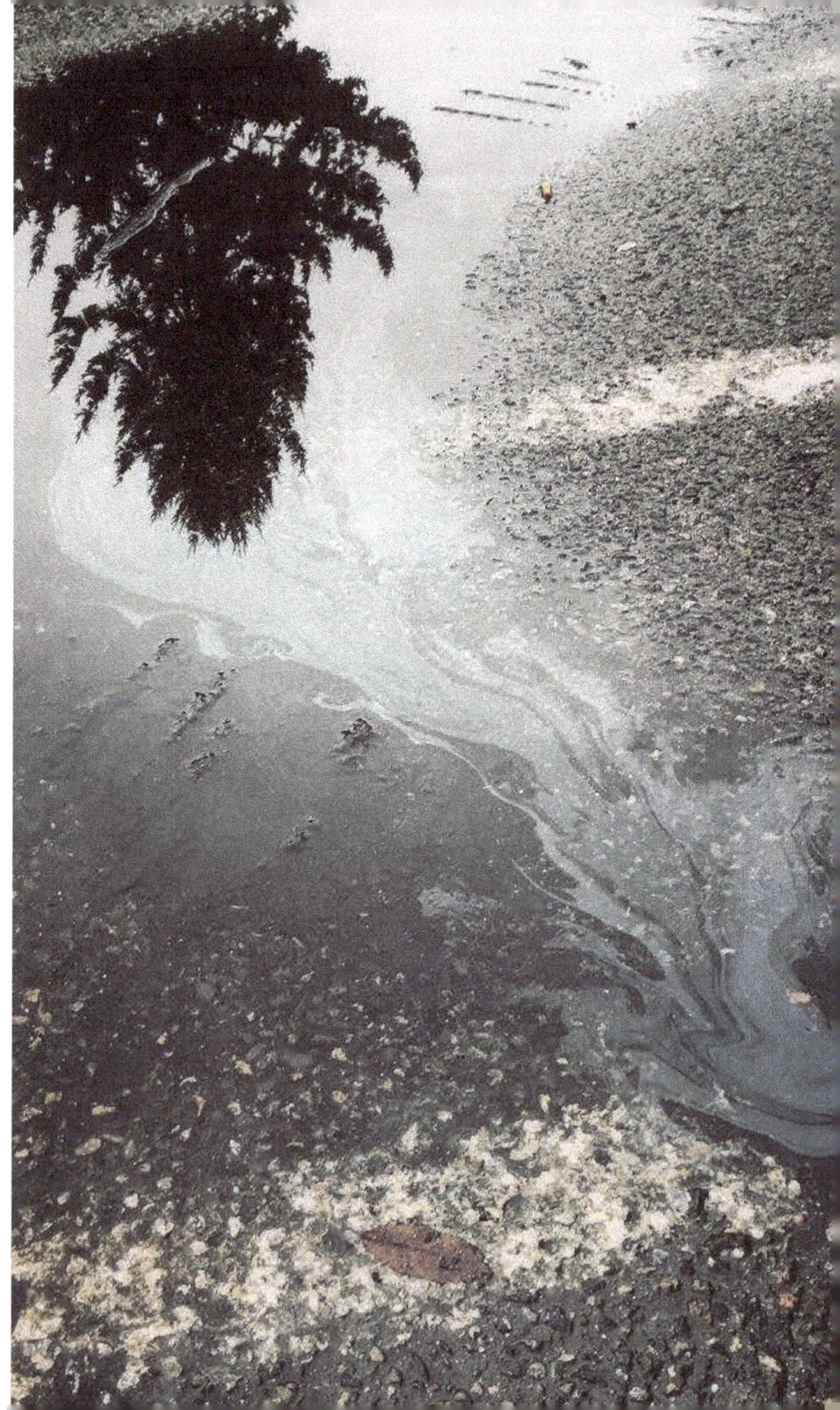

# A CLOSER LOOK
## oil and water

Disastrous oil spills in the ocean capture our attention, but everyday leaks into city storm drains contribute a tremendous amount of pollution.

When it rains, storm water collects oil and other pollutants as it moves downstream. The untreated water empties directly into the Puget Sound via rivers and street drains. Its negative impact on marine life and habitat must be addressed.

Residents can decrease their impact on the Puget Sound by making small changes, like using a car wash, which reduces the amount of chemicals introduced into local waters.

Lawns contribute a lot of chemicals to the Sound. Fertilizer and weed killer are washed away by rain and enter storm drains. Again, these drains empty directly into the Sound.

Lawns require a fair amount of irrigation, too. Drought tolerant and native plants are water-wise and less needy.

FOG

Wake
and see the cool, marine
air drifting by
like so many
nameless ghosts.

They carry away
midnight fears and
yearning,
their cold kiss,
living diamonds on
spider webs.

    *Stranded Moon jellyfish, Aurelia aurita*

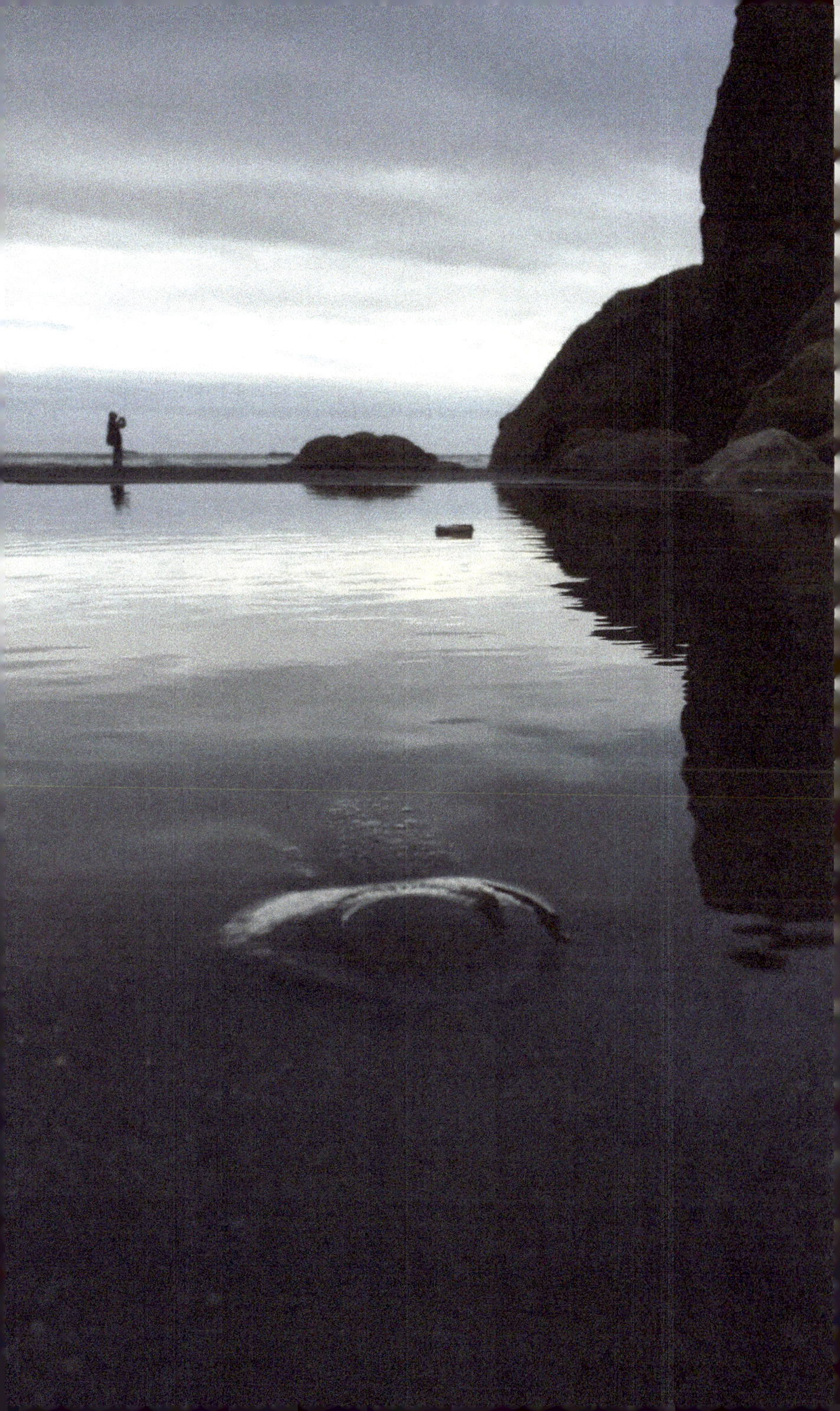

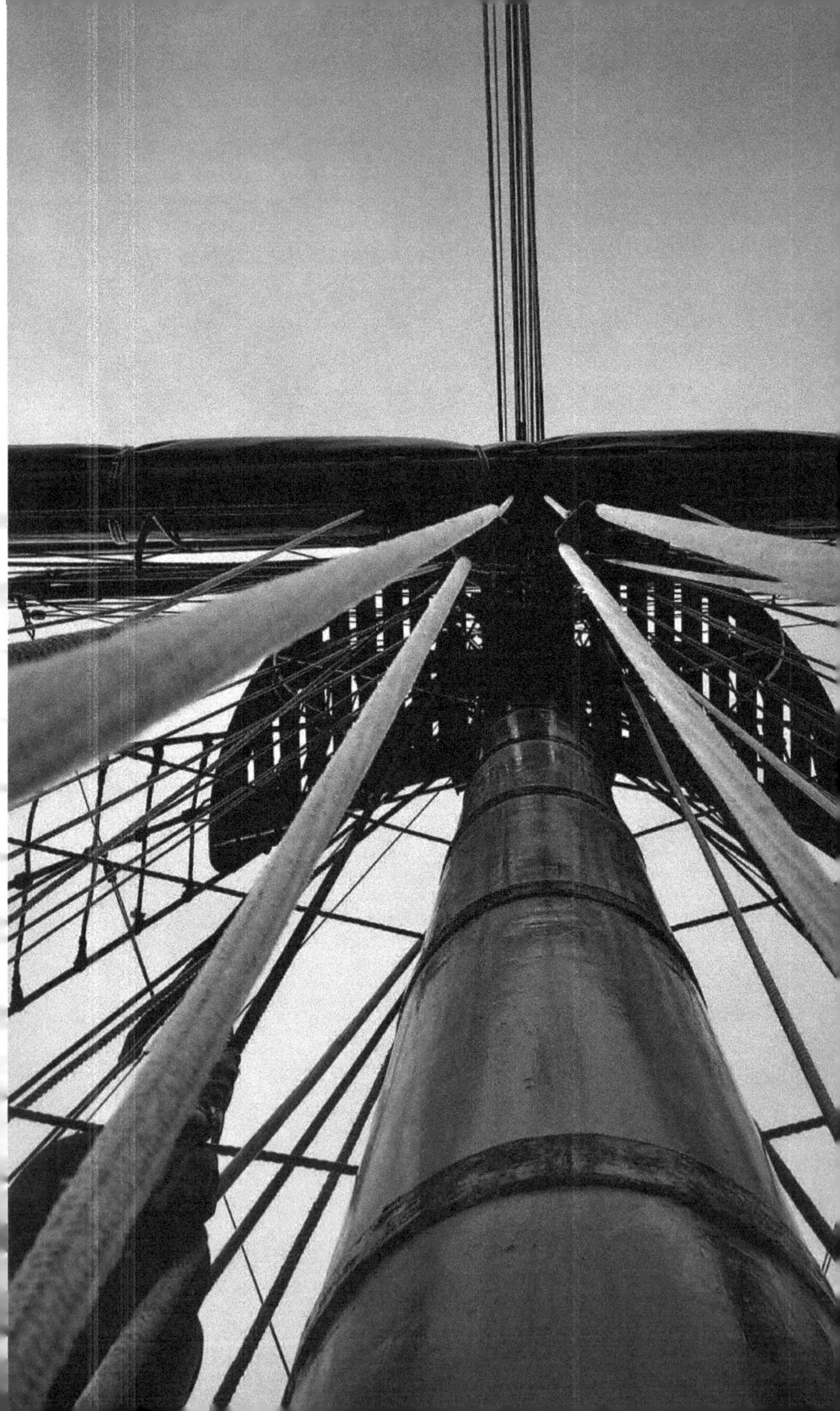

# A CLOSER LOOK
## *shipwrecks*

The area where the Columbia River empties into the sea is known as *The Graveyard of the Pacific.*

The clash of fresh and saltwater currents and shifting sandbars hidden just below the waves combine to create one of the world's most treacherous shorelines. Below are a few of the many ships that met their fate there.

* 1792 *Chatham* British tender
* 1798 Small boat from the *Hazard* American brigantine
* 1811 Small boat from the *Tonquin* American ship
* 1813 *Raccoon* British sloop of war
* 1829 *William and Ann* British barkentine
* 1830 *Isabella* Hudson Bay Co., British supply brigantine
* 1839 *H.M.S. Sulpher* British Royal Navy ship
* 1841 *U.S.S. Peacock* U.S. Navy ship
* 1846 *U.S.S. Shark* U.S. Navy survey schooner
* 1848 *Maine* American whaler
* 1848 *Vancouver* British barkentine
* 1849 *Josephine* British brigantine
* 1876 *Dreadnought* sloop
* 1906 *Peter Iredale* British
* 1909 *The Alice* French
* 1913 *Rosecrans* American steamship oil tanker
* 1922 *Iowan* freighter and *Welsh Prince* British Steamer
* 1930 *Admiral Benson* American steamship
* 1961 *Mermaid* fishing boat and *Triumph* Coast Guard Cutter

TACOMA TRANSPLANT

A certain slant of autumn light
low and drowsy
full of golden promise
reaches out its arms.

But the dust of day soon settles
into winter's long goodnight.

I know the season's end is on its way
with a gallery of charcoal rubbings,
where days wear down with leaden,
unrelenting rain.

Summer slowly slipped away
I don't remember when
I tasted my last kiss.

In the dark tonight,
I dream
of fresh born flowers,
their luscious pointed spears
poking through the soil.

Please, I pray,
come quickly!

But the rhythm of this town
tiptoes across my sheets.
Its never ending trade
subliminally whispers.



*Long Beach*

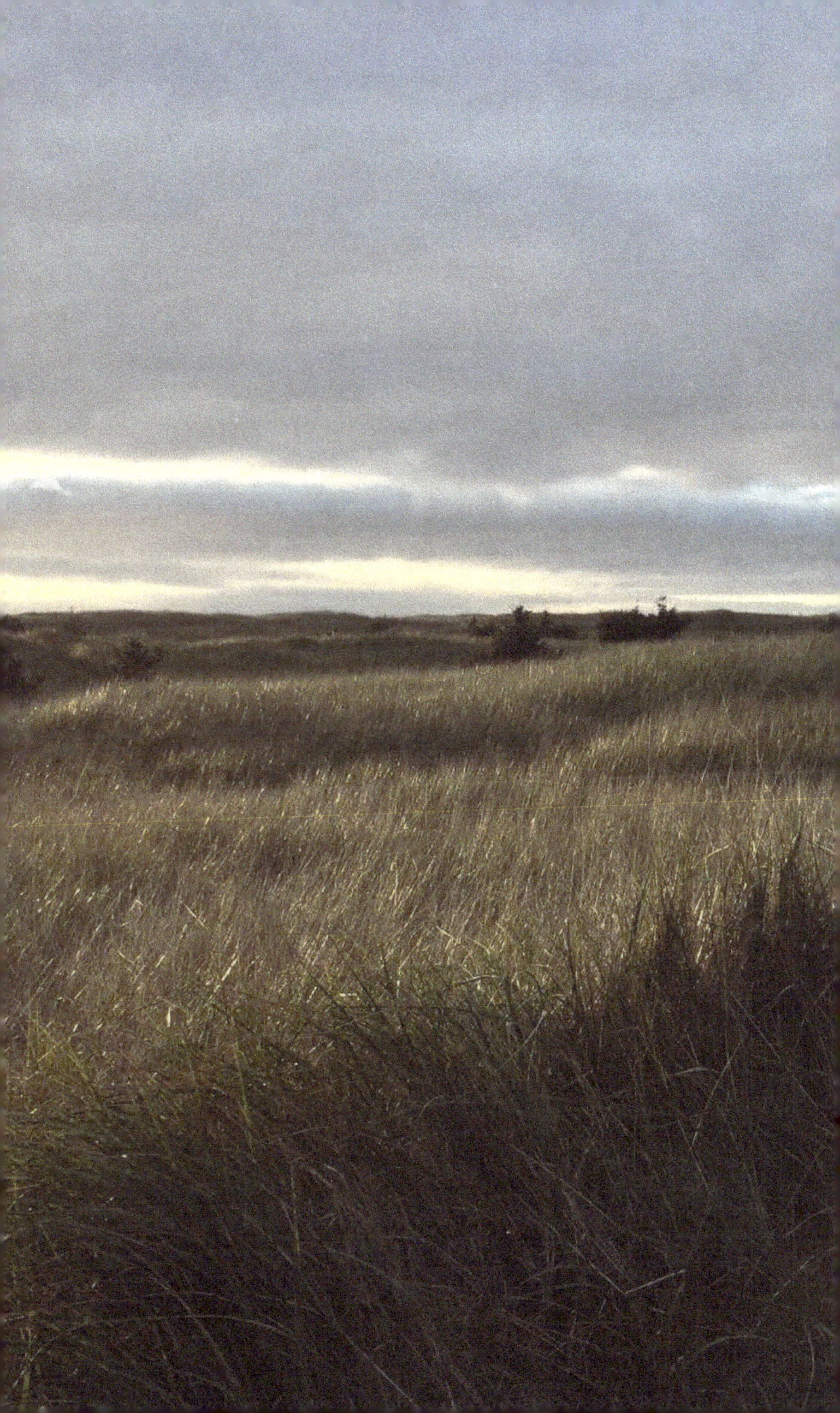

I'm bounded by the call of trains
hovering on misted cliffs,
humming past the Point.

I'm folded into foghorn purrs,
which are nudging me to sleep
floating on the murky,
churning waters of the Sound,
chanting ancient warnings,
or a siren song,
my lullaby.

Maybe I can cope
with the soft, delicious rain.
Besides, I've almost made it
and the garden's verdant voice,
is hiding just behind
the calendar's sharp corner.



*Raindrop on a maple bud*

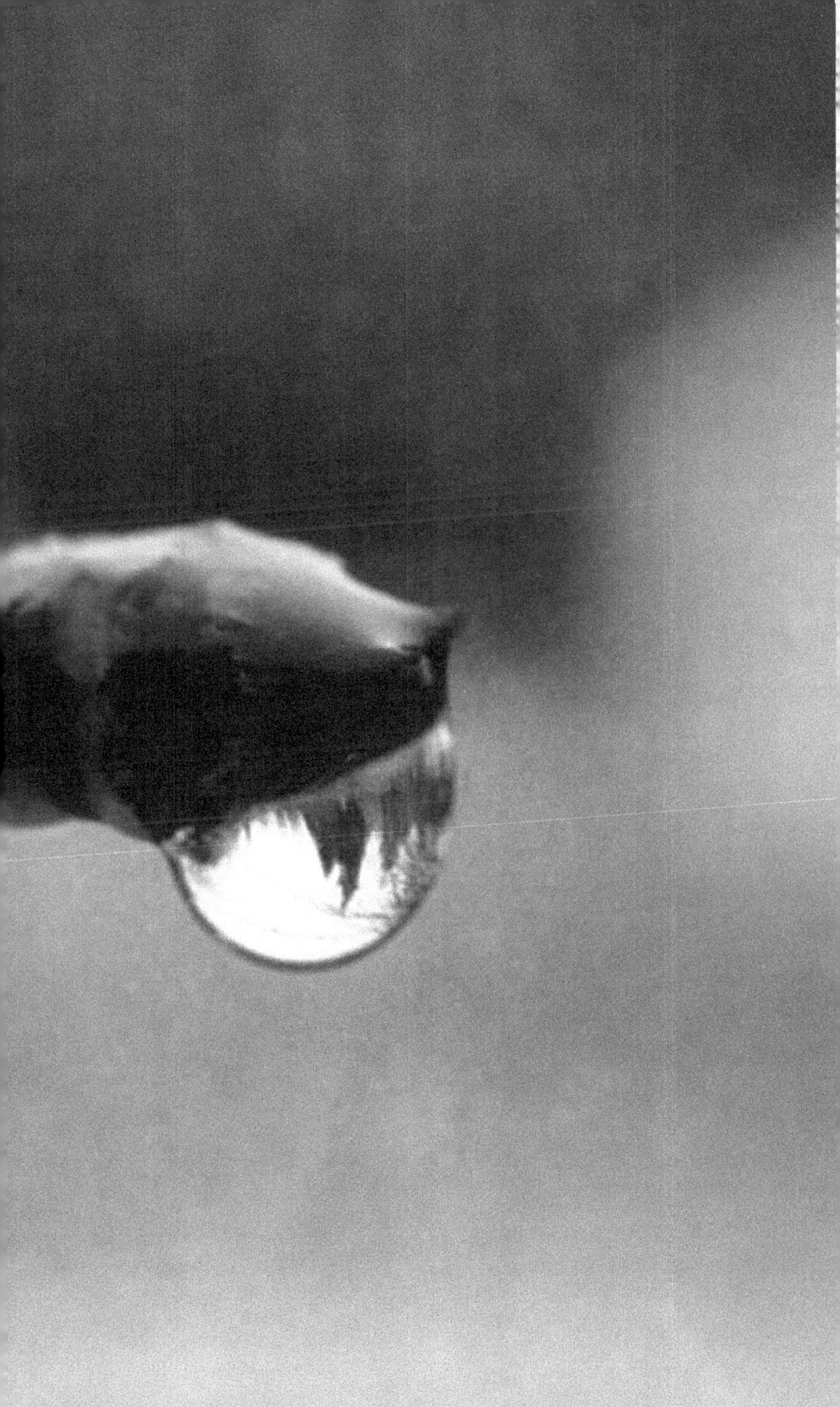

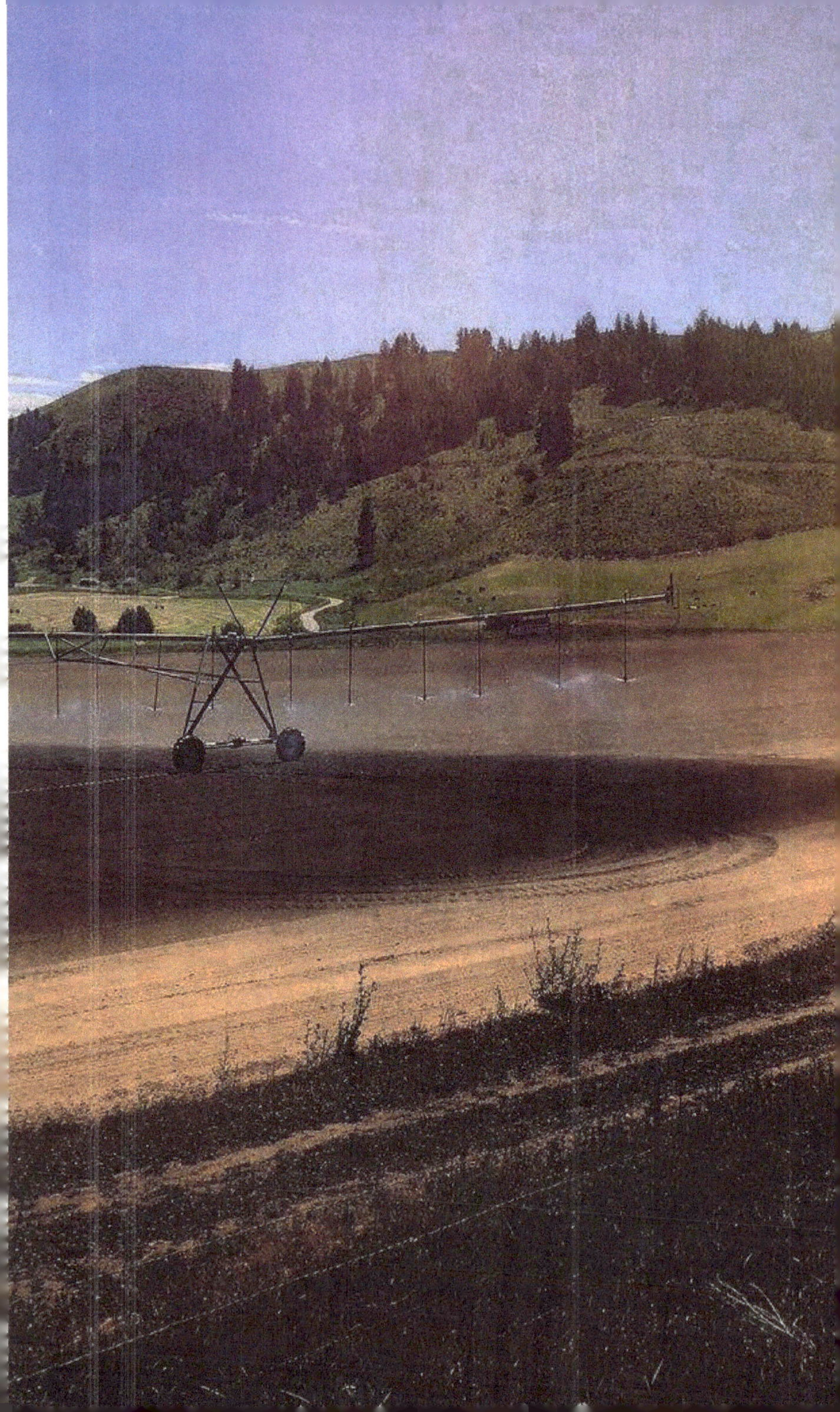

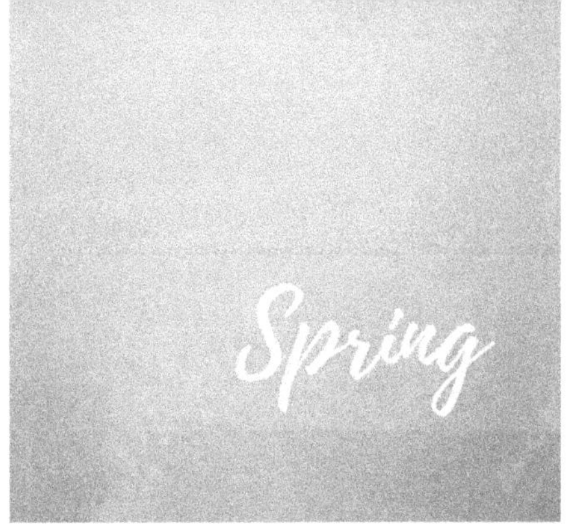



Washington is a study of contrasts. Split down the middle by the Cascade Mountain Range, the state has two distinct regions. Marine air coming off the Pacific creates cool, wet weather. This precipitation is blocked by the Cascades and creates a rain shadow, which makes Eastern Washington much drier.

The enormous inland body of water known as the Puget Sound or Salish Sea helps to moderate the temperature. Many are surprised to learn that Western Washington's climate is similar to the Mediterranean's with warm, dry summers and mild, wet winters. Supplemental irrigation is necessary in June, July and August.

Meanwhile, Eastern Washington experiences more extremes. The dry, hot weather makes it a perfect place for growing wine grapes and other crops.

## BEACH GLASS

I'm searching for the perfect piece
of tranquil broken
glass.

A fragment of sky
worn smooth,
worried by countless waves.

I'll pluck it from its
restless bed and
bring it home,
my fingers searching
for sharp edges.

I'll rediscover it
click-clacking
in the dryer's heat
and remember the day,
not too long ago,
when I was someone
else.

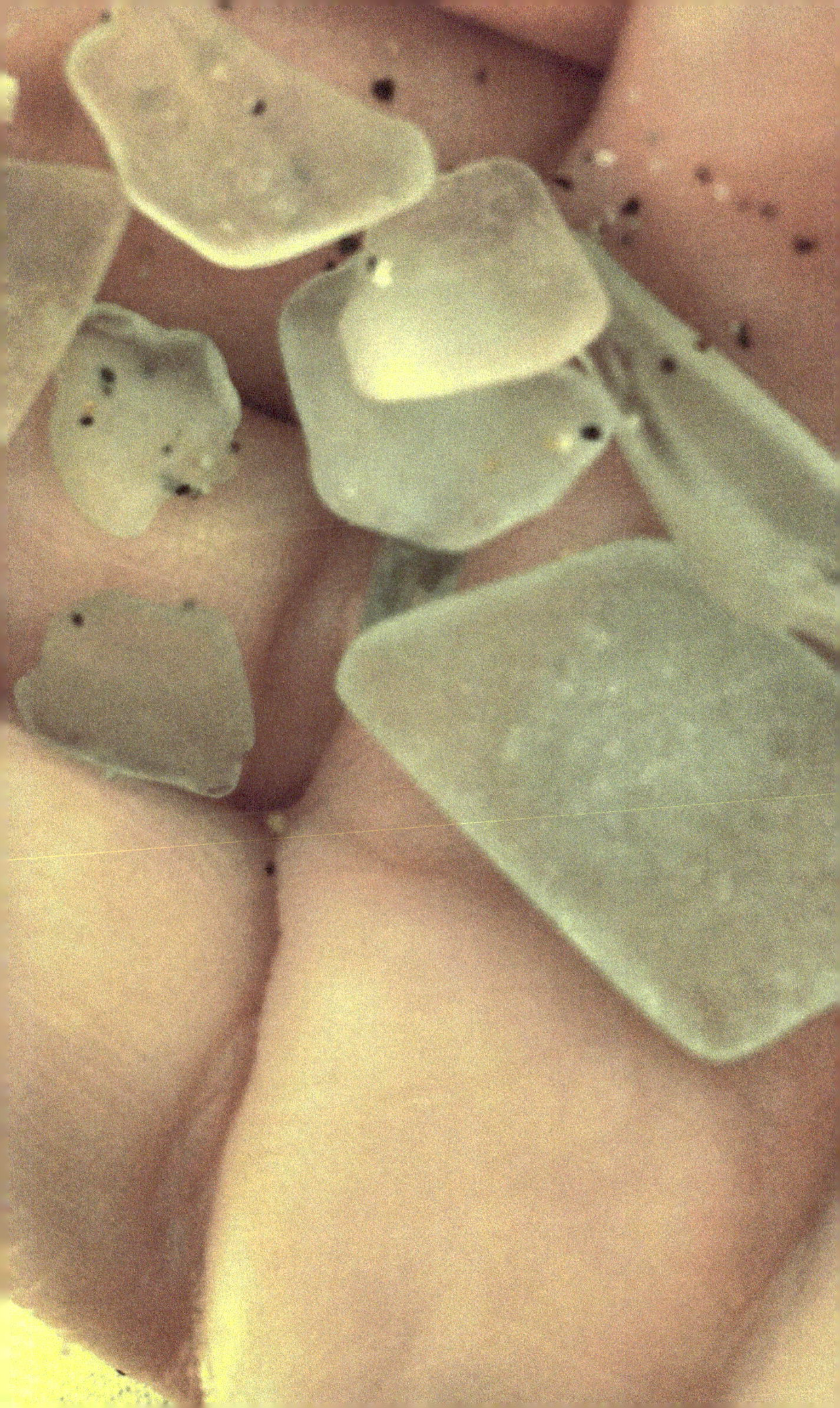

OVERPASS

Such beauty missed,
we pass it by
unnoticed, on our way
to wherever.

But our eternity awakens,
that great span of time,
if we'd only glimpse the
rushing rivers just past
the concrete byways
that nature burns to
cover, its green knuckled
fingers wrapping wrapping
wrapping up and over
up and over. Obliteration
in our blind sight.

I thank God
for this.



*Columbia River Gorge*
*(Next page: Lake Quinault)*

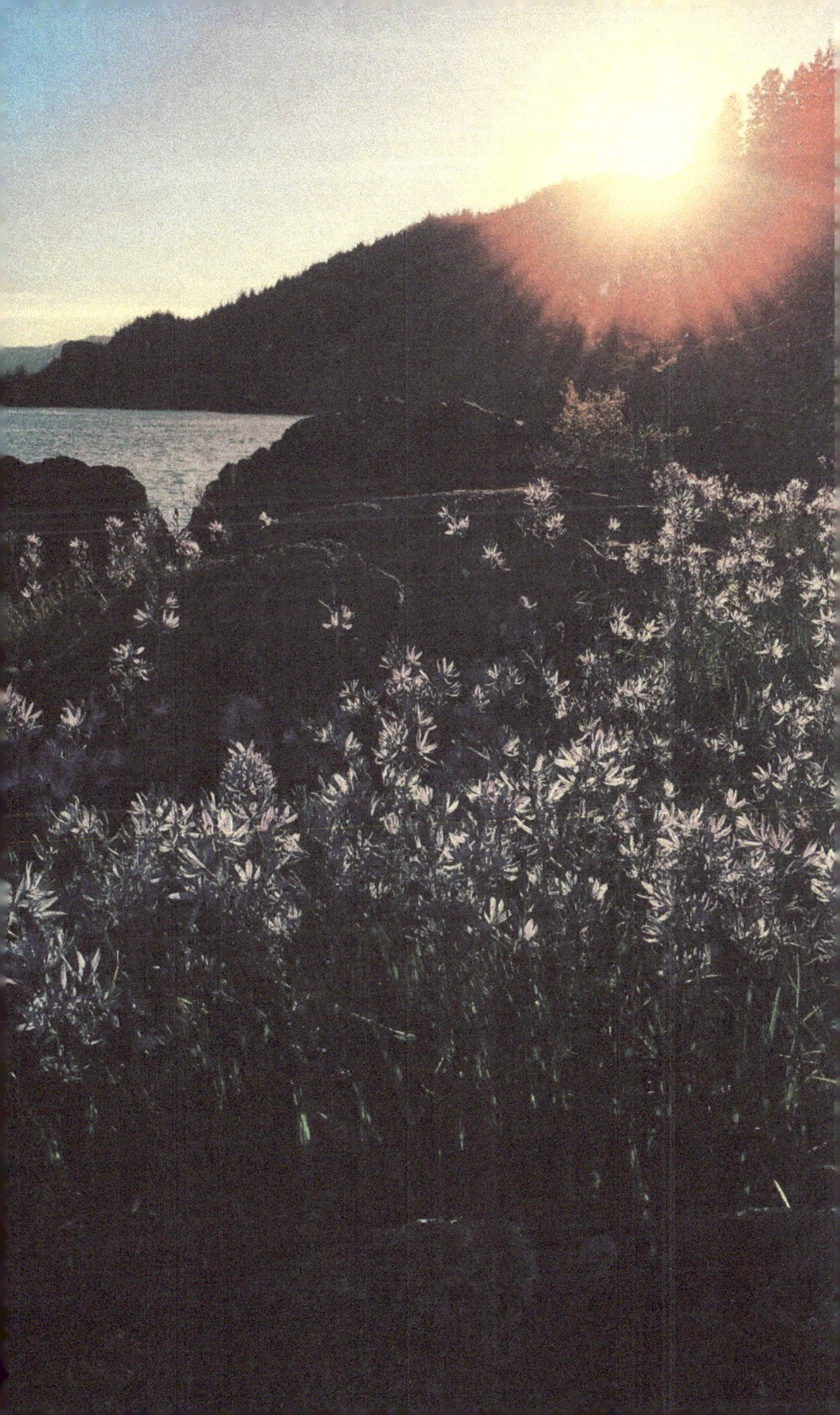

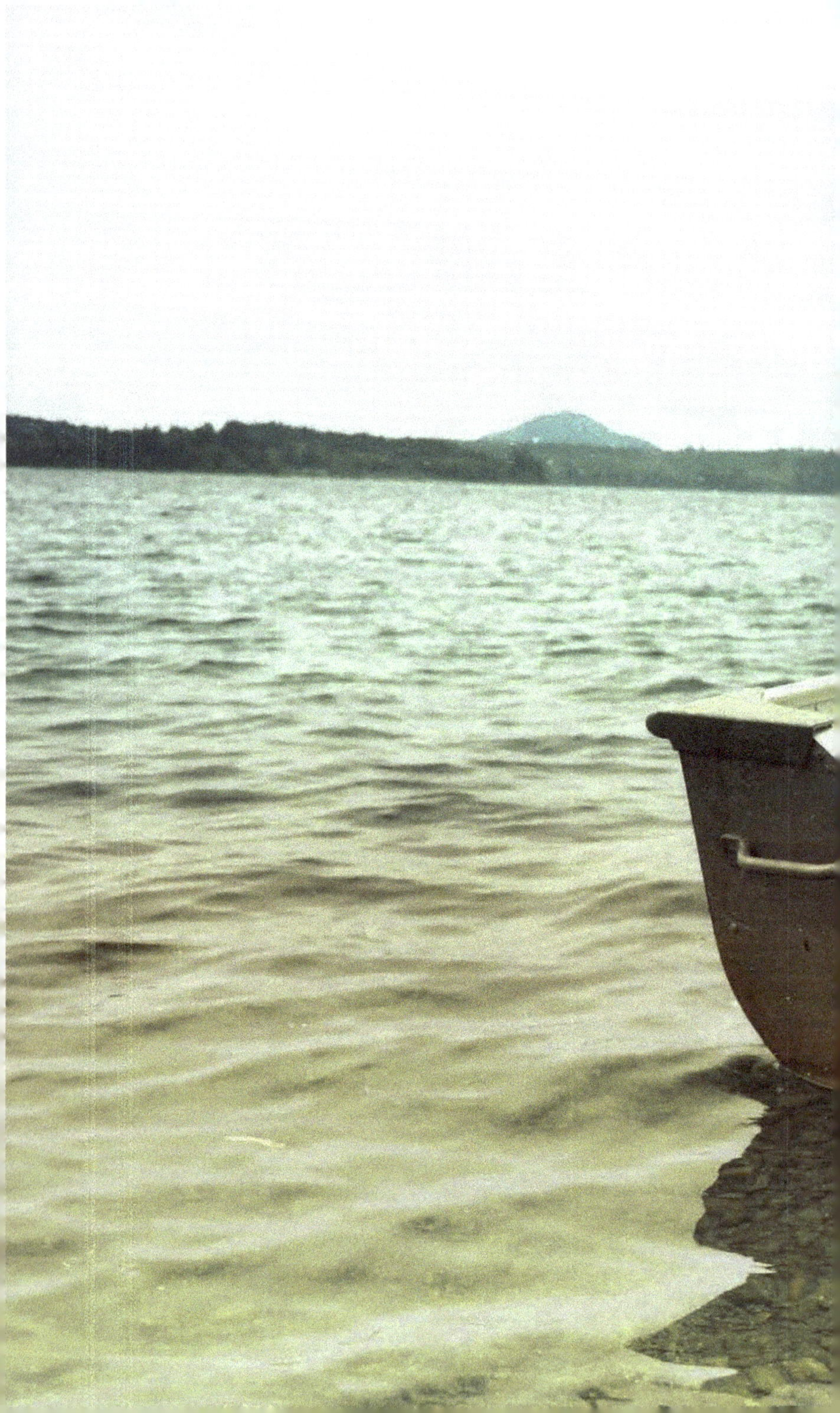

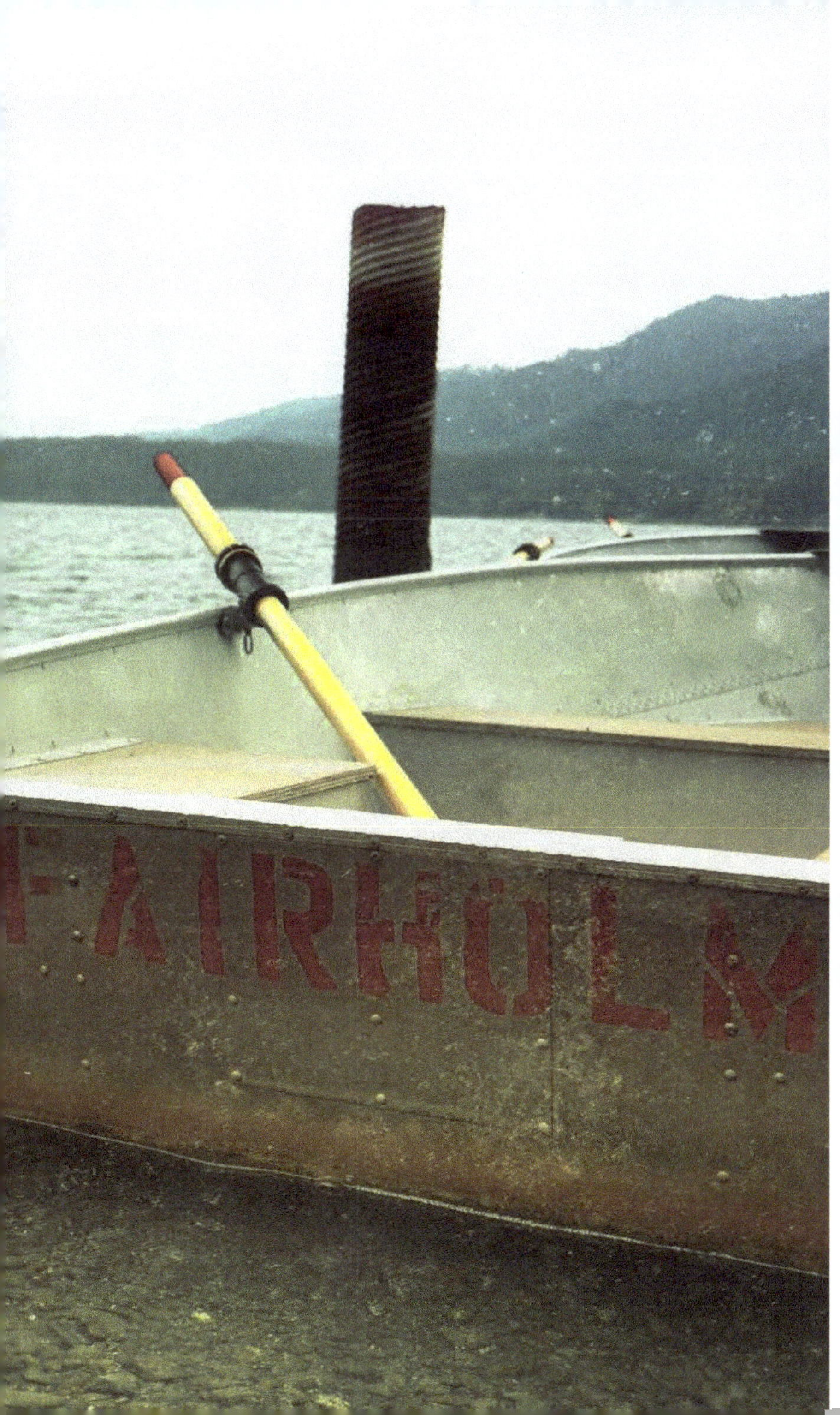
FAIRHOL K

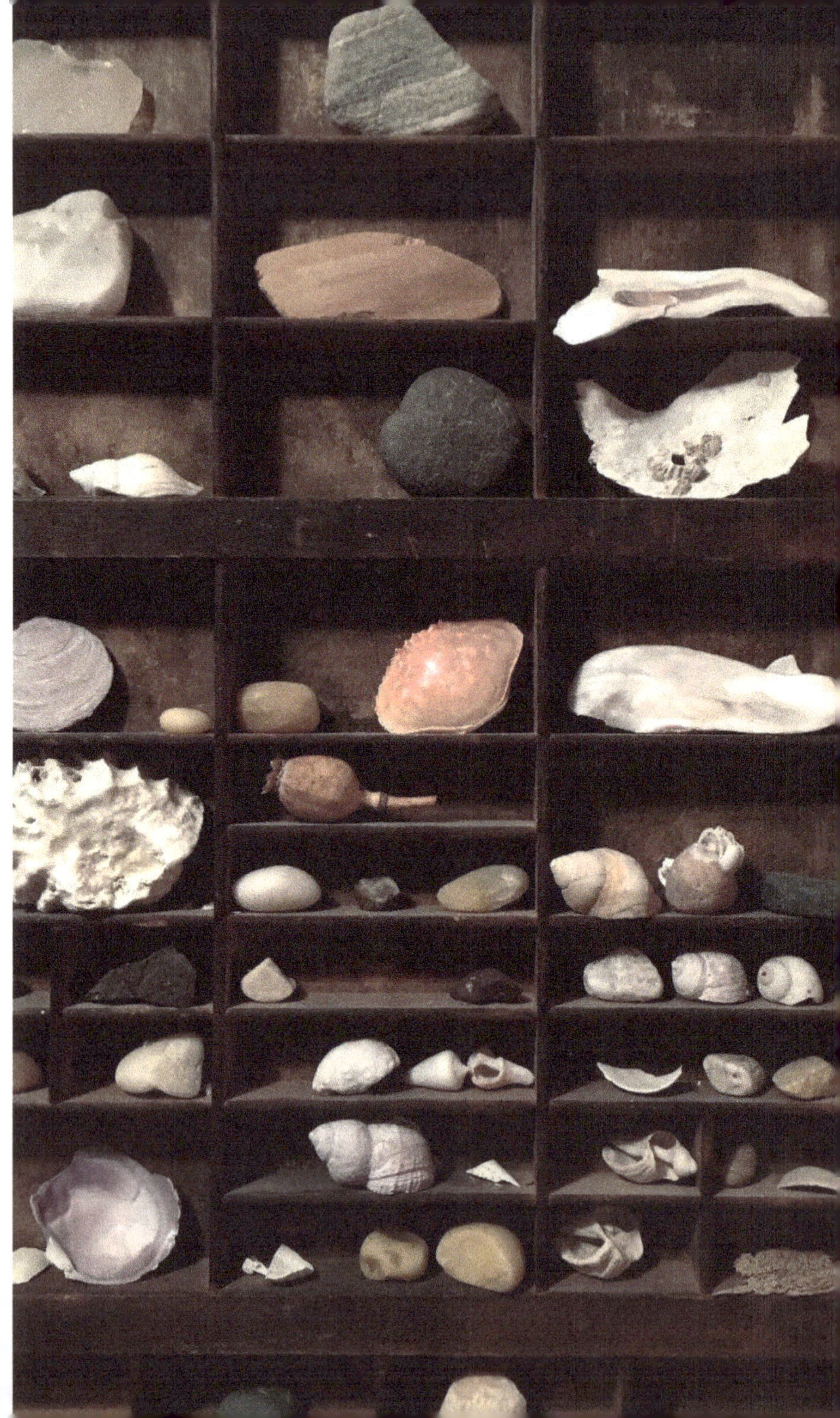

# A CLOSER LOOK
## *marine mammals of the salish*

The inland waters of Washington are home to many sea creatures including: Dall's porpoise, Harbor seals, Gray whales, Humpback whales, Minke whales, Orcas, Steller sea lions, river and sea otters.

There are three resident Orca pods in the Salish Sea. The Southern Resident Killer Whales (SRKW) are experiencing a population decline. Scientists are working hard to figure out what's happening. UW researchers have proposed three hypotheses: 1) Decline in Chinook salmon, their primary prey. 2) Disturbance from whale watching boats. 3) Exposure to pollution like PCB and PBDE.

PCB's and PBDE's are chemicals in plastic and flame retardants that are shown to be endocrine disruptors, which means they influence hormones. They are in our water and have been discovered in fat and breast milk. Studies are ongoing and we've yet to comprehend the dangers of long-term exposure.

SEMIAHMOO BEACH

The sea spits up its seeds
spent rocks
smoothed by ceaseless
ebb and flow
ground down offspring
of their mountain mother
who watches from a careful distance
witness to the tumble of her babes,
which waves lick and lap
refining features.

An endless sieving tongue
sifts and launders
tames the tower - Earth's revolt
extension of internal flux.

It cultivates the broken boulders,
weaves a bed of bones.

The sea inhales the mountain and
exhales it into bits.

*Quillayute River jetty near La Push*

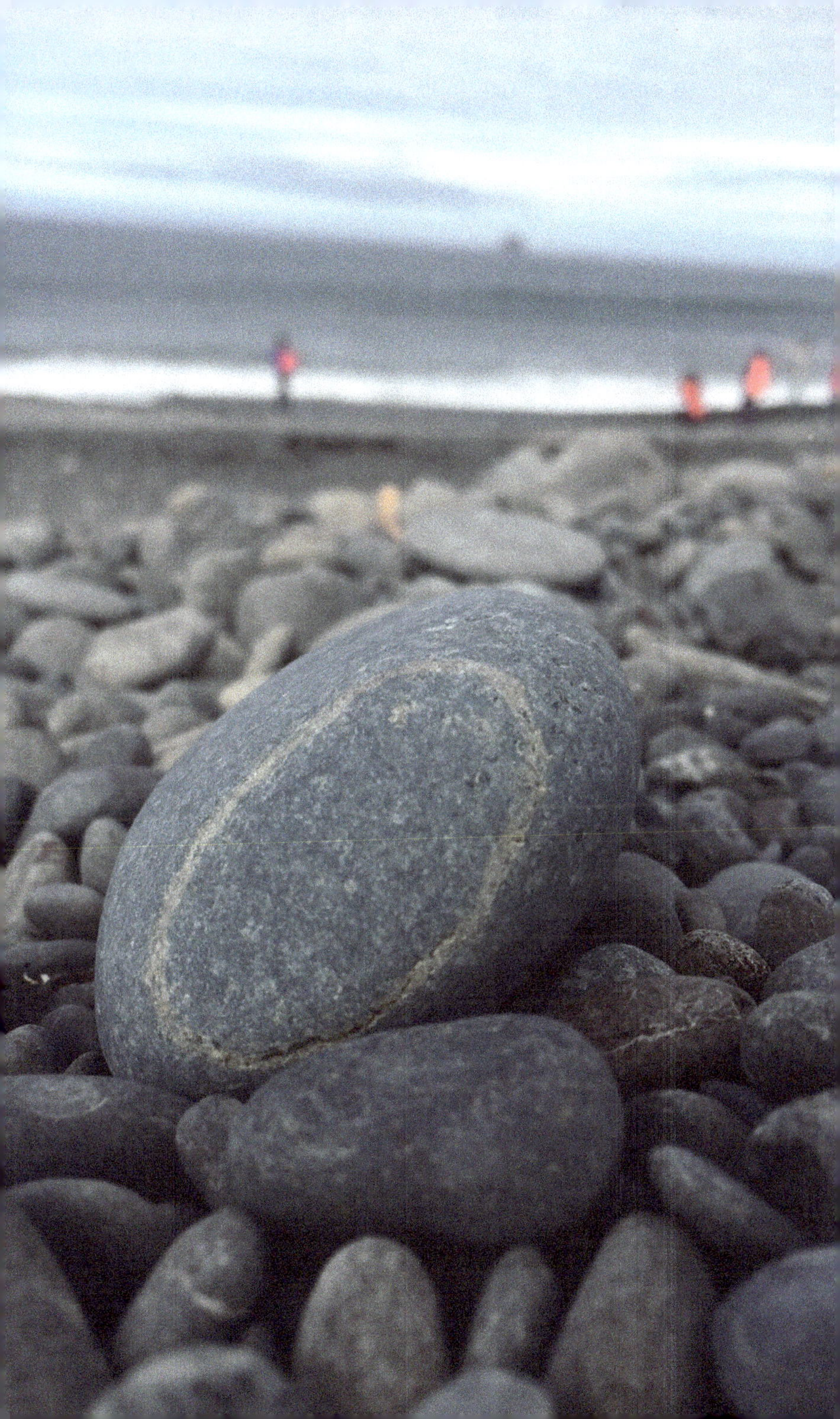

# A CLOSER LOOK
## *dams*

There are 1166 dams in Washington state, with over 60 in the Columbia River Watershed. Dams are built for flood control, to make river navigation safe, for irrigation and to generate power.

Mossy Rock is the tallest dam in Washington. It's on the Cowlitz River and supplies 40% of Tacoma's electricity. The famous Grand Coulee Dam in Eastern Washington provides a tremendous amount of power and crop irrigation. It is the largest producer of electrical power in the USA.

The energy dams produce is considered 'clean,' though they interfere with anadromous (sea-run) fish trying to return to their headwaters, which include salmon, trout, striped bass and sturgeon. Fish ladders, like Seattle's Ballard Locks, help fish bypass dams to spawn, but not all fish ladders are successful.

Dams can harm the environment for several reasons. They alter the course of rivers; lead to the erosion of deltas; create warm water, which is harmful to fish reproduction; and trap sediment behind them that is necessary for salmon spawning.

The Elwha (1910) and Glines Canyon Dam (1926) were built for the growing Olympic Peninsula and city of Port Angeles. Unfortunately, they lacked a safe passage for migrating fish and blocked over 70 miles of habitat. Sadly, the dams also flooded the homeland of the Lower Elwha Klallam Tribe.

Once the Elwha and Glines Canyon dams were finally deemed inefficient and detrimental to the environment, they were decommissioned. After two decades of planning the largest dam removal in US history, the Elwha's demolition began September 2011. It took 6 months and was followed by the Glines Canyon dam removal. After 100 years, the area is quickly recovering and fish are returning to spawn.

The Elwha River's delta is reshaping itself, supplied by the tremendous amount of sediment that was released. Sandy beaches are coming back, and with them, healthy shellfish beds and a restored estuary. The river is growing wild again.

*(Next page: Grand Coulee Dam, Grand Coulee)*

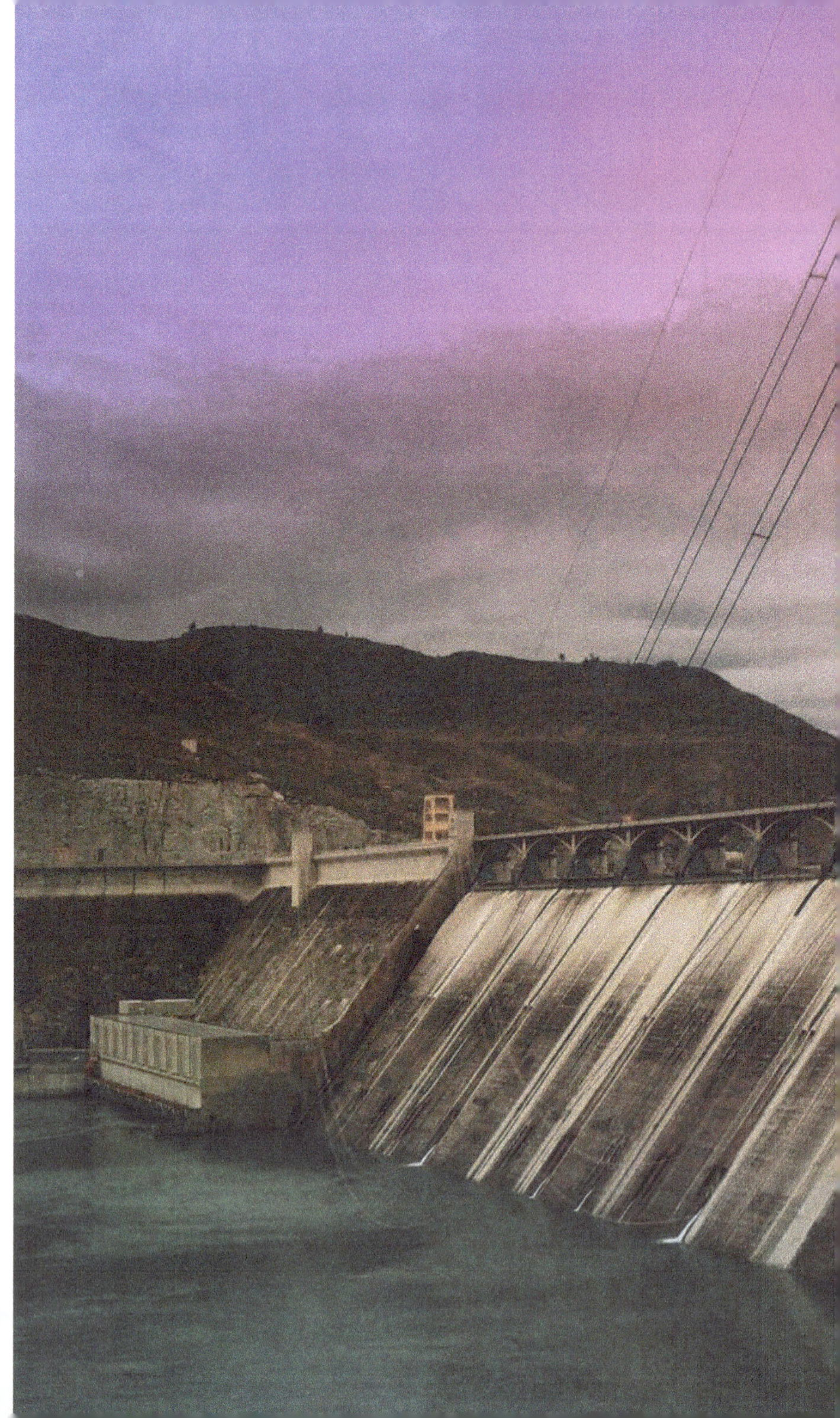

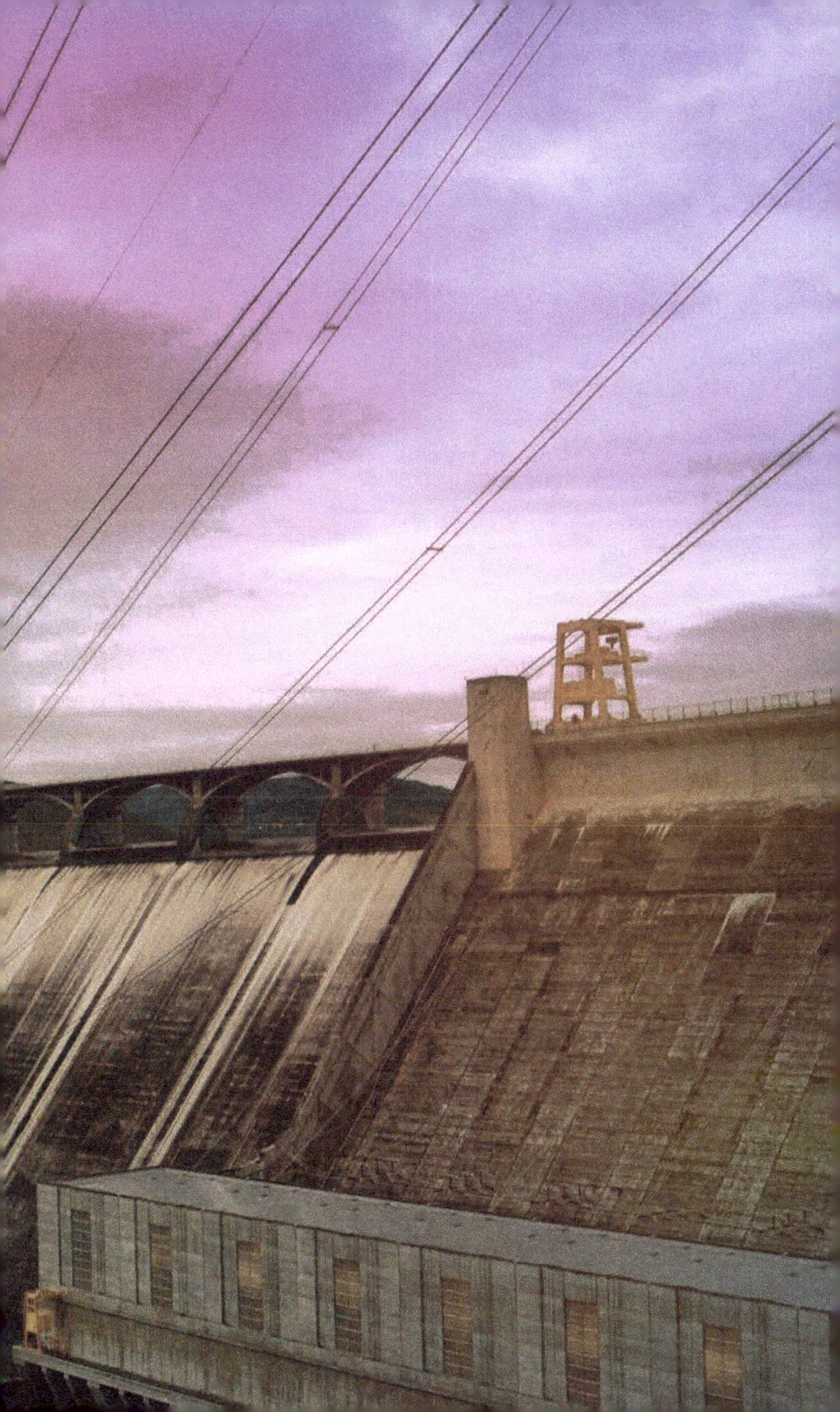

SALMON

The rivers are still,
thick with silence
in their drowsy, patient wait
before the fall.

Even now, 100 years have passed
and fish return
to toss themselves

                                                            up

                                        up

                        up
the concrete bier
but never over
never breachable
with abdomens full of
living pearls,
soft spheres
pulsing.

Home
Home
Home

is all they hear.
Every muscle twitches,
contracts this truth.

Native stories live like mists,
like shy ghosts on lonely shores.

"This place, once so full of fish,
we crossed the river on their backs."

"A sound came to me at night,
like hundreds of oars slapping the water.
The salmon had returned."

My heart is with the man,
that guards a quiet pool,
full of quick silver flashes.
It's too far to travel, he says,
up the river, past the dams' fish ladders
and death defying leaps,
to come to this fern-lined pond
of fanning gills
and be sacrificed.

Something buried deep
also calls us

Home
Home
Home

and we are never closer
than at the water's edge.

*(Next page: The Salmon Chief" blessing the catch by Virgil "Smoker" Marchand. The Spokane Tribe named Spokane Falls, "Stluputqu" meaning "swift water" and the fish they caught sustained many families. The salmon are now blocked by several dams and no longer run. In 1890, the WA Power Co. built the Monroe Street Dam. It's the longest running hydroelectric plant in the state.)*

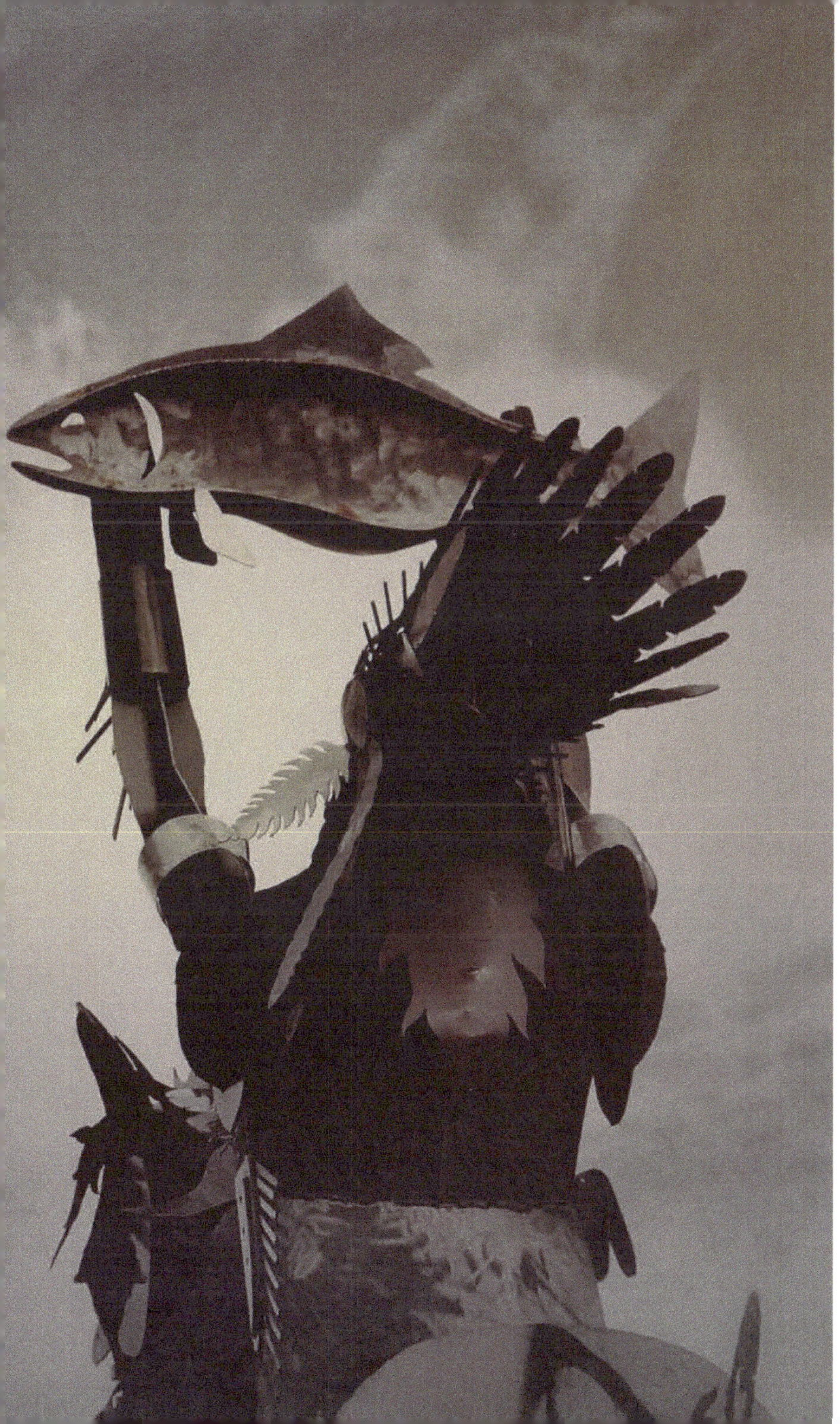

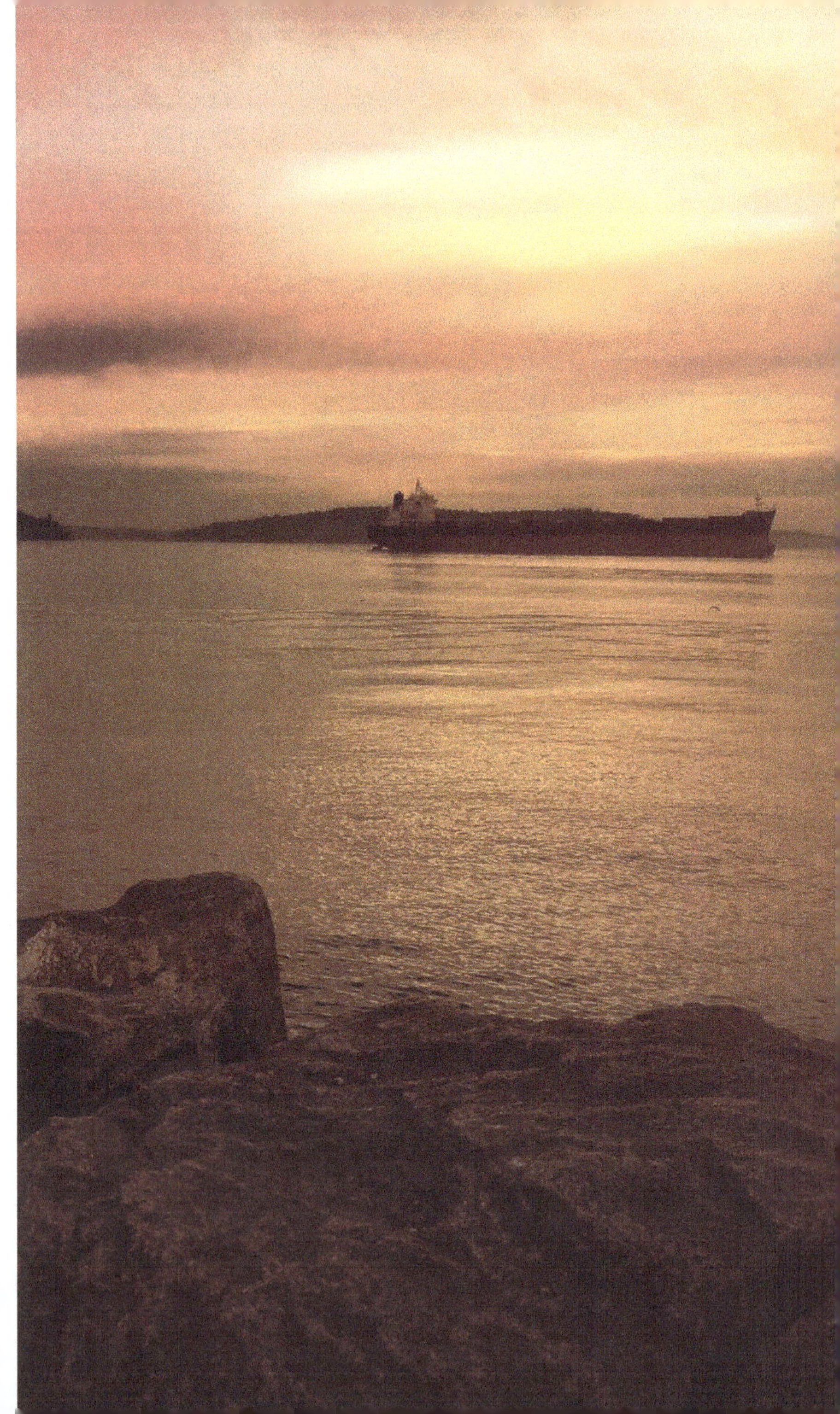

# A CLOSER LOOK
## *the puget sound*

The Puget Sound is a large inland body of water with 2,500 miles of coastline giving Washington its unique contours. When it includes the waters contiguous to British Columbia it's called the *Salish Sea*, after the Native peoples who first settled the area. About 14,000 years ago, a glacial ice sheet that extended down from Canada began to retreat, leaving behind this deep, lowland basin, which covers about 10,000 square miles.

A tremendous amount of nutrient-rich water flows from the Pacific Ocean and enters the Salish Sea through the straits of Juan de Fuca. Four times a day, strong tides churn seawater with sediment-rich freshwater pouring in from rivers. They meet in *estuaries*, which are areas where salt and freshwater mix. The Puget Sound is the second largest estuary in the United States after Chesapeake Bay.

All of this action creates a fertile environment for a diverse population of animals. The delicate ecosystem must be monitored as thousands of people living nearby have a tremendous impact. 75% of Puget Sound pollution comes from storm water that washes over roads and rooftops, which drains directly into the Sound.

*Commencement Bay, Tacoma*

# LUNGS

*Phytoplankton is a microalgae that floats in the sunlit part of the ocean and provides food for sea creatures. If it grows out of control, it can form toxic algae blooms, which has widespread effects in the food chain.*

The ocean breathes
her lungs a distillation
of Earth's ethers.

Whales breach and churn
the sea, mixing
phytoplankton's
green geometry
in spirals, cubes and cones,
the building blocks of life.



*Sea Nettle jellyfish*
*(Next page: a smack of jellyfish)*

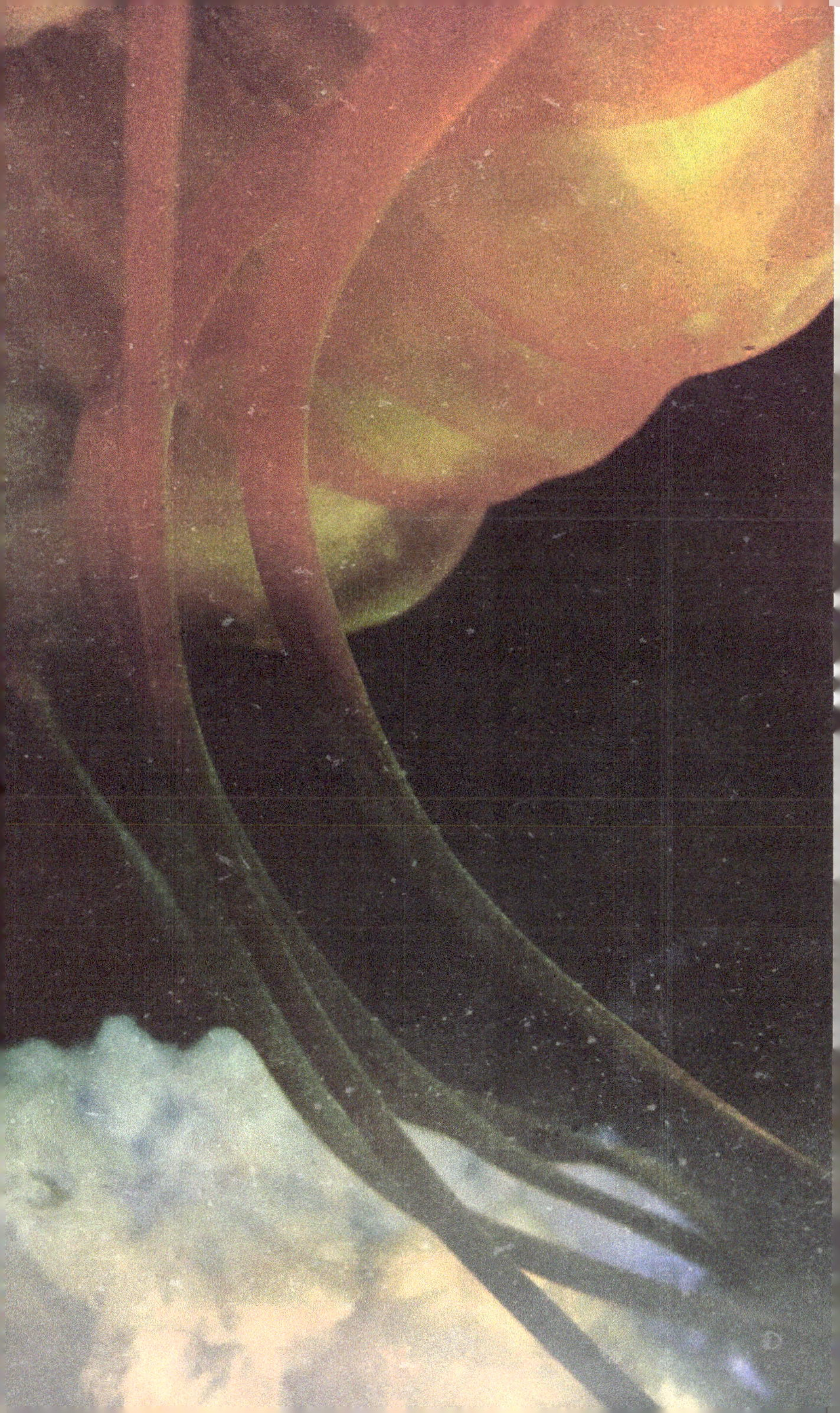

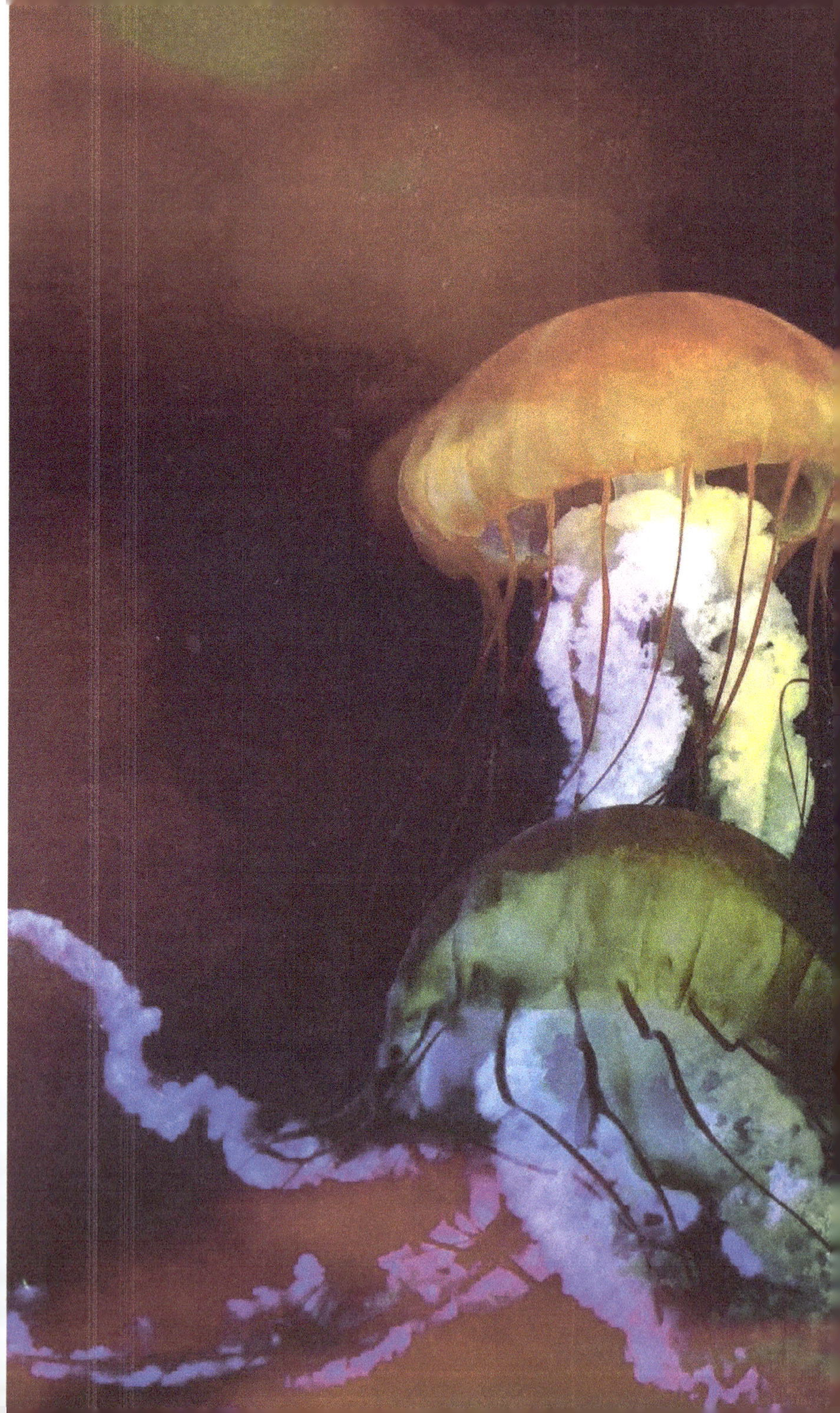

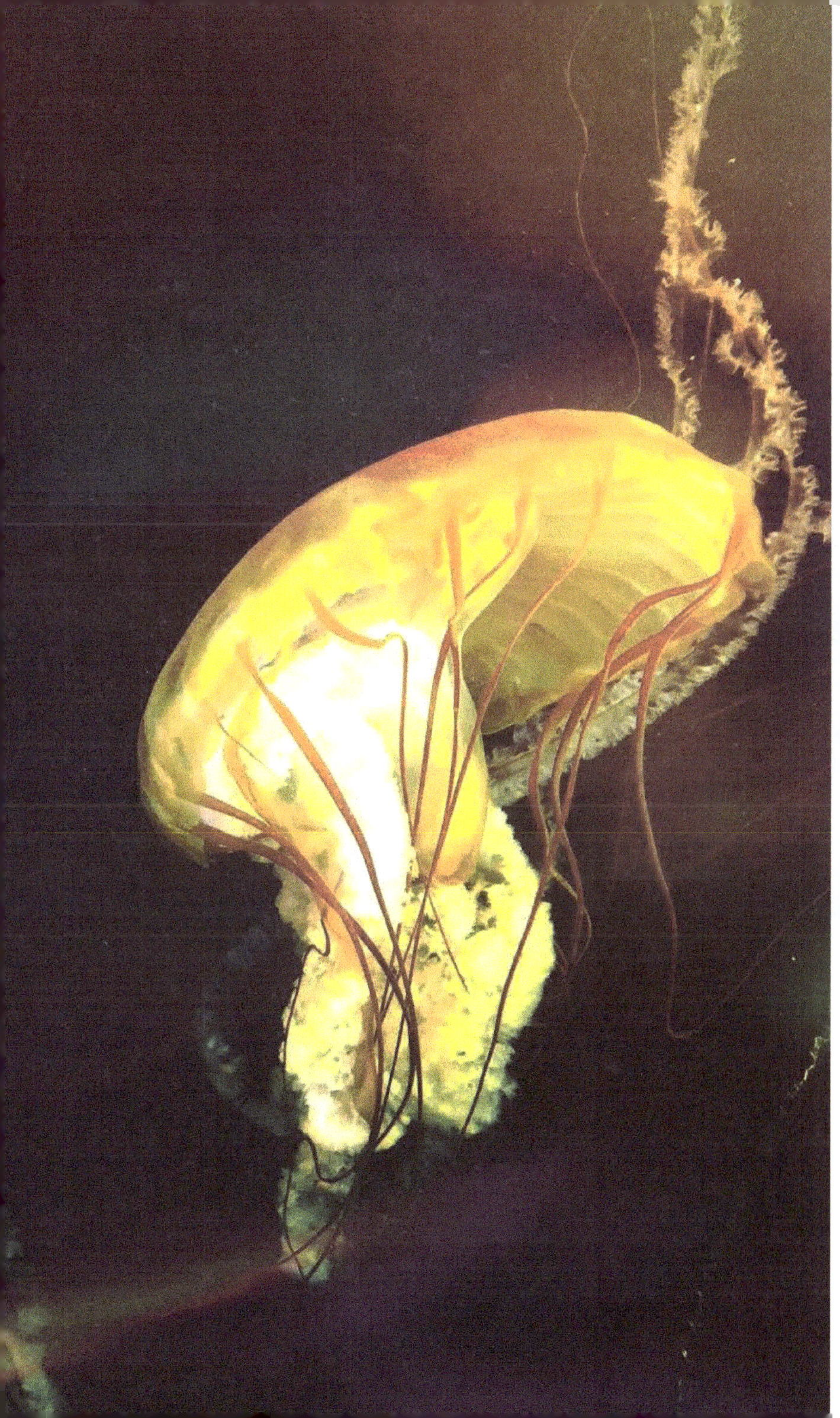

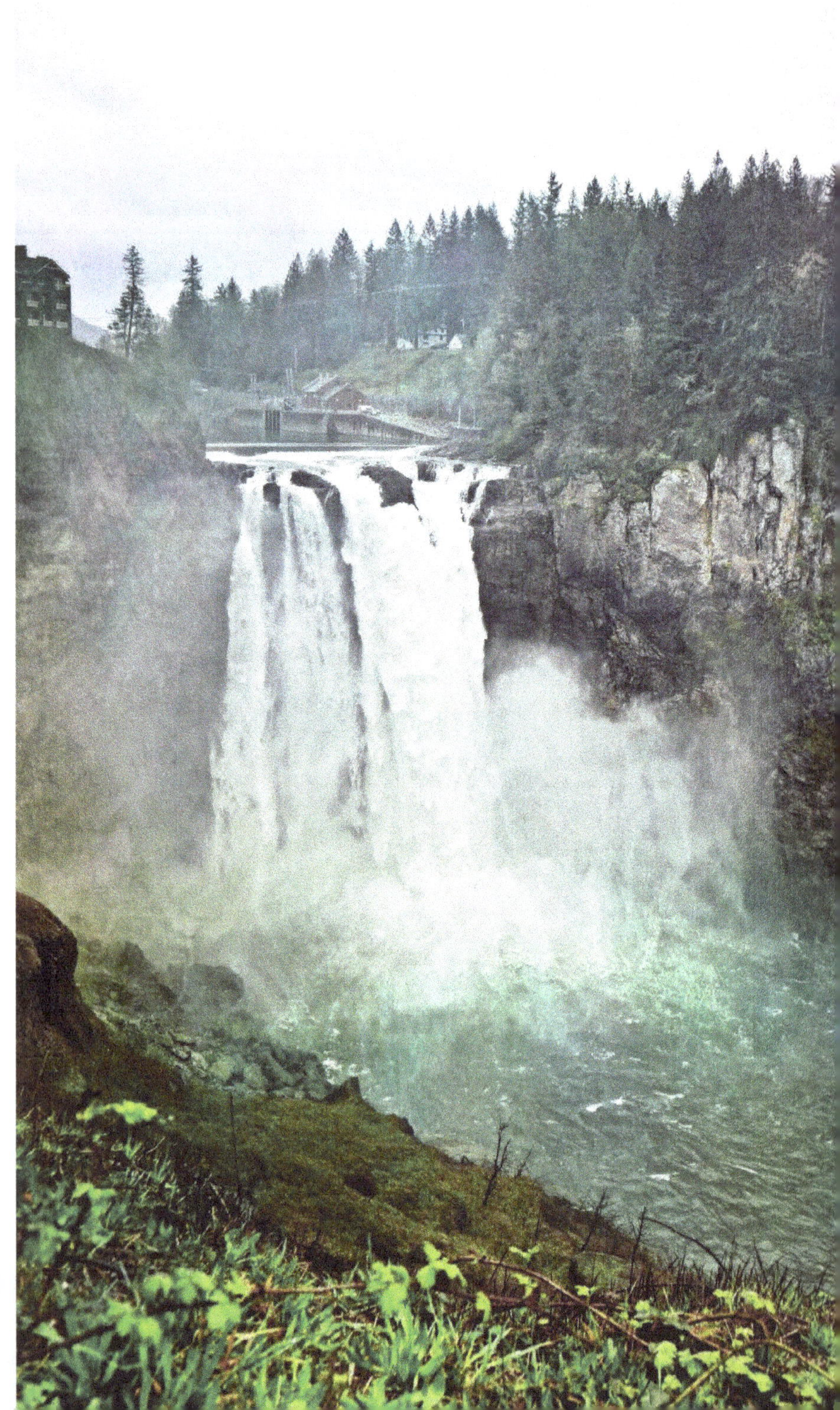

# A CLOSER LOOK
## *snoqualmie falls*

* Snoqualmie Falls is considered a 'Wonder of the West' at 270 feet, which is 100 feet taller than Niagara Falls.

* Waterfalls and rivers fed by glaciers appear milky and gray-blue because of glacial rock erosion.

* "Snoqualmie is the English pronunciation of *"sah-KOH-koh"* or *"Sdob-dwahibbluh,"* a Salish word meaning 'moon.' The Native peoples in the valley below were known as the 'people of the moon.'

* According to the Snoqualmie, a Coast Salish people, the falls carry prayers up to the Creator in the mists, which connect Heaven and Earth.

* The daredevil Mr. Blondin successfully walked a tightrope over the falls in 1889. A year later there was a fatality when another daredevil, Charlie Anderson, parachuted in from a hot-air balloon. As the horrified crowd watched, a gust of wind sent him toward the falls and into a boulder.

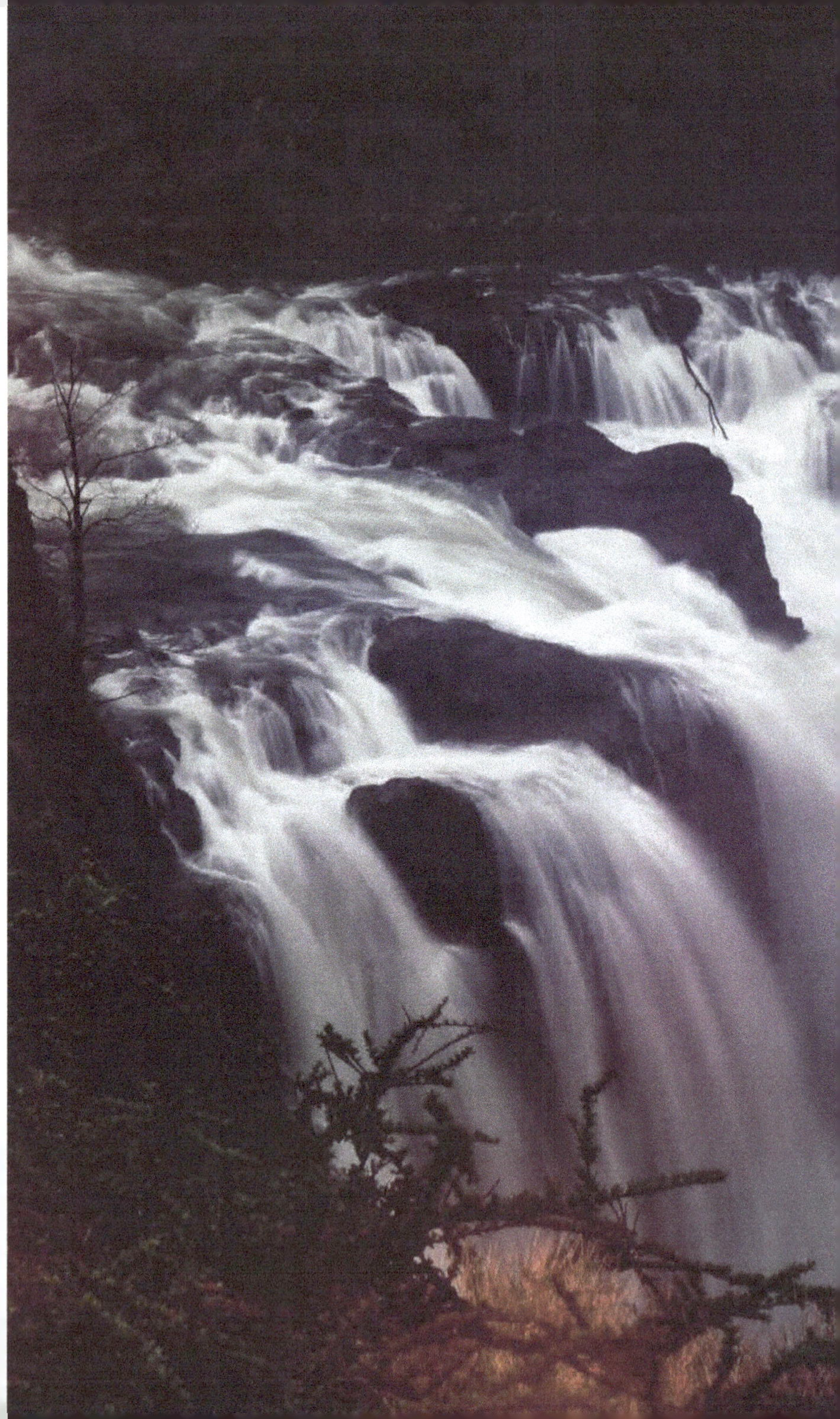

SNOQUALMIE


Go visit the Falls
in the dead of winter
when the tourists
and thin-skinned
stay inside, safe
and dry.

It will be quiet
enough to glimpse
the sacred and
imagine the prayers
that live like mists.

It will be still enough
to hear the heaven-bound
hymns of
rock and water.

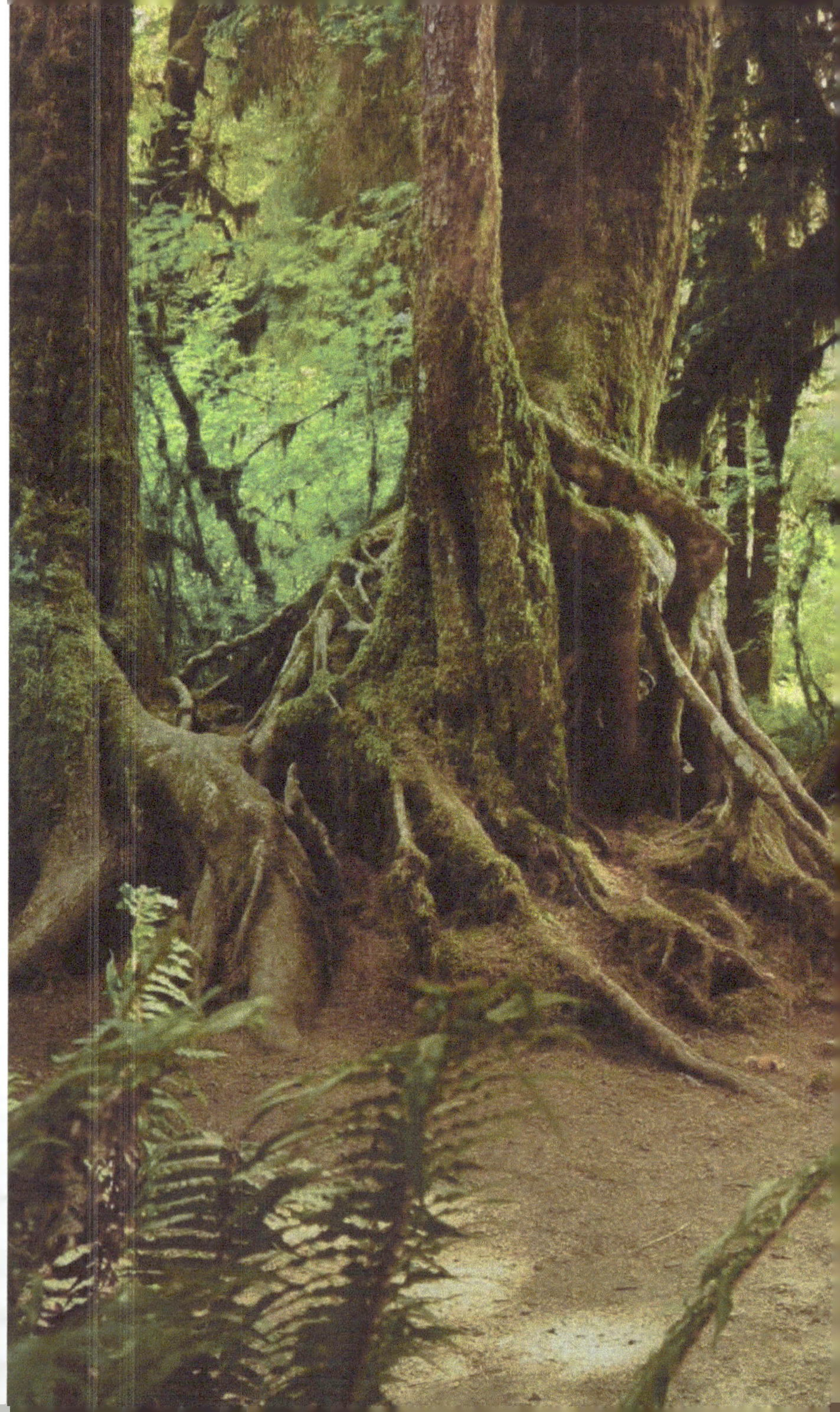

# A CLOSER LOOK
## *hoh rainforest*

The Hoh Rainforest is located on the Olympic Peninsula and is one of the world's largest temperate rainforests. There are actually four rainforests in Washington: Hoh, Bogachiel, Queets and Quinault. They're called "temperate" because they have a long, rainy season and a dry summer with abundant fog.  140" - 170" (12' to 14') of rain a year is common. Compare that to Tacoma's annual 39" (US average is 37").

Many moss and lichen live in the rainforests, requiring the moist atmosphere to grow. Moss is an *epiphyte,* a plant that grows on another plant without harm. They survive on the moisture and nutrients in the damp air.

There's a lichen that looks like lettuce called *Lobaria oregana* that grows in the rainforest. It enriches the soil and provides food to animals. It's very slow to return in logged forests.

The long strands of lichen that drape from old-growth trees are called, *Alectoria sarmentosa,* commonly known as 'witches' hair.' Deer will eat it if their food source is covered in snow. The lichen only grows in pure air and can be used for monitoring air quality.

## PURPLE MOUNTAIN MAJESTY

*Mount Storm King is a summit in the Olympic Mountain Range*

I know you
think you're immune
to miracles,
but come with me.

Let's skirt the edge
of an ancient
wild wood.
I'll show you a melancholy
sea that lives in mists.

Let's meet underneath
the tall and twisted trees
in green shade and
shadows.
Let's breath in this
silent,
sacred light.
I'll crown you Storm King
and be your
Seaweed Queen
in this last Eden.

*Cape Flattery is the northwestern-most point of the
contiguous United States and part of the Makah Reservation.*

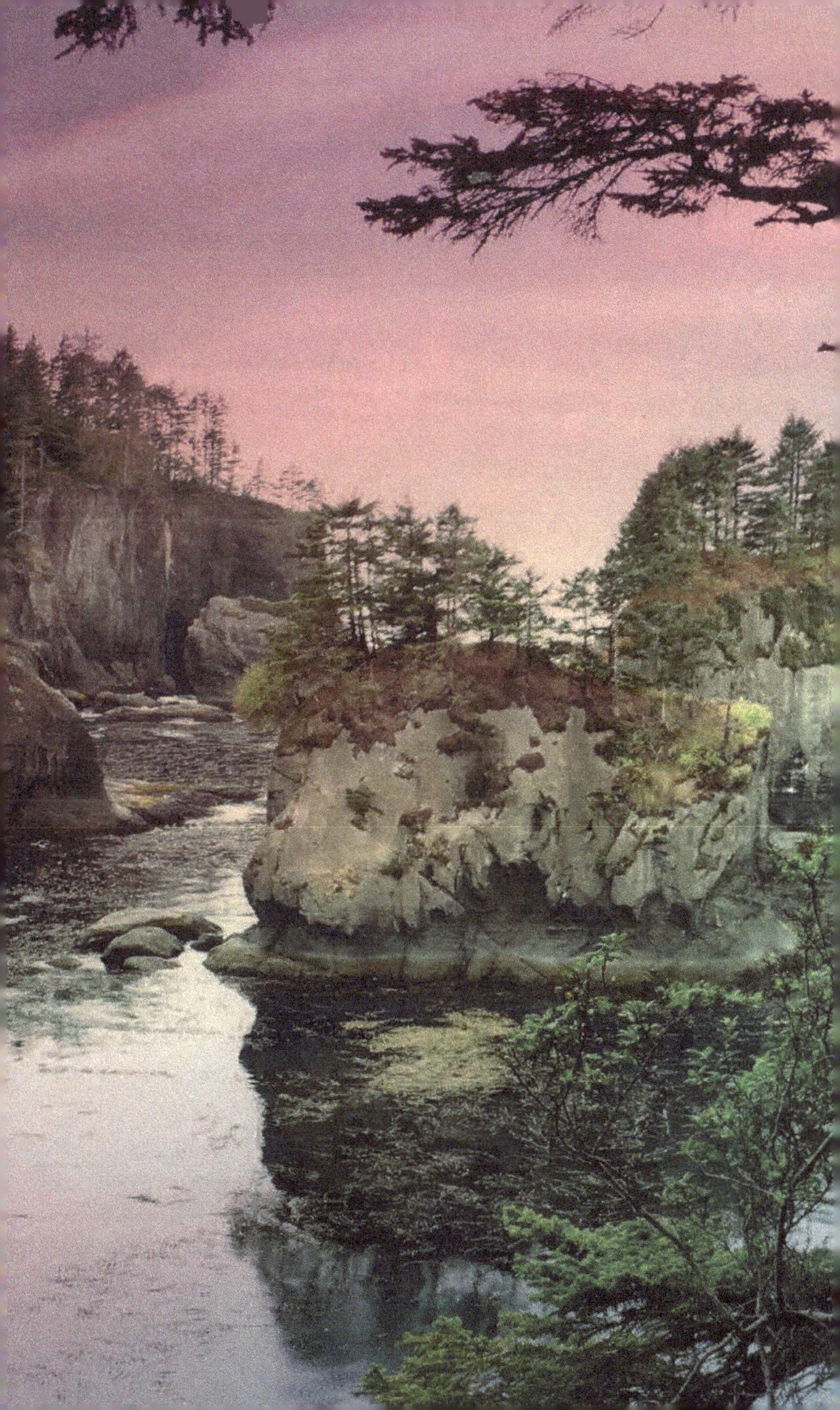

# UNDERWATER WORLD

The mighty river finds the bay
where creatures meet to hunt and play.

Seals and otters put on a show
while an alien world waits below.

Eelgrass sprout like a forest of trees.
Anemones sway in the current's breeze.

A sudden squall stirs the ocean.
Shadows drift in calm, slow motion.

When whales float by, they glide with grace,
weightless in the liquid space.

A moon snail glows in the dark blue sea
as sea stars scatter the wet galaxy.

Where seagulls dive and fish fly by
the heavens spin a twin night sky.

*Sea star*

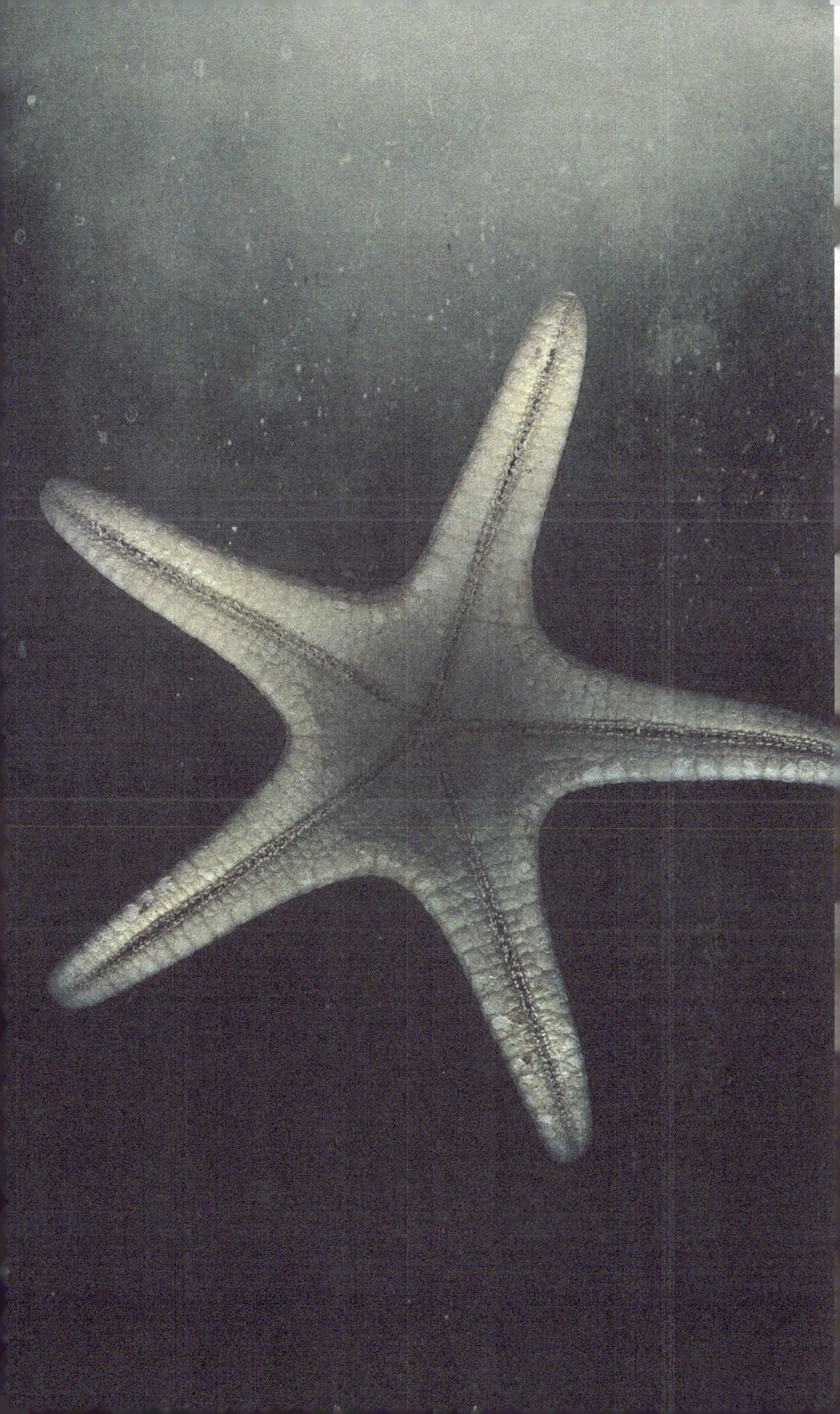

ETERNAL

Our oasis is
shrinking
and the butchery
tools have all been
sharpened.

A pause before
the mirror reveals
a quiet, hidden
grief.

We cling
to dead, dark things.

But the light is there,
it's all around us
in snowflakes and stardust –
in you.

 *Point Defiance Park, Tacoma*

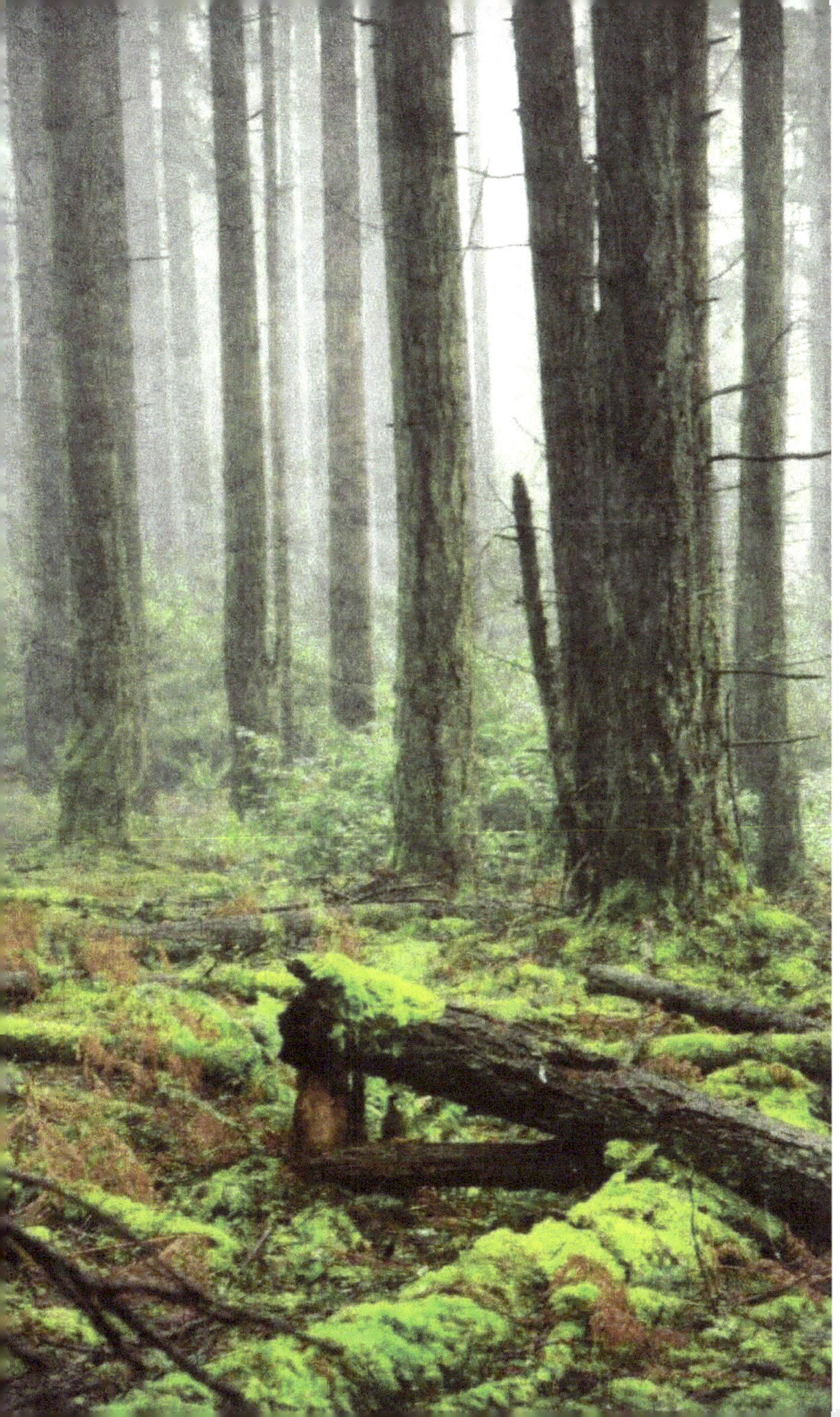

# A CLOSER LOOK
## canoes

Long before it was called the Puget Sound over 300 tribes lived in cedar-planked longhouses along Washington shores. Today, the tribes are collectively known as Coast Salish. Their language and culture were diverse, but one thing connected them: water. Water was central to transportation, food and ceremony. Distances were even calculated by how far a canoe could travel in a day.

The Salish were hunters and gatherers with a focus on salmon fishing. As expert mariners, they traveled waterways in beautifully crafted dugout canoes. Each one was made from a western red cedar log. Some of the larger canoes could carry up to 100 people, while most were much smaller.

The designs were also specific for whether the canoes were used inland or on the open ocean for whaling. In rough water, seal-skin bladders were tied to the canoe's sides to keep them steady.

Crafting a canoe was a spiritual process, from selecting the wood to cutting the tree down and shaping it. The craftsman prepared for it by fasting and prayer.

A great deal of ceremony was involved as each canoe was considered a living thing with a spirit. A skilled carver could make two large canoes or four small ones from a typical tree trunk; it could take two years from start to finish.

When European explorers arrived, the Coast Salish people sometimes traded services with them, ferrying early mountaineers out of the Olympics via the waterways and rivers to the sea.

The culture surrounding the canoe has had a revival thanks to Tribal Canoe Journeys, which are organized by the Indigenous peoples of the Pacific Northwest. Every year a different Nation hosts and thousands of people participate. Once the canoes arrive at their host shore, the families ask permission to land, usually in their native language. In 2016 the theme was, "Don't Forget the Water."

## THE SALISH SEA

We take for granted
this blue water
the mountains furred in
moss and cedar,
the ocean's exhalations,
her immortal majesty
and silent passages
where deceptive depths
crush and quiet bones
where splintered wood and
salt-brined skin
are nothing in this scheme, but small acts
of courage and defiance.

Our native tongues are gone
and we have lost our way
with words that don't add up.

This long forgotten language,
is carried on the waves,
echoes glimpsed between
the squalls.

Intone these names
and know what's lost
when you forget
the birch bark
boats are gone,
mingled with the forest floor,
but strong trees once again.



*Quileute tribal member fishing the Quillayute River*
*(Next page: Dungeness Spit)*

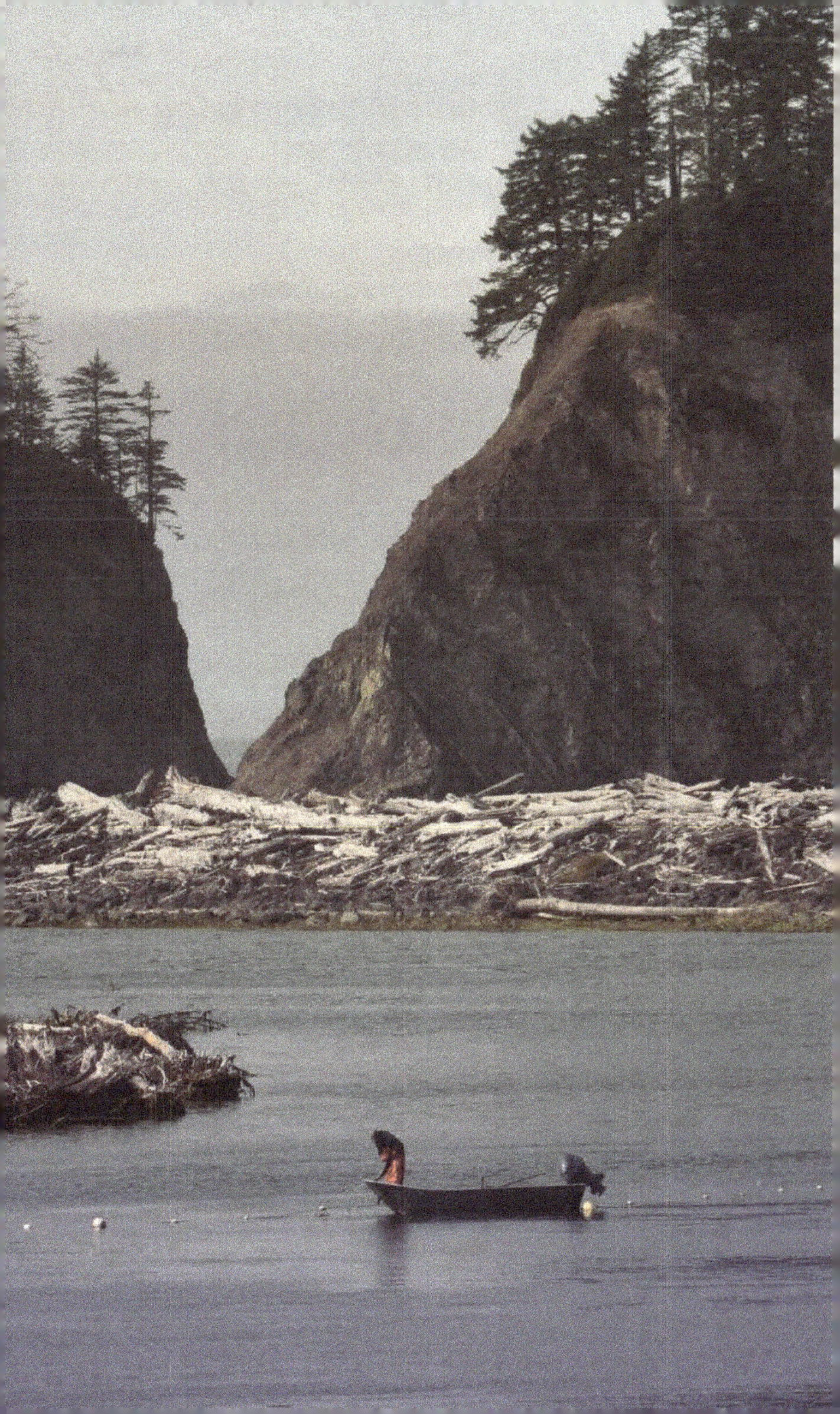

Lummi, Nooksack, Klallam, Skagit, Samish,

Swinomish, Sauk-Suiattle, Tulalip,

Snohomish, Duwamish, Snoqualmie,

Muckleshoot, Sammamish,

Puyallup, Nisqually, Sahewamish,

Skokomish, Suquamish,

S'Klallam

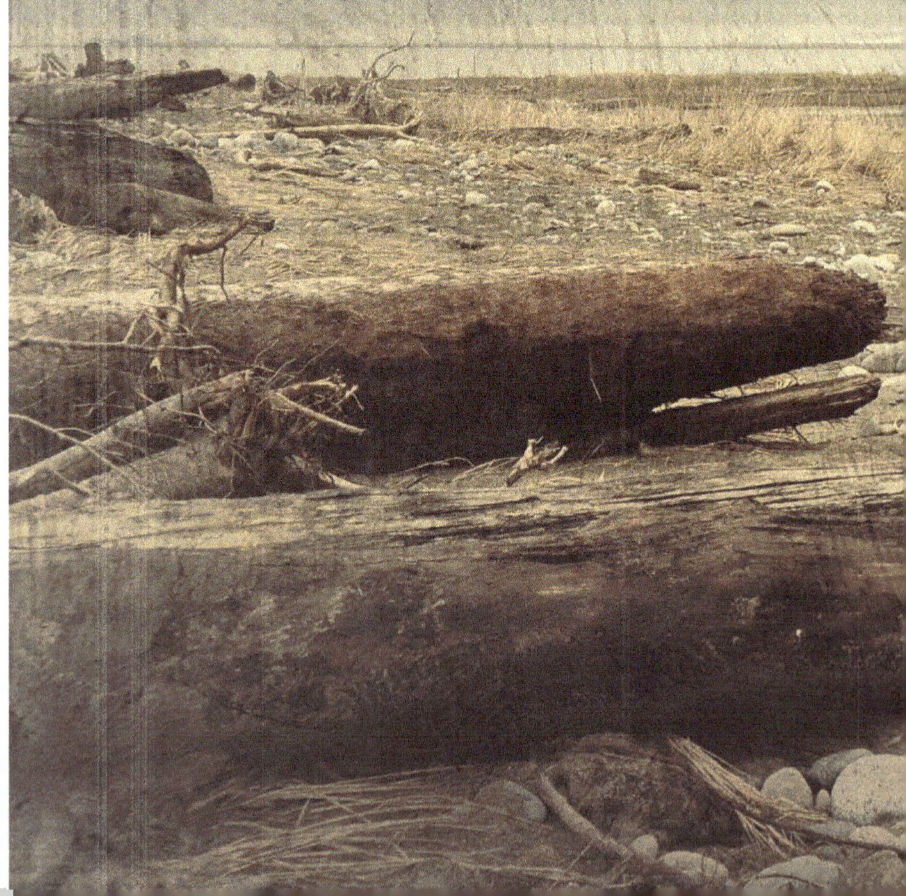

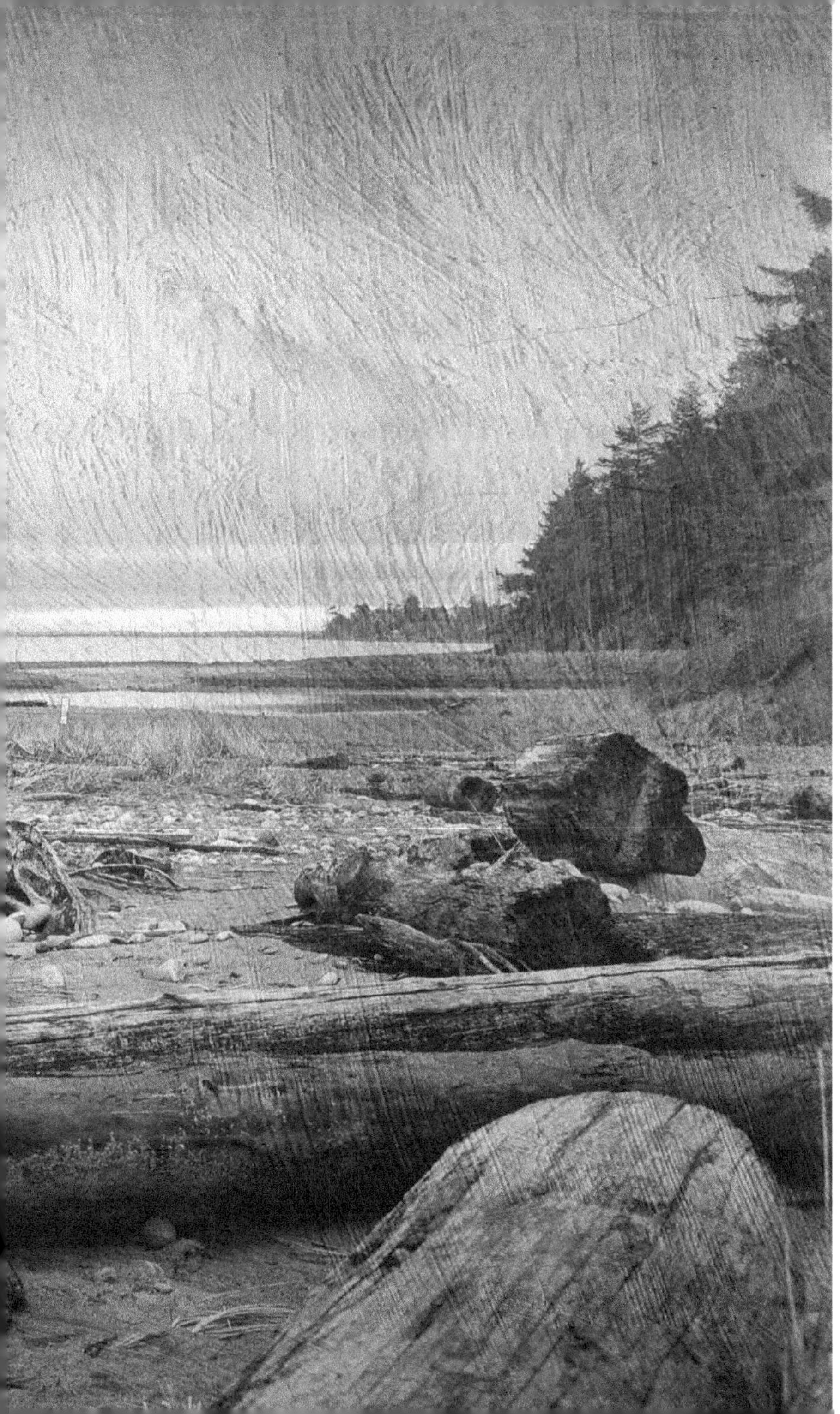

# HAWSER

*A thick rope or cable for mooring and towing a ship.*

Washington beaches
show their
age.

A wind and water
reincarnation
is slow and lives
beyond remembered
generations.

Their karmic
liberation plods
forward in crumbled
rocks orphaned
from the mainland,
they cast off.



*Ruby Beach, Olympic National Park*

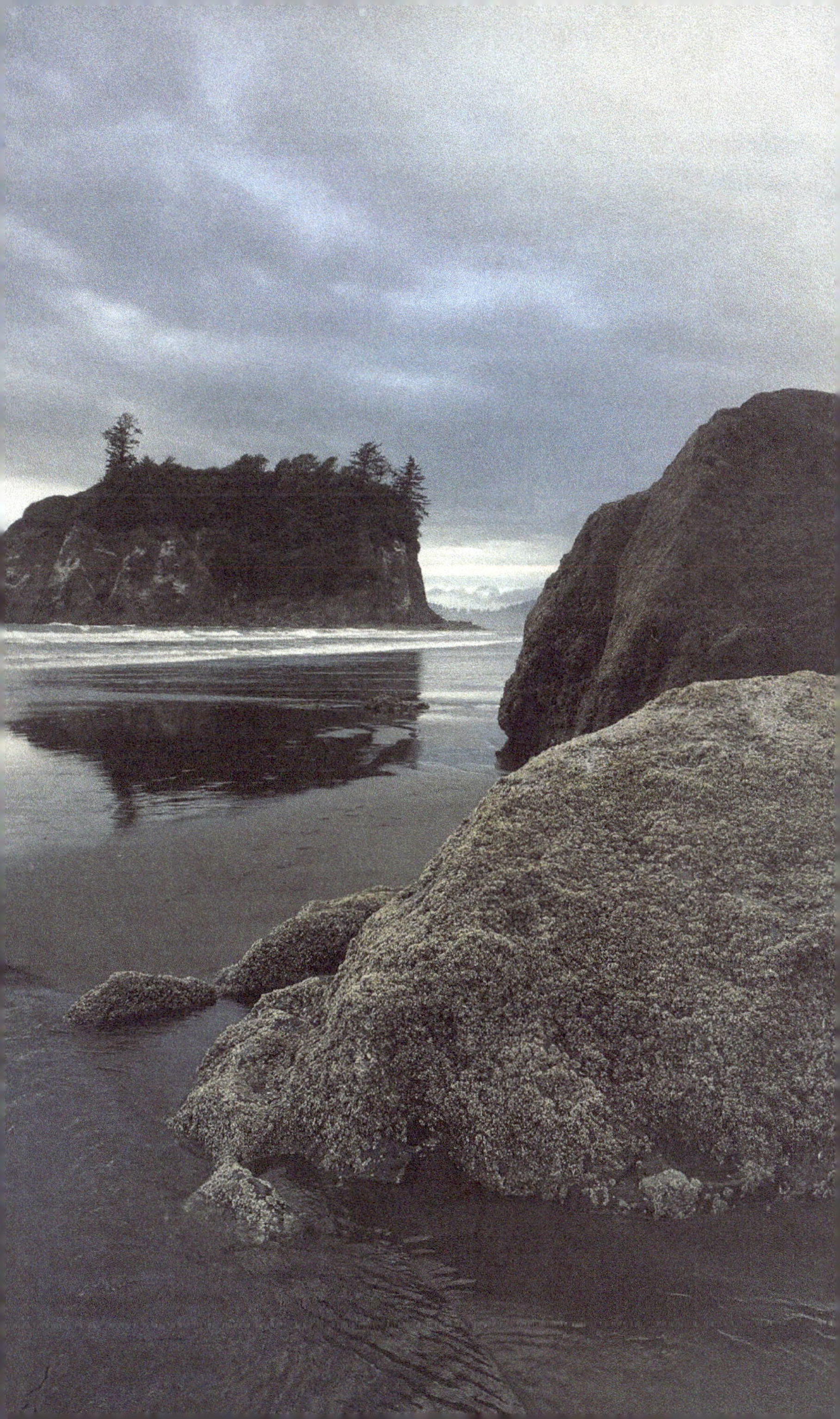

# DRIFTWOOD

The sea's
detritus,
sun bleached
bones,
mysterious
fossils of
unknown origin
all gather here.

Somewhere up
river, the water
pulled them in and
they saw more
in an hour than
100 years tied
to shore.

Most driftwood begins its journey inland,<br>
where fallen trees sweep downriver to the sea.<br>
(Next page: Tacoma Narrows Bridges from Gig Harbor)

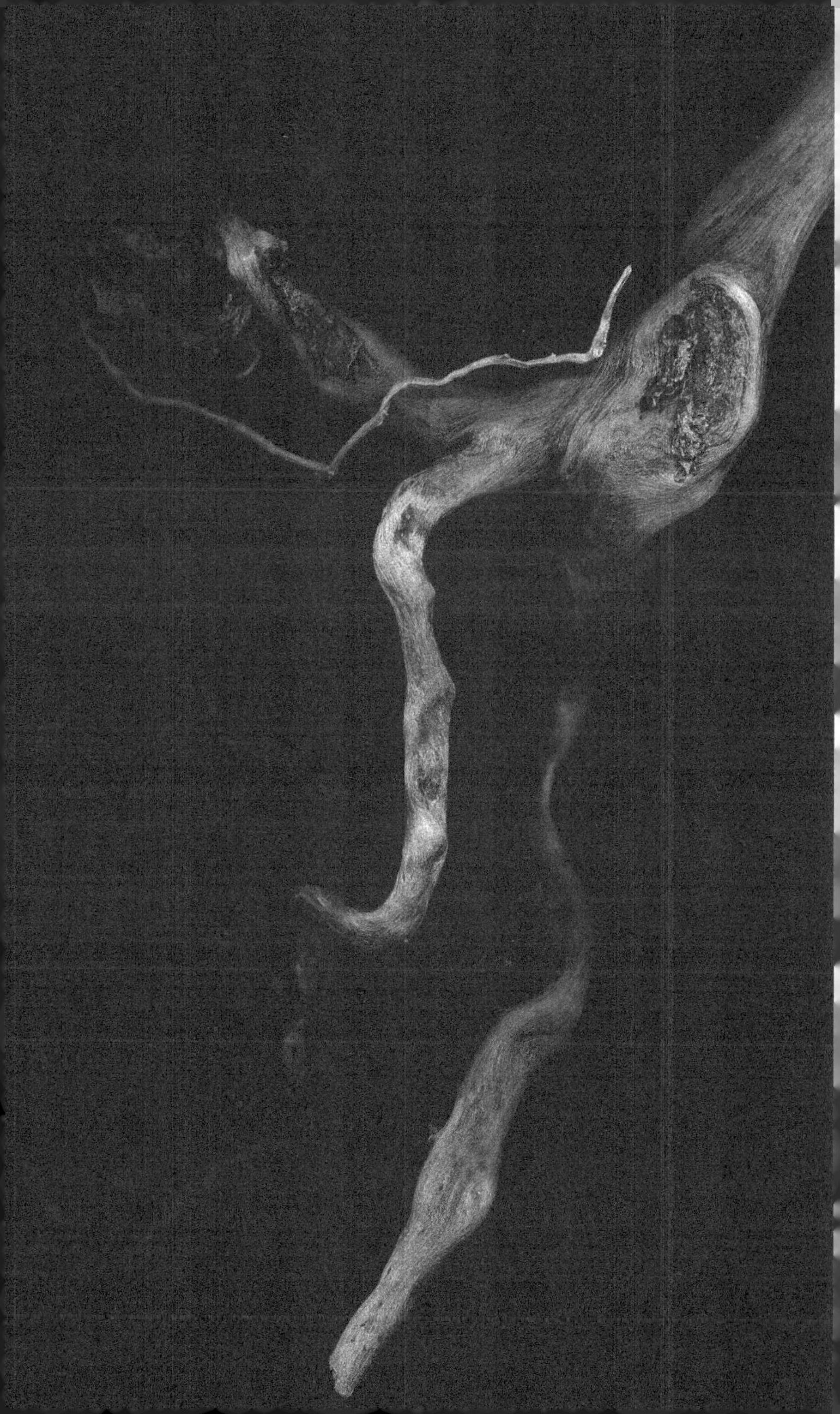

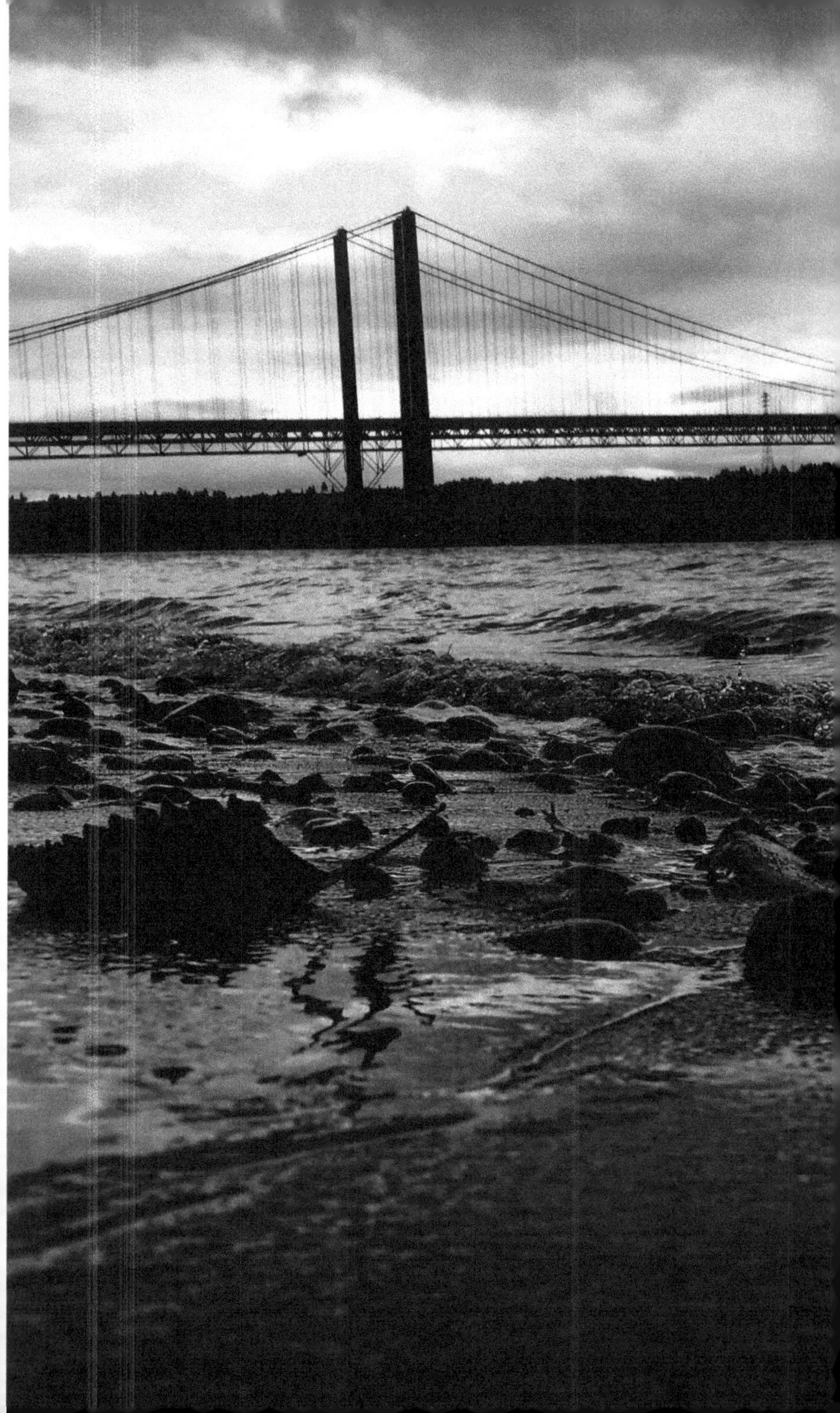

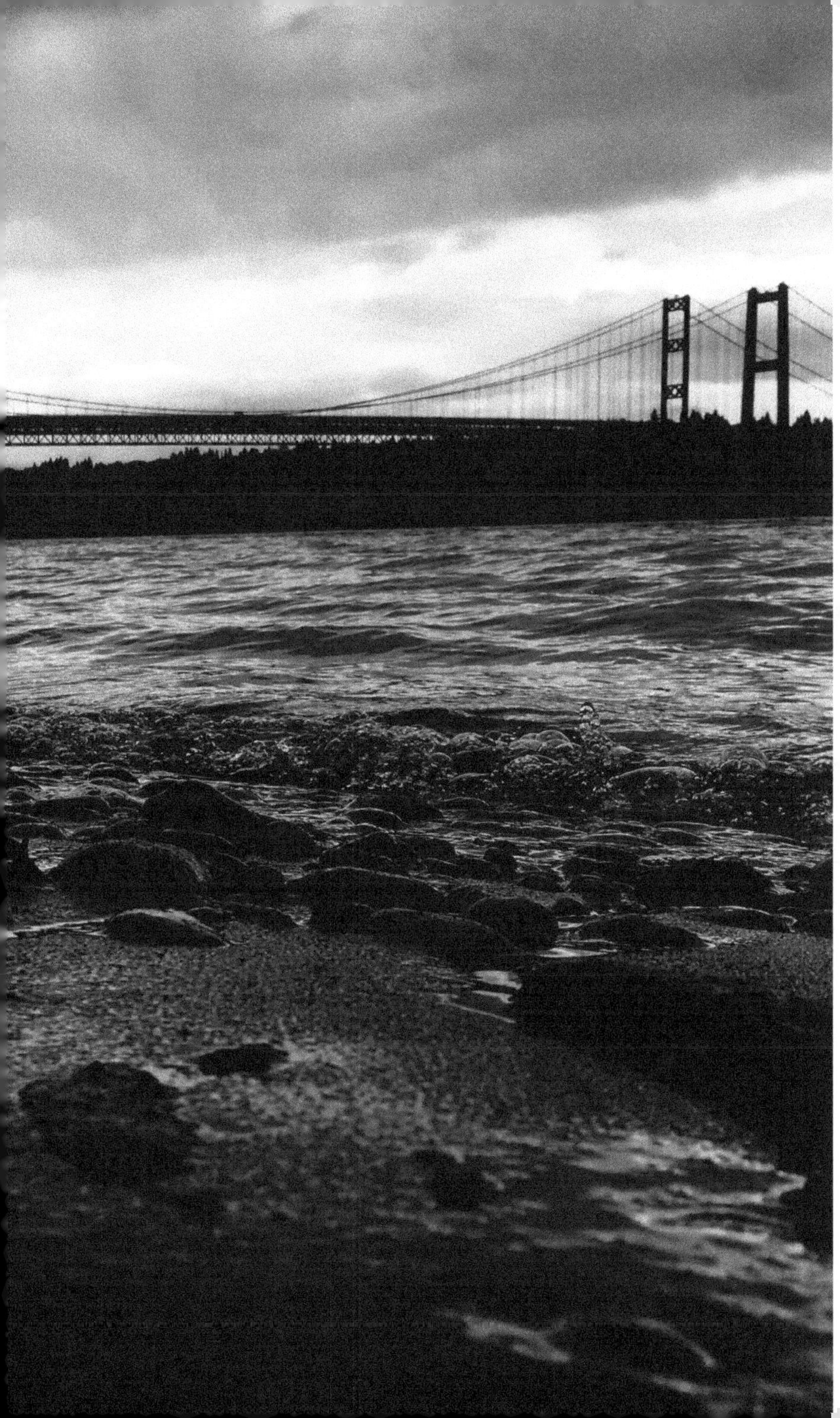

## LAST DANCE

*"Galloping Gertie" was the nickname given to the first suspension bridge that spanned the Tacoma Narrows. The bridge opened July 1, 1940 and collapsed into the Puget Sound November 7th because of a design flaw known as aerostatic flutter, which made it susceptible to twisting in the wind.*

Under the rumble
and din
far below the girders
and struts
a silent blue
inverted sky is
spangled with
stars.

And an octopus picks
his way through the bones
of an old, nervous bridge
that danced its way
to the bottom of
the sea.

*Closeup of a starfish arm*

# A CLOSER LOOK

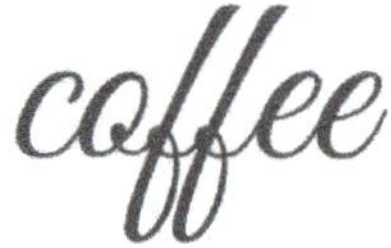

* Seattleites consume more coffee than any other city dwellers in the United States.

* Coffee cupping, AKA coffee tasting, is a popular practice in Washington where enthusiasts gather to judge the taste and aroma of coffee. Similar to wine tasting, flavor profiles are discussed along with mouth feel, aroma, color, proper brewing technique and, of course, taste.

* Dark roast coffee has less caffeine than light because roasting burns off caffeine.

* Coffee with cream cools 20% slower than plain black coffee.

* In 1511, coffee was banned in Mecca and then by Italian clergy. However, Pope Clement VIII loved coffee so much that he lifted the ban and baptized it.

* The Specialty Coffee Association of America provides a Coffee Taster's Flavor Wheel and lists strict water standards on their website. Coffee is, after all, 98.75% water.

Dungeness Bay

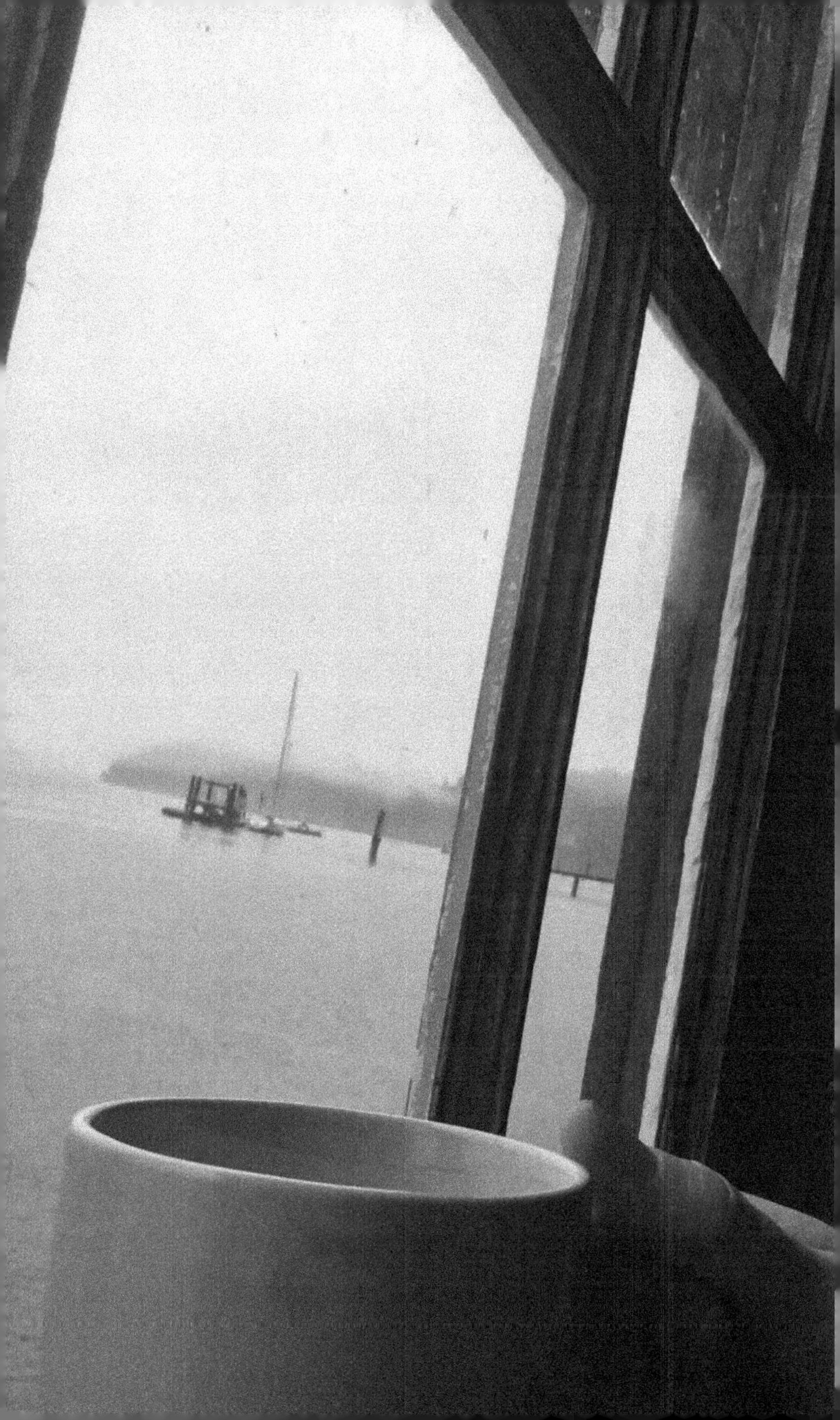

## A WAKE

I've known obliteration
and I just want to wander home
hidden in the dark wood
where sunlight cannot penetrate.
I've asked for your wet blessings,
but I'm still made of dust.

Why is it so hard
to walk down to the river?
Why are we so hobbled
seeking out these mysteries?

This is the prayer of all things
pulsing –
to return
like salmon
to our headwaters.

*Mussel shell*

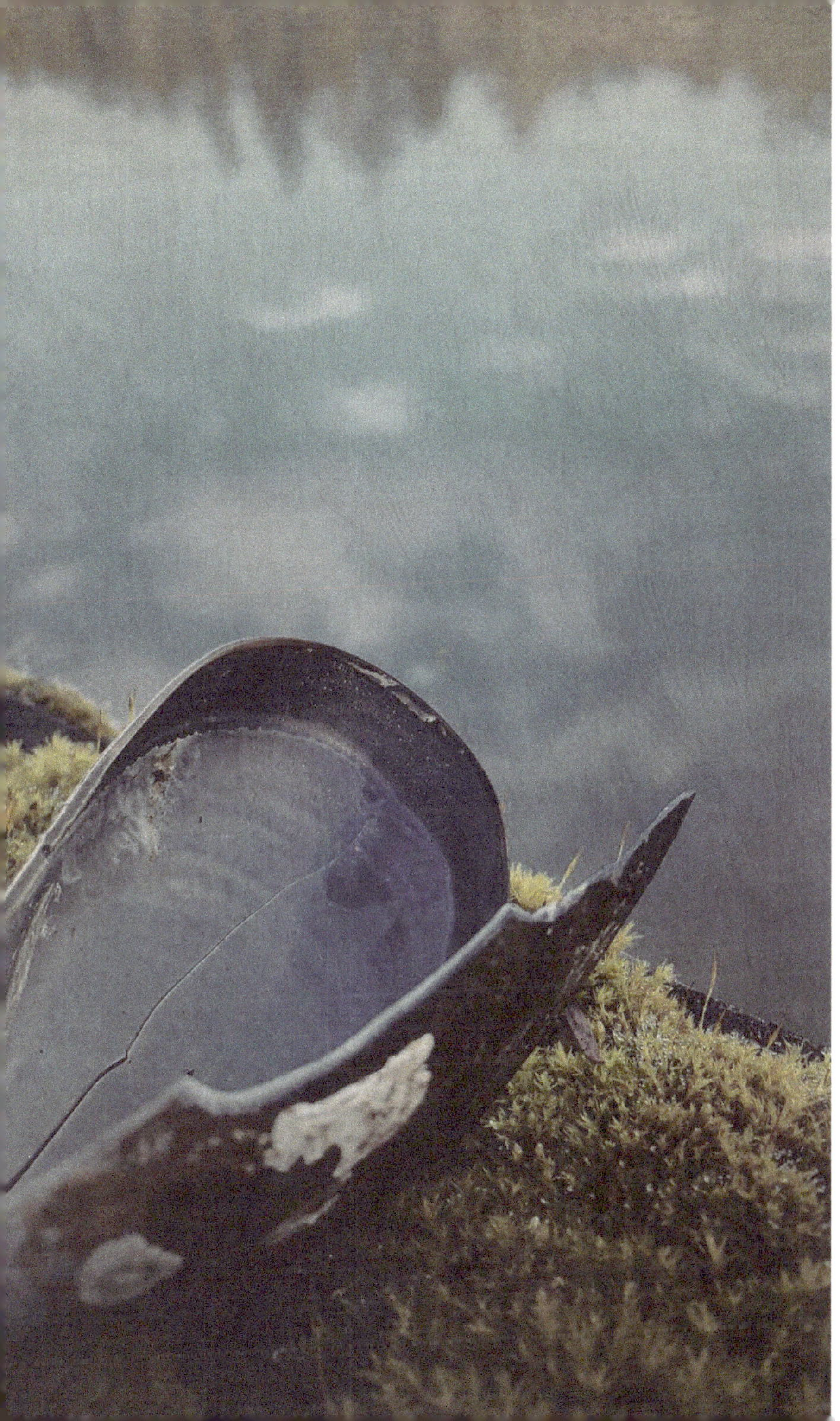

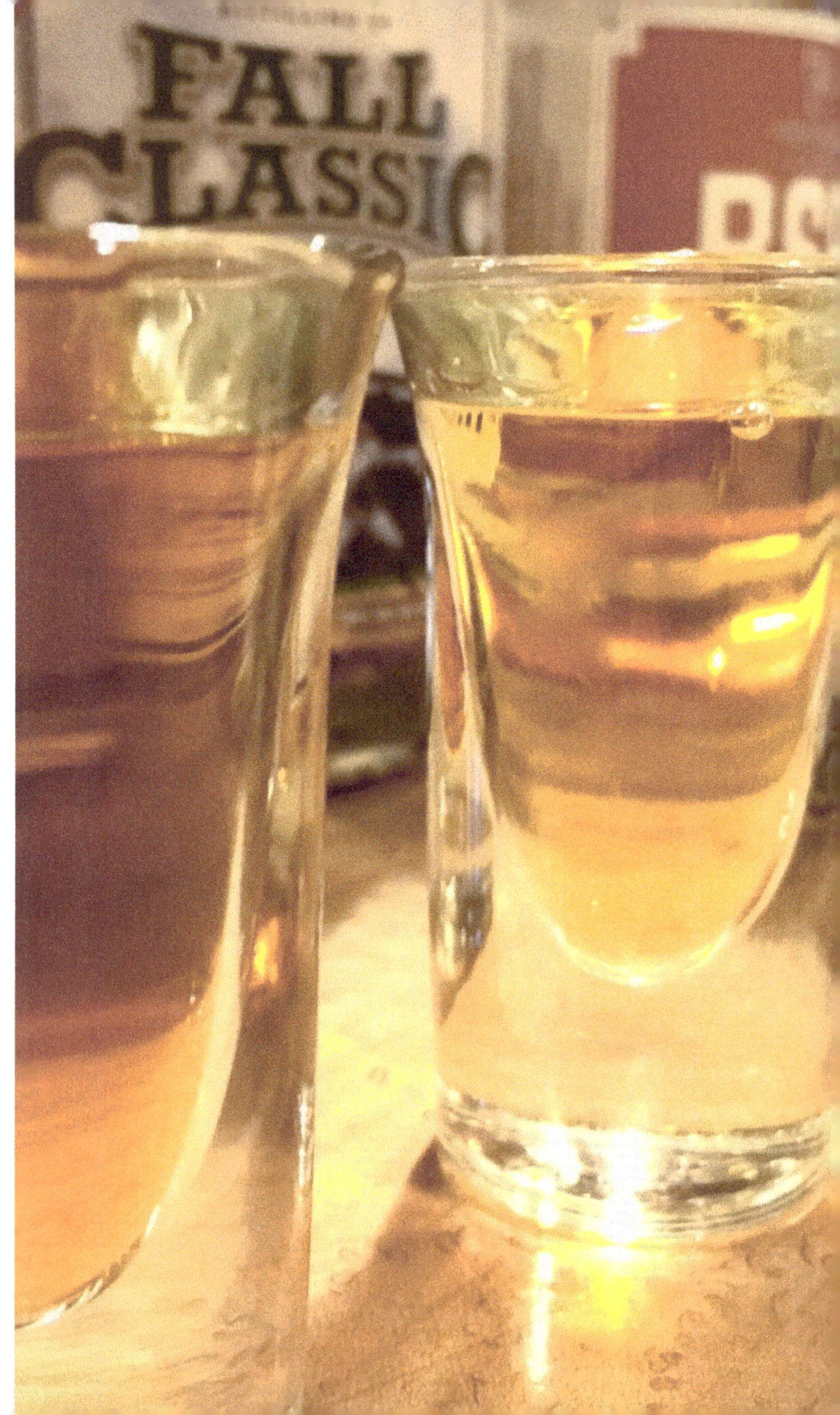
FALL
CLASSIC

# A CLOSER LOOK
## breweries and distilleries

* Washington ranks #7 for the number of craft breweries in the U.S. with 340 in operation.

* Tumwater's Olympia Brewing Co. (1896-1983) was famous for using local, artesian water in their beer. Their slogan was, "It's the Water." This same water can be found at the Artesian Commons in Olympia for public use. The well is about 90' deep and 10 gallons flow per minute. Some residents use it as their primary water source.

* The fertile Yakima Valley is responsible for over 77% of the United States hop crop. The desert climate and plentiful water from the Yakima River ensures its success.

* Local distilleries make interesting use of water. A Graham farmer delivers his artesian well water for Tacoma's Old Soldier Distillery to use in their whiskey. They trade him *wash* from the distilling process, which adds nutrients to his hay. The Chambers Bay distillery stores bourbon barrels in a secret boathouse where the constant rocking aids the aging process. Gig Harbor's Heritage Distilling Company has several artesian wells and the pure water is the foundation of their spirits.

*Heritage Distilling Company, Gig Harbor*

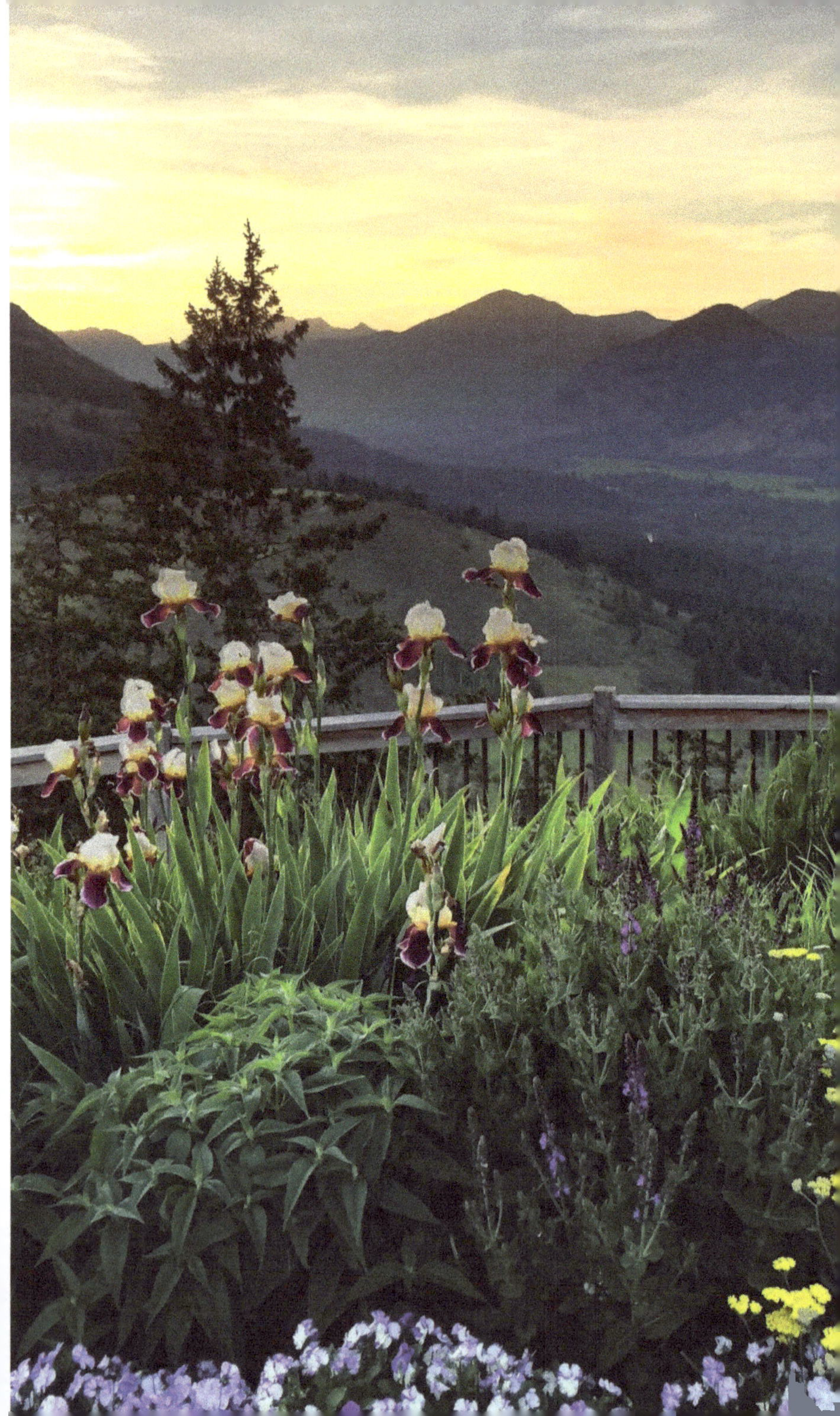

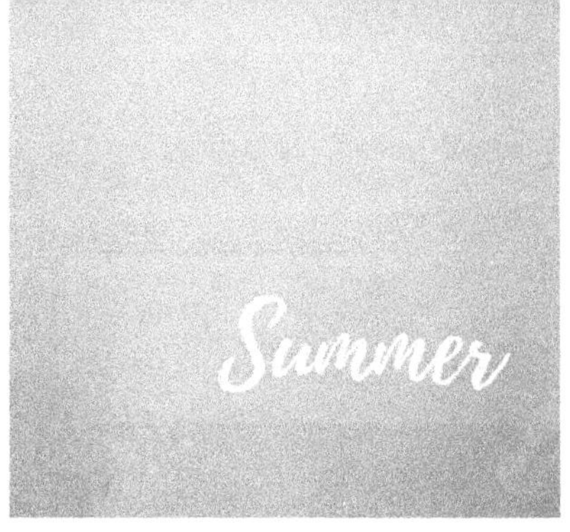


Washington summers are warm and generally dry. And thanks to all the rain for the past eight months, everything is green! This is the season for road trips, visiting the shore and harvesting crops.

Eastern Washington's grain, fruit and vegetables are ready to be shipped and sent around the world. They're transported from the fields several different ways.

Barges on the Columbia-Snake river system handle 40% of the nation's wheat exports. Tacoma and Seattle have natural, deep-water bays, which make them excellent, world class ports. Goods are loaded onto trucks, trains and ships via *intermodal* yards.

In 2015, Washington experienced a drought, which many were surprised could even happen. It occured because of a low snow pack from the previous year and a record-setting hot summer. The state emerged from it thanks to plentiful rain and snow.

*Winthrop*

FRESH

All nature
is born again
in the rain,
especially when it
comes at night,
quiet as cat feet,
and you wake
to see leaves
and flowers,
the garden shed
and even your black
rubber boots, transformed
into something new
that reawakens
something old and
familiar.



*Vineyard in Walla Walla*

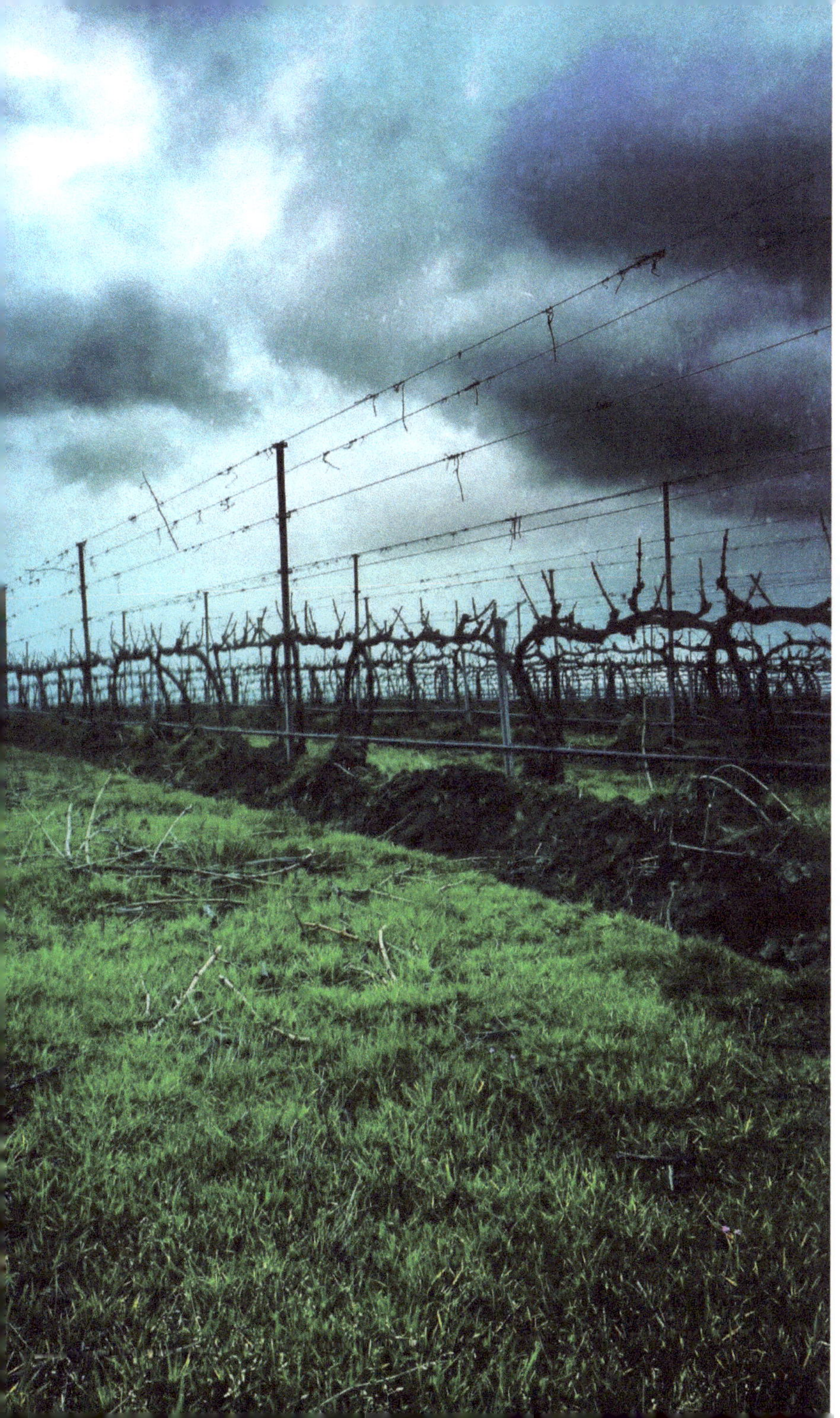

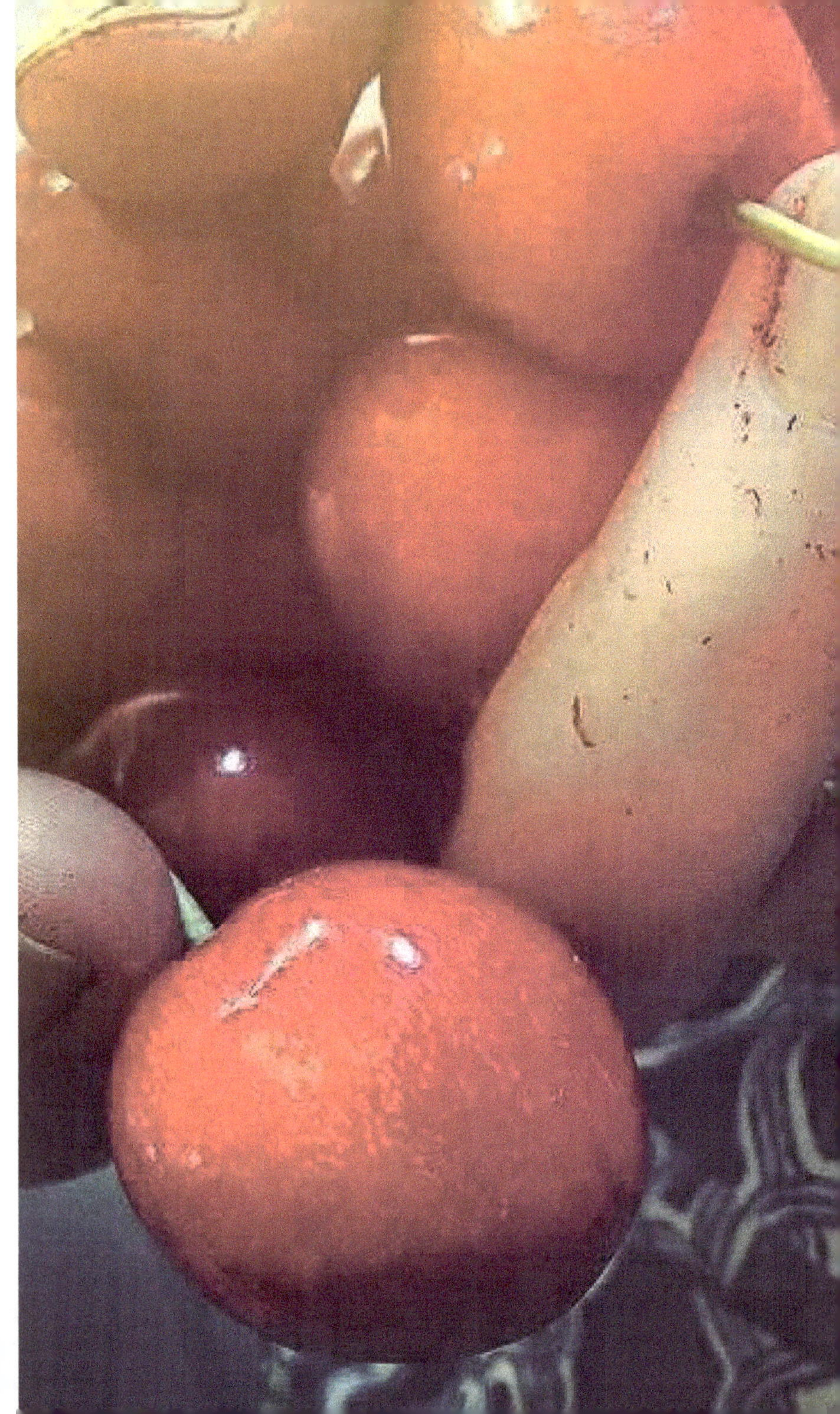

# A CLOSER LOOK
## *agriculture*

* Washington ranks #1 in the United States for 11 crops including: apples, raspberries, hops, spearmint oil, peppermint oil, wrinkled seed pods, sweet cherries, pears, Concord grapes, carrots and green peas.

* Agriculture in Eastern Washington consumes the most amount of water in the state with over 1.8 million acres of irrigated farmland. Put another way, it accounts for nearly 80% of the water consumed in the state. For example, in the town of Prosser 6-8" of rain falls a year and an apple orchard requires 42." Even with this huge amount of water consumed, it's still only 4% of the renewable water available in the Columbia River Basin.

* Water for Washington's crops is sourced from the Columbia, Snake and Yakima river watersheds. All three rivers join near Tri-Cities where they become one and head to the Pacific Ocean as the Columbia.

## THE GREEN MERMAID

The city sleeps
on the water
Pacifica – my found
Atlantis.

Kayaks wait patiently
to sliver through the
blue.
Ferries, water taxis,
boats and paddle boards
all part of the show
all dancing on the
shimmering Sound
threading the water
into unseen and
easily loosened
knots.

*Seattle from Alki Beach*

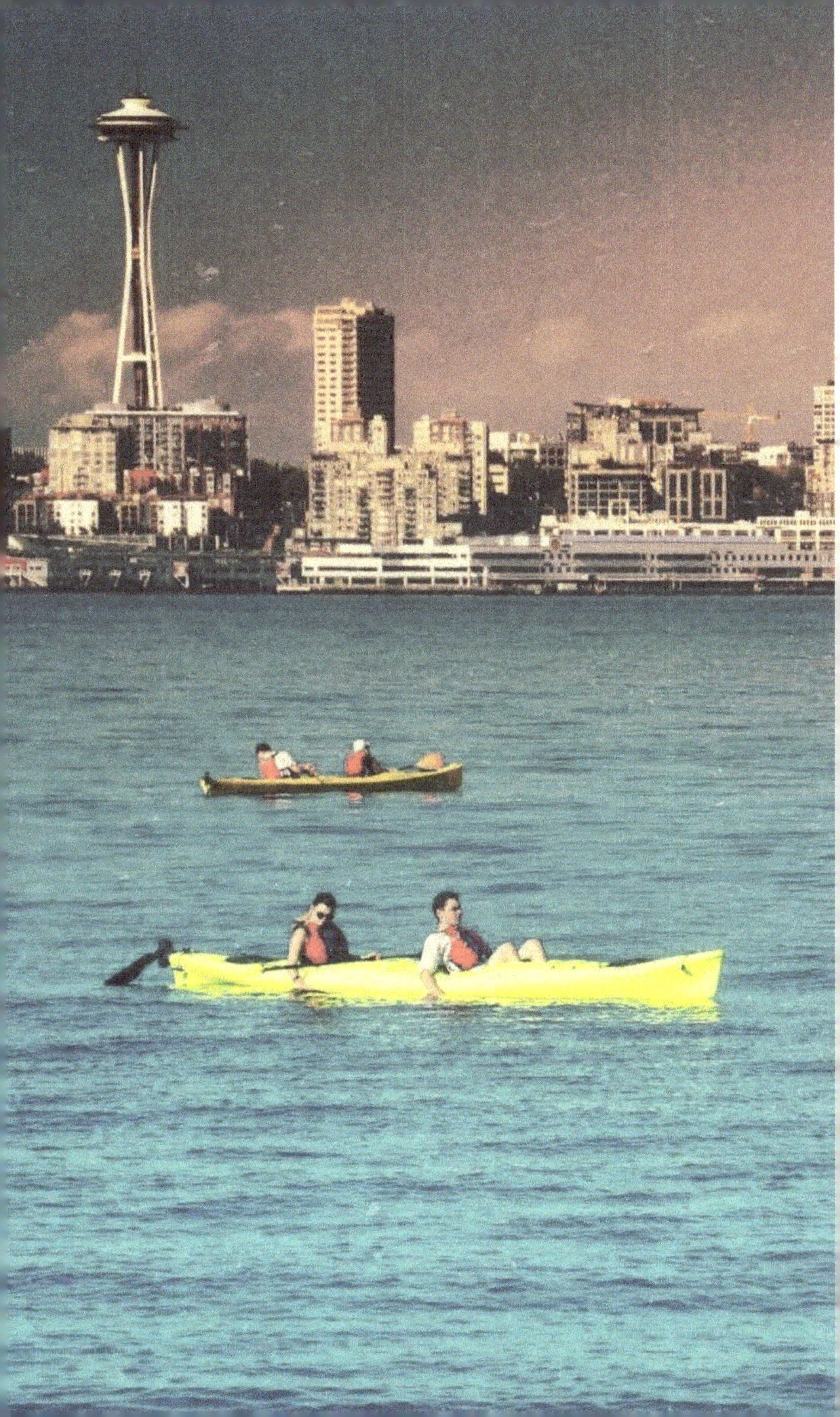

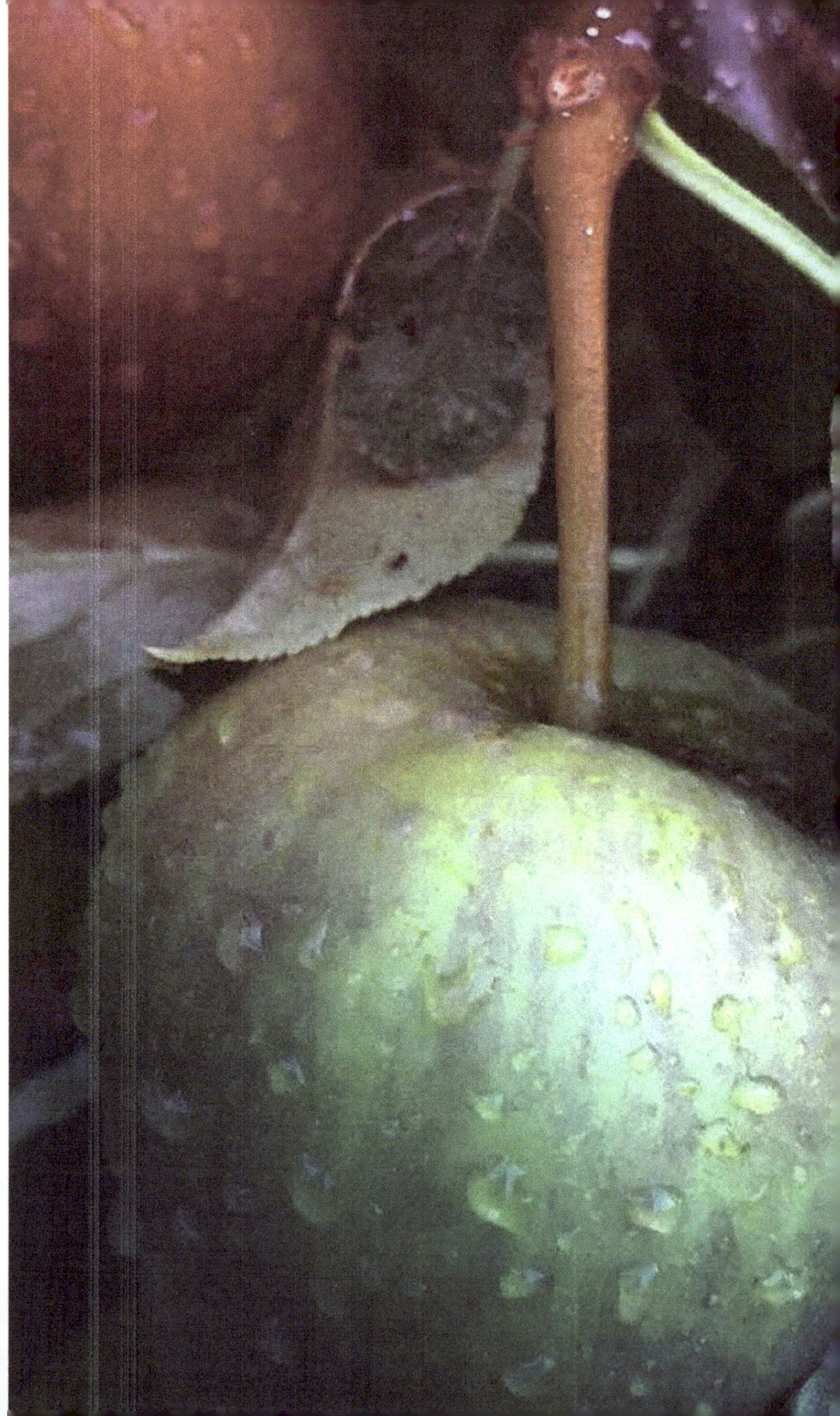

# A CLOSER LOOK
## *apples*

*   The apple became Washington's official state fruit in 1989. They are its biggest agricultural crop with over 10 billion produced every year. Each one is handpicked.

*   If you put one harvest year of Washington's apples side-by-side, they would circle the earth 29 times.

*   6 out of every 10 apples eaten in the United States are from Washington.

* The majority of apple production occurs in Eastern Washington. The Columbia, Yakima and Snake River watersheds irrigate the orchards.

* Apples originated in Kazakhstan and were carried along the Silk Road trade route. Crabapples are the only apple native to North America.

* Growers recommend that you refrigerate apples to keep them crisp and tasty.

* Apples are rich in antioxidants, flavanoids and fiber. Their phytonutrients and antioxidants may help reduce the risk of cancer, hypertension, diabetes and heart disease.

TWO STATES AWAY

I came from a land of long summers
and soft seasons, where groves woke to the sun
and the lemon, orange and grapefruit
trees bowed to the ground
heavy with fruit, their citrus scent
drifting over aqua pools on hot afternoons.

Bright, wet swimsuits,
rinsed and wrung out,
hung in backyards and bathtubs,
dripping chlorine water.

Days of gauzy clothes
brushed bare arms and thighs
warm with honey nights.
Linen, cotton, something cool and light,
so the air would taste of skin.

Here, the legend Pacific
came ashore and its blond beaches
spread out, indifferent.

Oil derricks pumped the flanks
of Signal Hill's forgotten forest.

Surfers watched for waves
above skimming rays,
schools of fish, sharks and dolphins.
Everything was kissed with salt,
with sun.

*Wollochet Bay, Gig Harbor*

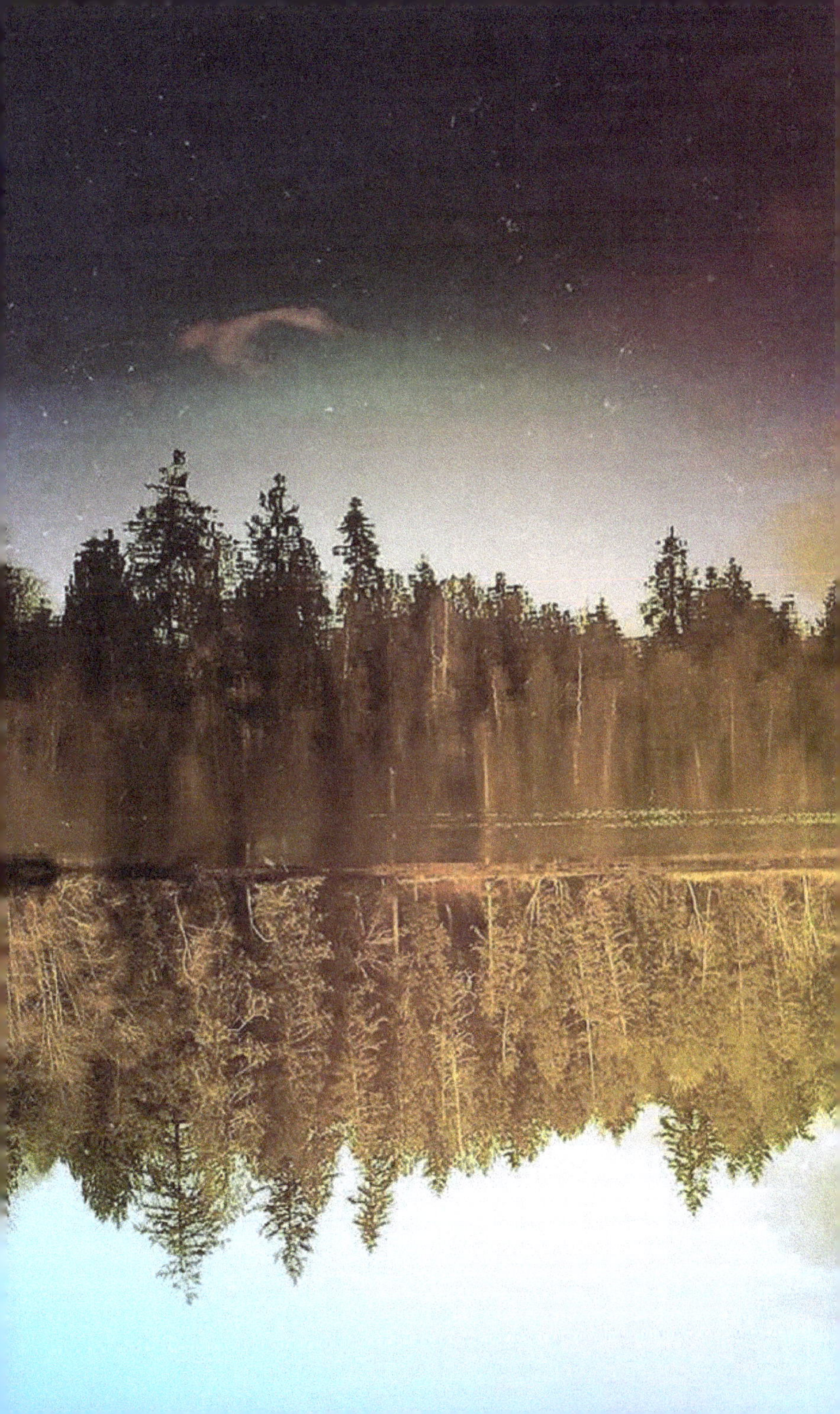

At the close of summer,
that sun grew fiercer
in its arc across the sky.

The Santa Anas whipped fires into frenzies
swept up scrub brush and scoured hillsides
until there was nothing left but
hard packed dirt and the odor of
weedy herbs drifting
in the charred air.

Beautiful, but dead missions
in their tucked away places
filled with Hitchcock lore,
waiting patiently for the devout,
the trinket seekers
and kept silent when photographers
delighted over a palm frond shadow
on a plaster wall.

Now, I live in a land so wet, so ripe with life
fir trees sprout like weeds.

Inlets, bays, harbors, coves, lagoons
they carve the green-flanked landscapes
into shelters.

The Sound itself, is a long
sinuous curve of relief
from the open ocean
lapping gentle shores, like an endless lake.
opening to its headwaters.

We are almost cut in two by the Salish Sea
Here, half the world is underwater.

Clams lay snug in the sand,
a strange-shaped fruit,
waiting to be plucked
from the shoreline's orchards.

Oysters in briny beds
plump up in their calcified shells,
hiding iridescence in the dark,
as seals dart in the murky water
popping up to blink and
dip towards passing kayaks.

Far below the white capped waves,
tentacles tumble over Gertie's
rusted struts in a never-ending caress
of her too skinny skeleton.

Rich dark soil spreads out beneath
a sleeping volcano,
testifying to its belly's fire.

I live in a land so wet, so ripe with life
fir trees sprout like weeds.

*(Next page: Ruby Beach)*

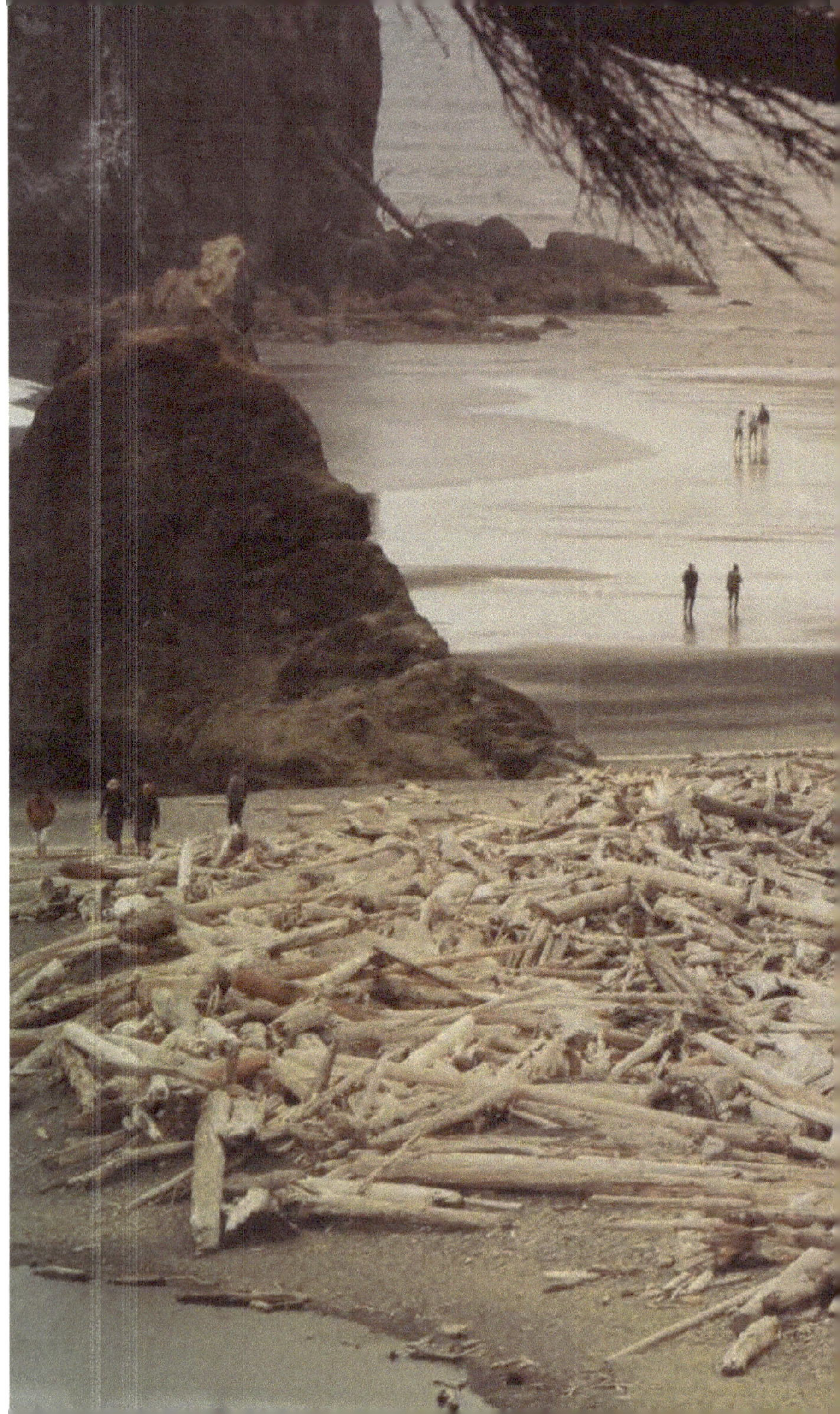

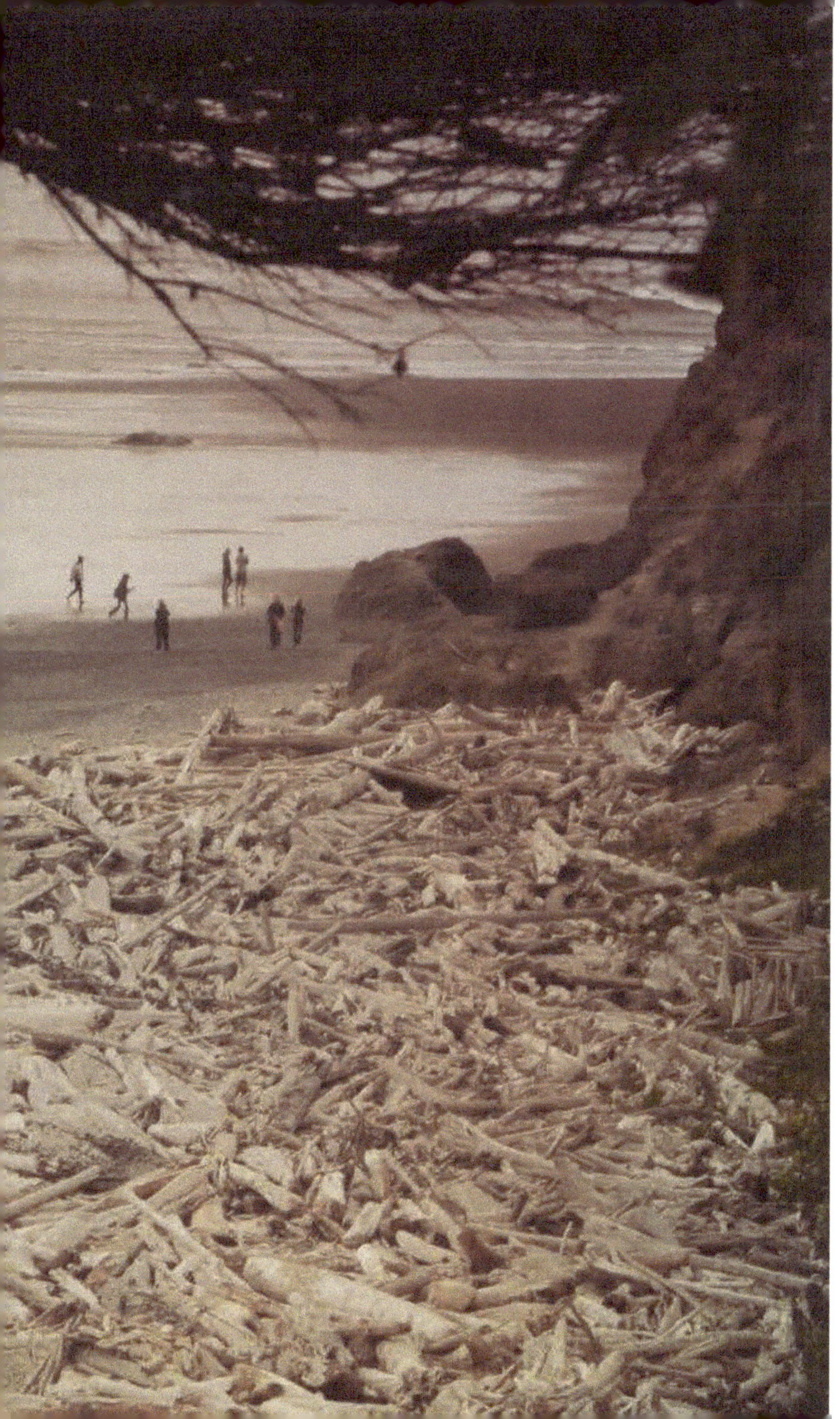

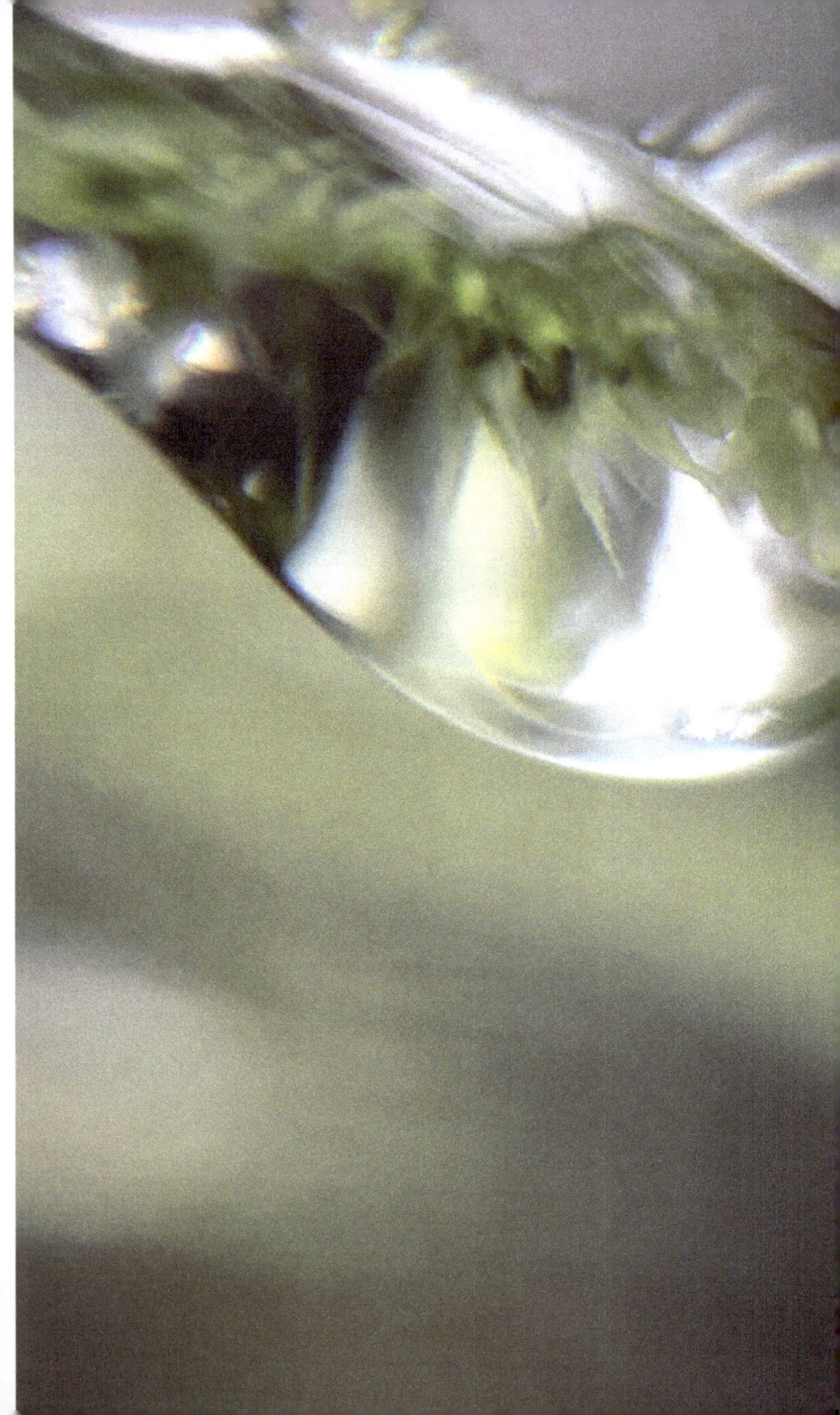

DRIP

Each drop
perfection
the tremulous
sphere
a fragile mirror
reflecting as it falls
a single silent

witness.

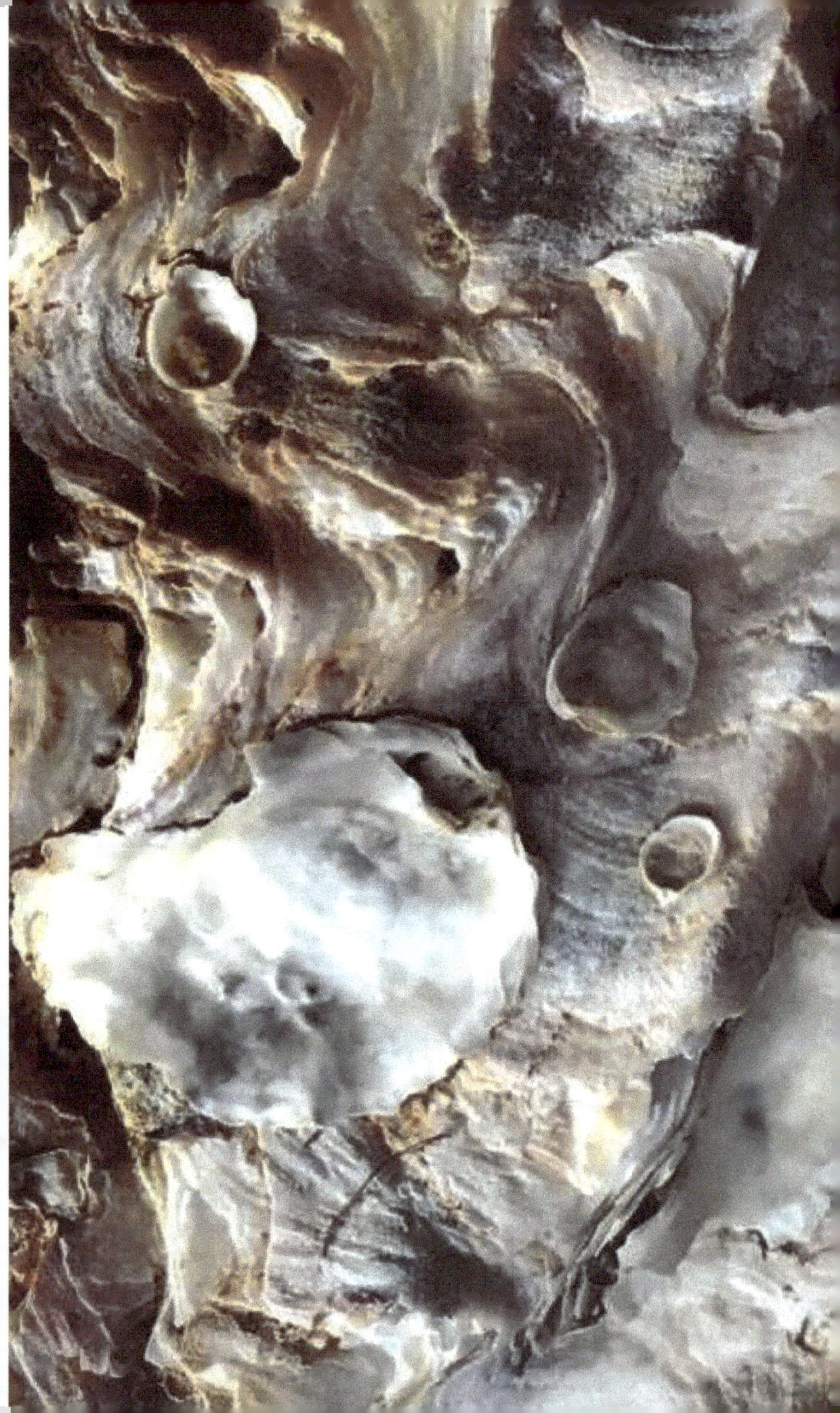

# A CLOSER LOOK
## *shellfish*

* Washington produces more shellfish than any other state, about 75 million pounds per year.

* 98% of the oysters grown in Washington are Pacifics. The Olympia oyster is the only native species and their numbers are a fraction of what they once were. They are small and have a coppery taste.

* 20 million pounds of Dungeness crab are caught each year – half on the coast and half in the Sound. They take their name from Dungeness, WA. The crab became the "state crustacean" of Oregon in 2009. Surprisingly, Washington does not have a state crustacean.

* Geoduck (pronounced "GOO-ee-duck") are enormous clams that weigh an average of 2 lbs and can live for more than 140 years!

* Shellfish are filter feeders, removing algae and other particles from water. One oyster can filter 25 gallons per day. Poisons can quickly accumulate in their tissues, so whatever they eat, we eat. Yet another reason to keep our waters clean.

*Closeup of Pacific oyster shell*

## DOES THE SEA EVER CALL YOU?

Does the sea ever call you
down?
Promise its secrets?
That magnetic pull, those slippery
riptides bring you
to the shore,
to stand and cast your eyes
across hypnotic undulations,
the endless waves repeating
a chant your saline pulse cannot
resist.

Does the sea ever call you
down?

No?

Me either.

    *Fried Egg jellyfish, Phacellophora camtschatica*

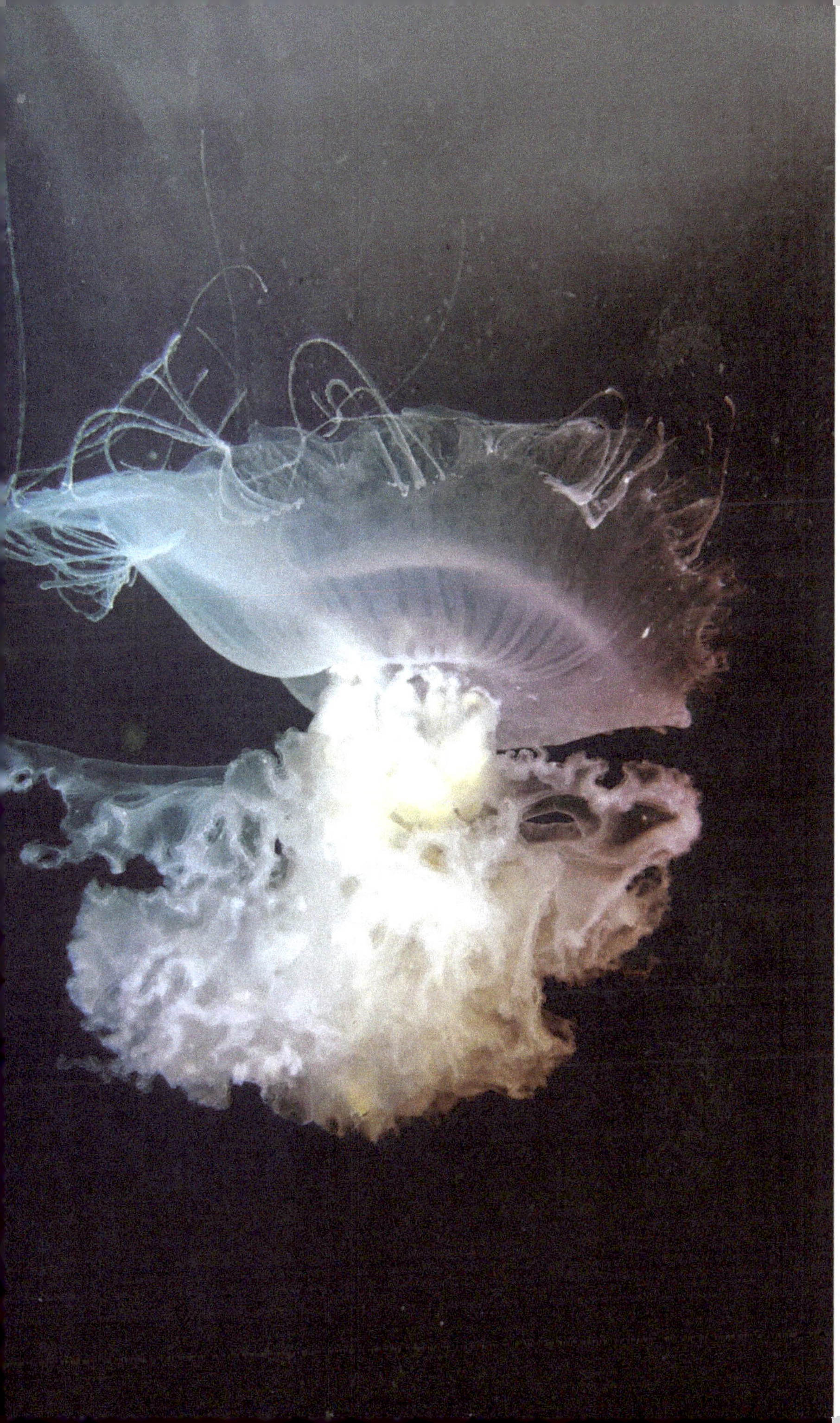

# A CLOSER LOOK
### *native anadromous salmon*

There are only five species of Pacific salmon in North American waters, but it can be confusing because they have multiple names.

1. Chum are also called Calico or Dog, because of the teeth the males grow while spawning. Chum means, 'variegated coloration.'

2. Chinook can be called, King or Spring, and are the largest but least populous salmon.

3. Pink are also known as Humpbacks or Humpies, because of the humps they develop as the males enter their spawning stage.

4. Coho, which are also known as Silver, are the second least abundant compared to Chinook, but one of the most sought after species.

5. Sockeye are also known as Red.

*Salmon inside the fish ladder at Bonneville Dam*

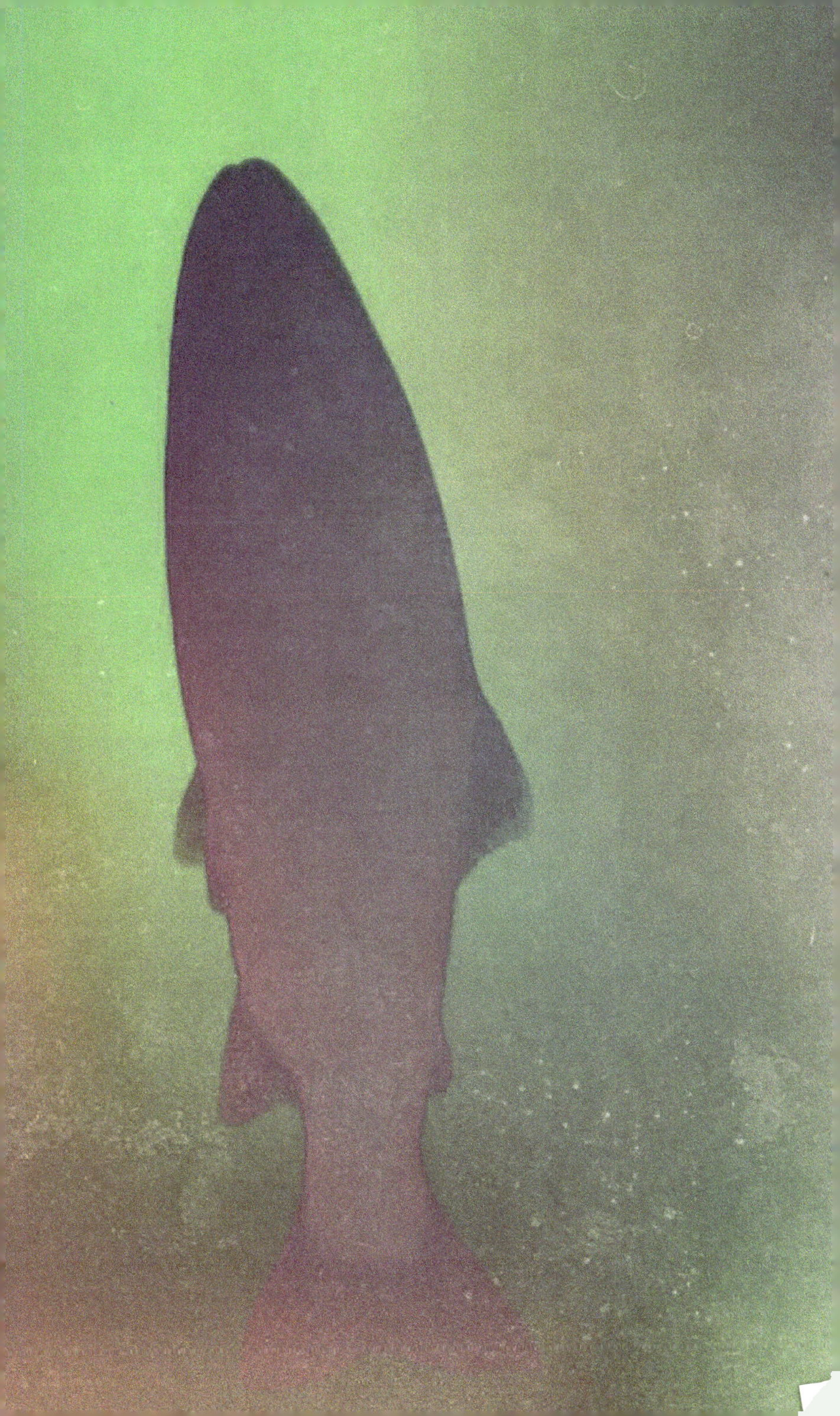

# BITTER END

*A nautical term referring to the end of the anchor rope tied on deck. It is marked so sailors know when the water is too deep to set anchor.*

I knelt on
smooth river
rock, on slick
mud flats and
miles of sunset
sand. I knelt at
the redwood's base
on the forest floor,
knees dirty and sore
from supplication,
searching for redemption
and a way back in
a single photograph.

This I bring to you –
a numinous landscape
where gods conspire
and consummate
and the moment I remember
we are not here
long enough.

Rialto Beach

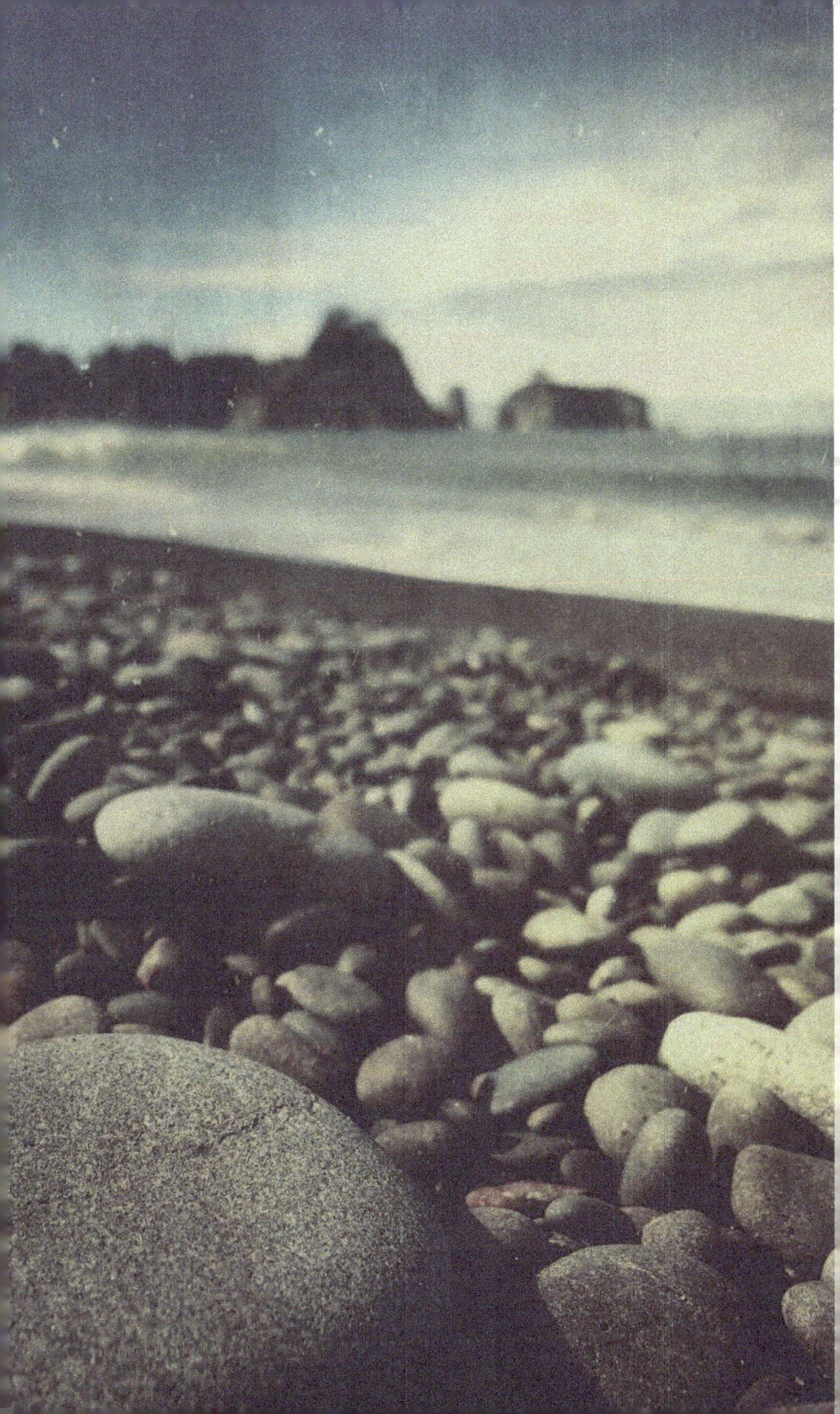

# A CLOSER LOOK
## the mighty columbia

* The Columbia River is the fourth largest river by volume in the United States. It drains 259,000 square miles, including all of Eastern Washington and the western slopes of the Cascades, between Mount Rainier and the southern border. That's about the size of France.

* On its way to the Pacific Ocean, the Columbia forms the boundary between Washington and Oregon. The river is not split down the middle, as one would assume. During the early days of statehood, Oregon claimed 2/3rds of it.

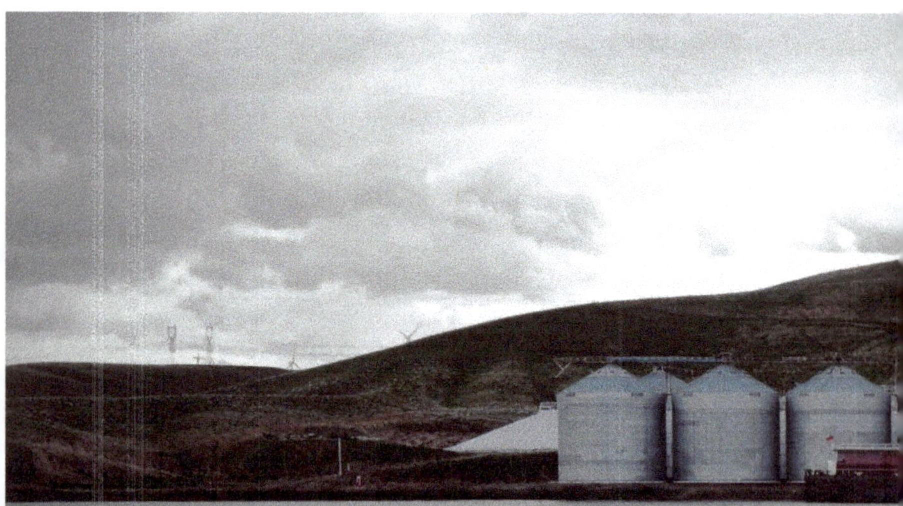

* The river provides water for Washington's extensive orchards, vineyards and hydroelectric projects.

* As the Columbia River meets the Pacific, it collides with the ocean's tides and deposits large amounts of shifting sediment, which makes the mouth of the river the most hazardous waterway in the world.

* Main tributaries of the Columbia include the Cowlitz, Pend Oreille, Snake and Spokane Rivers.

* River barges are able to travel deep into Eastern Washington because of the Columbia. They load grains and other goods near their source for shipping all over the world.

*River barge on Snake River*

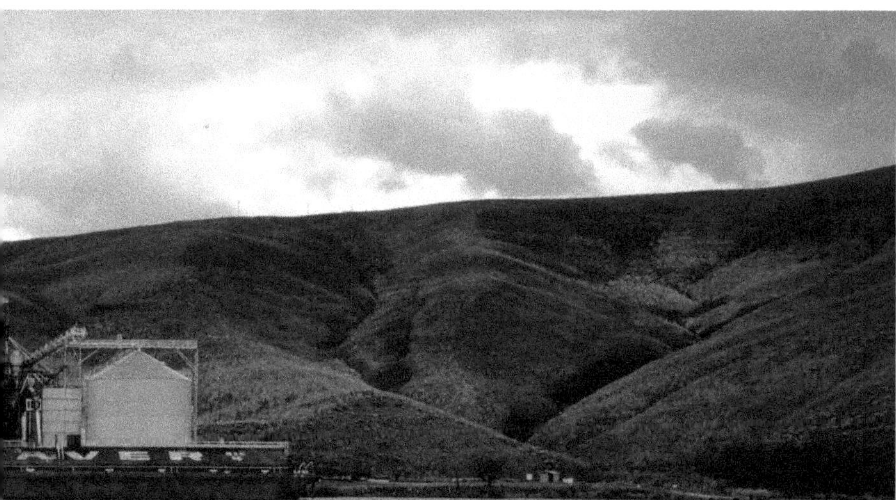

JUSTICE

The sea is all balance
all patient
retribution
gorging on the earth
reducing mountains to
rubble to sand to
dust.

The sea is all secrets,
nameless bones in
black water depths
lit briefly by phosphorescent
fish.

Lean in and lose yourself
in the glass ripples, then
you'll know.

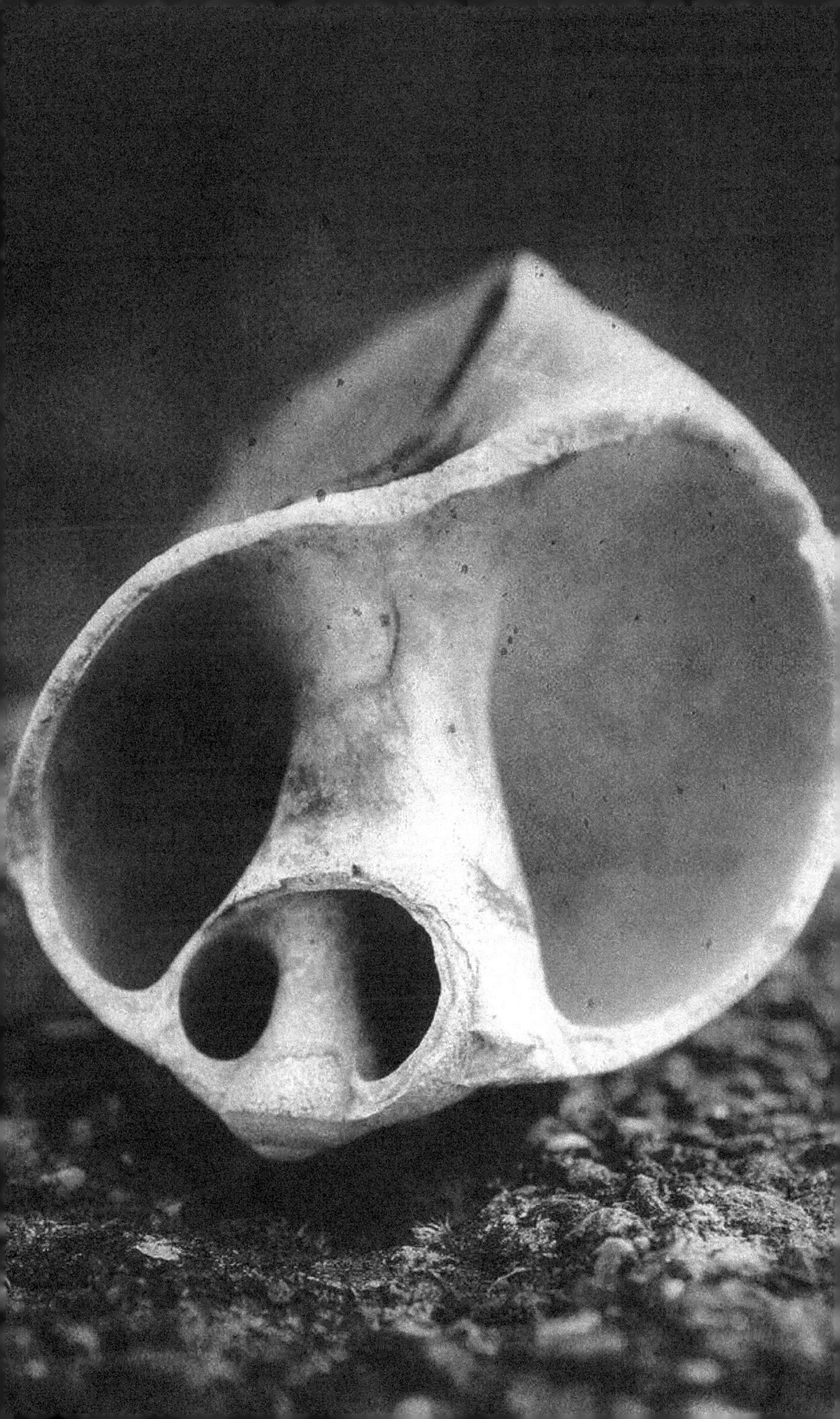

## PETRIFIED

*Petrified wood occurs when organic materials are slowly*
*replaced by minerals and become stone.*

The mineral-rich
waters are patient.
Cell by cell, they transform
tissue into stone, the dance
of life leaves
their bones white-hot,
baking in the sun,
under lava flows,
washed in torrents and revealed
tree trunks turned to
pillars, a testament
to what was once
a forest of green
breathing,

their autumn leaves and
emerald exhalations
long gone, whispers
in glacier-carved valleys,
in the sweet breeze against
your cheek.

　*Ginkgo Petrified Forest, Vantage*

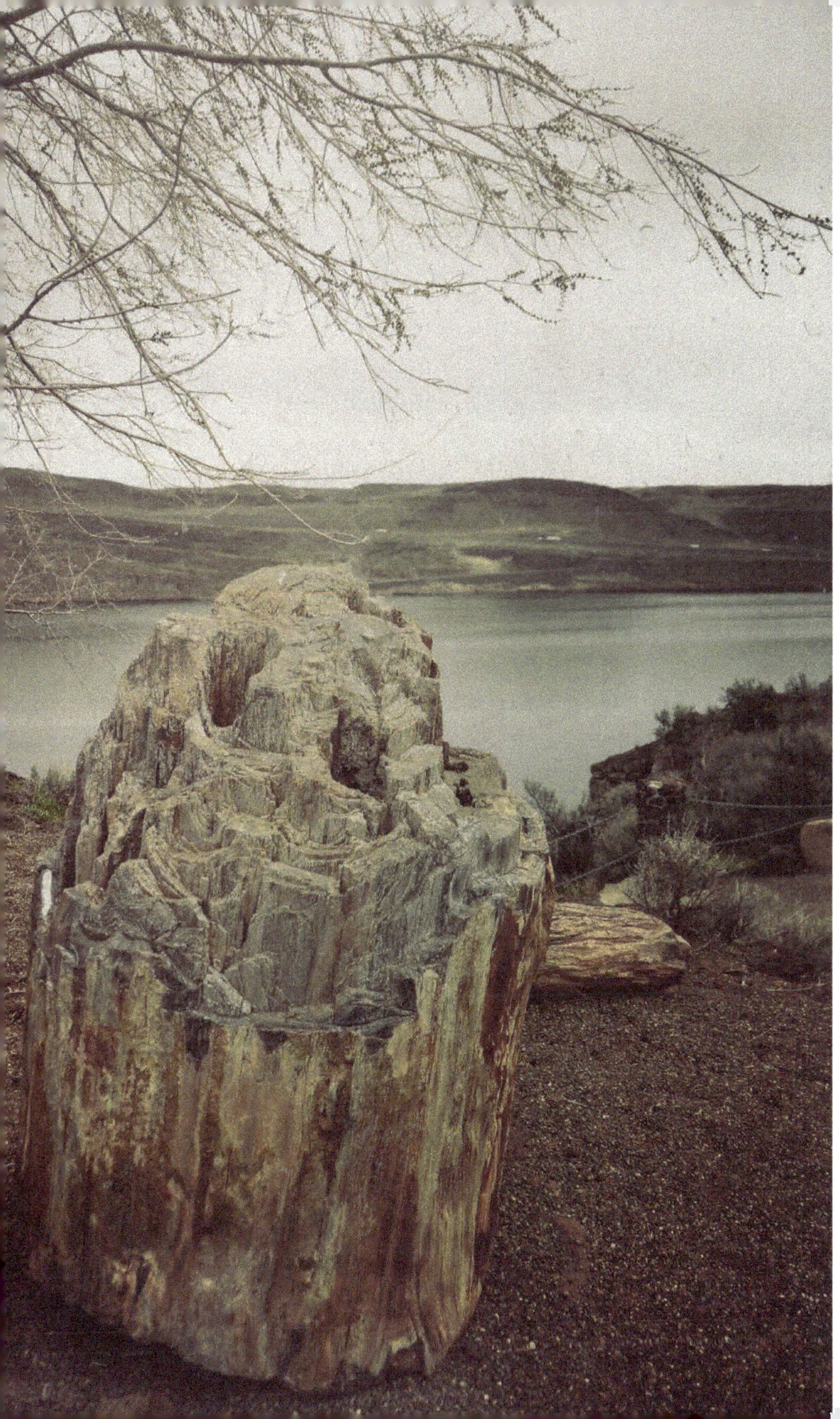

# A CLOSER LOOK
## the bretz floods

About 18,000 years ago, an enormous ice dam on Montana's Lake Missoula broke and water flooded Eastern Washington in a cataclysmic flood. It traveled down the Columbia Gorge and out to the Pacific Ocean. It is believed to have occurred several times over the course of 25 years as the ice dam refroze.

Along the way, it formed an unusual landscape, now known as the Channeled Scablands. This area includes the imposing Dry Falls and water-filled basins called, *kolks*, that settled in the valleys. These kolks were drilled out of bedrock by powerful underwater tornados within seconds.

The flow of water is estimated to have been 10 times the combined flow of all the rivers in the world and it all happened in less than 48 hours. The floods scraped the earth away, leaving volcanic bedrock.

*Sun Lakes-Dry Falls State Park*

Giant boulders were embedded in the ice that traveled with the flood. They were carried as far as Oregon and dot the landscape of the Palouse, where they're called, *erratics*.

*"I could conceive of no geological process of erosion to make this topography except huge, violent rivers of glacial melt water...It was a debacle which swept the Columbia Plateau."*

J Harlen Bretz

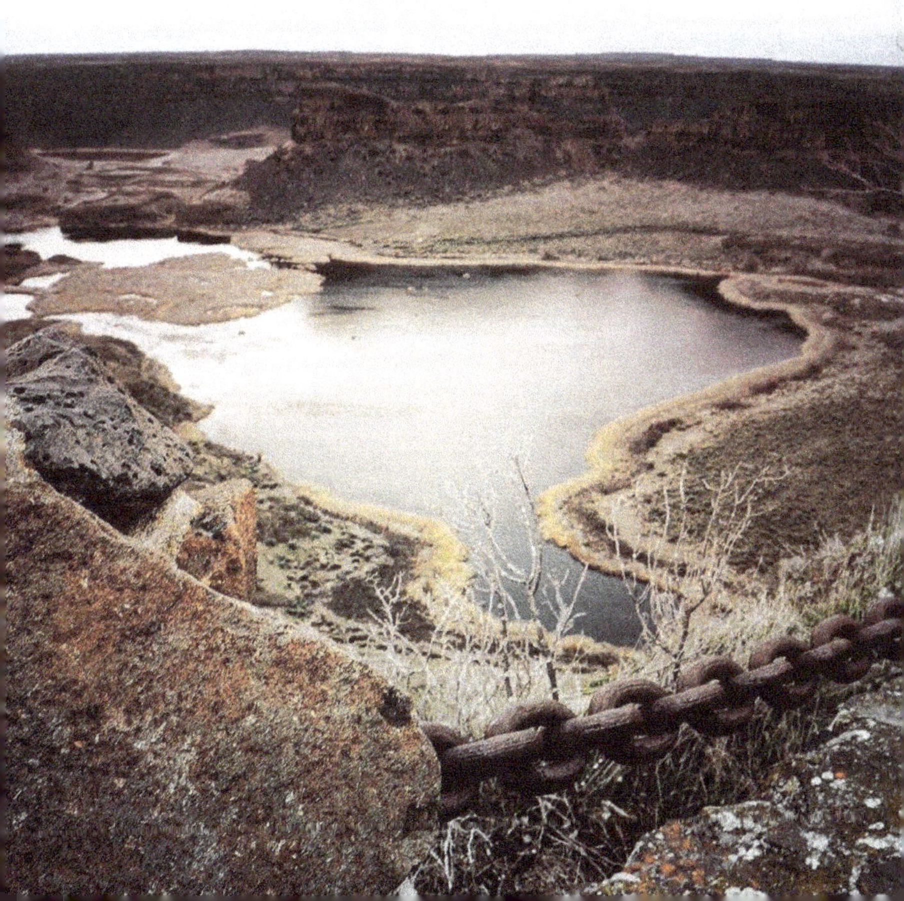

## FOSSIL

The geologist eyes time
in mortal drifts.
He knows the present is a
a small thing
caught between a quiet
yawn and future days
unfolding, the entire past
chained with promise
a tethered hope
a dubious wait.

He strains to hear the crashing
endless water of Dry Falls.
The deluge sends a shockwave
even after all these years
the land trembles.

He can feel the spray and
licks its mineral-rich breeze
from his lips, mud on his tongue.

Everything hangs together
in his mythology.
To speak of things long dead
his stoic tread in the field
threatens to widow him.

Still, he catalogs his findings.
Notes and numbers
are penned carefully.
The data is good.
It will outlast him.

But will the meadows he crossed
breathe his name?
Or will his memory be swift
and clean, unrecorded
in the strata.
Will chiseled crust reveal core samples
of his shadow?
Perhaps, bones worked into stone?

The geologists must all be mad
in discontented dreams worn flinty
to occupy this space,
to understand the irony,
the limits of their vigilant constructions
their data points and statistics
will  be a carbon line

50

feet

down.

*(Next page: Columbia River, Wenatchee)*

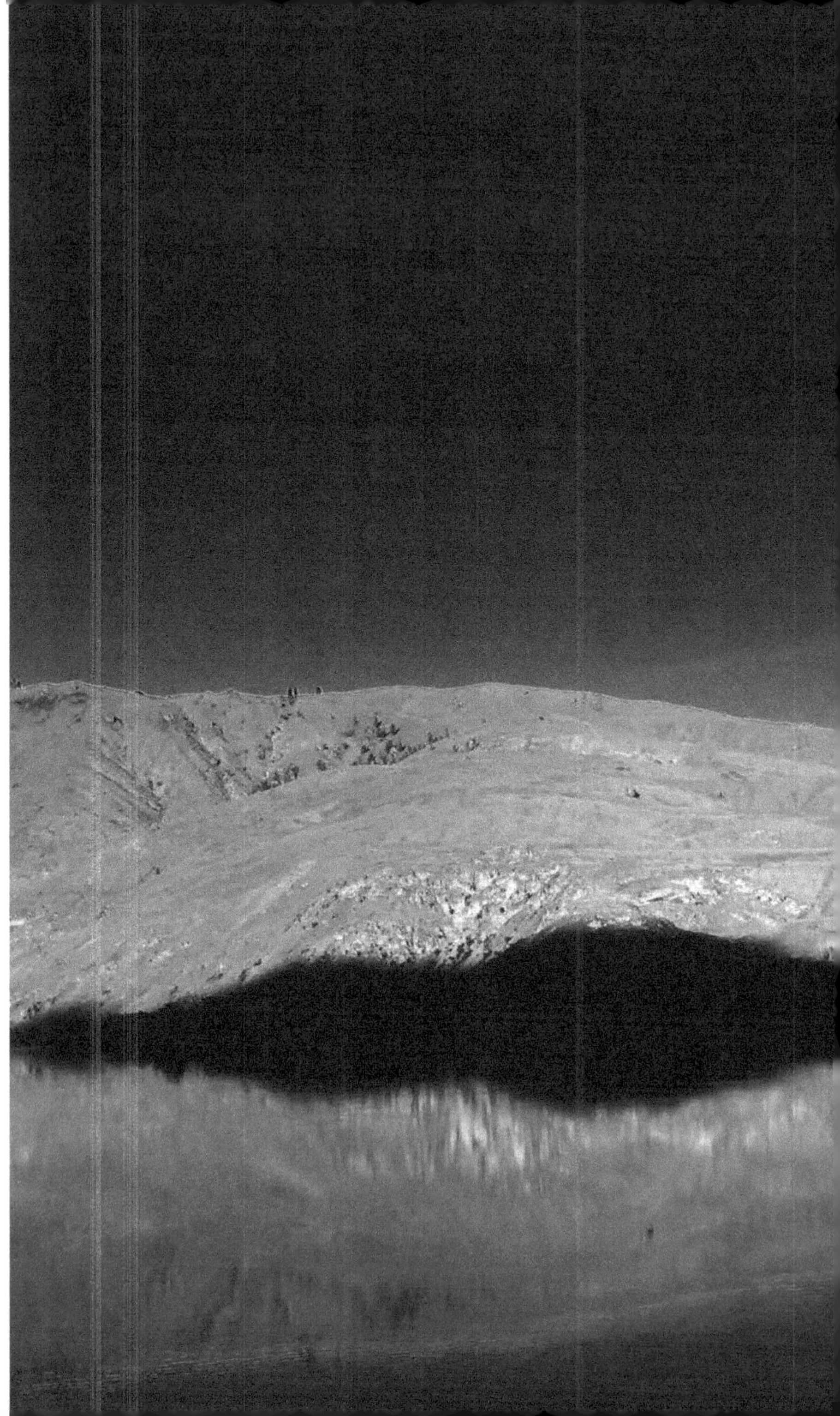

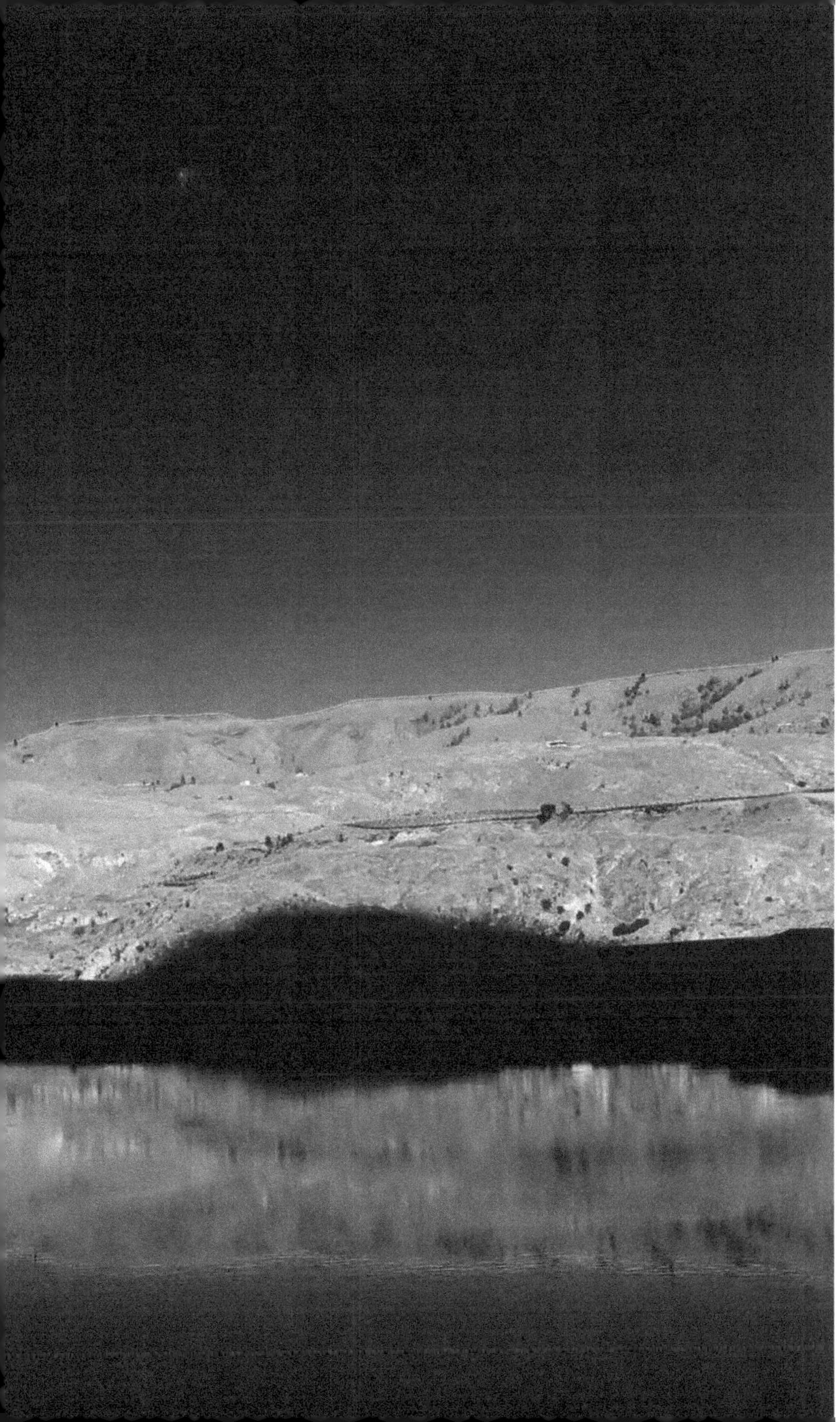

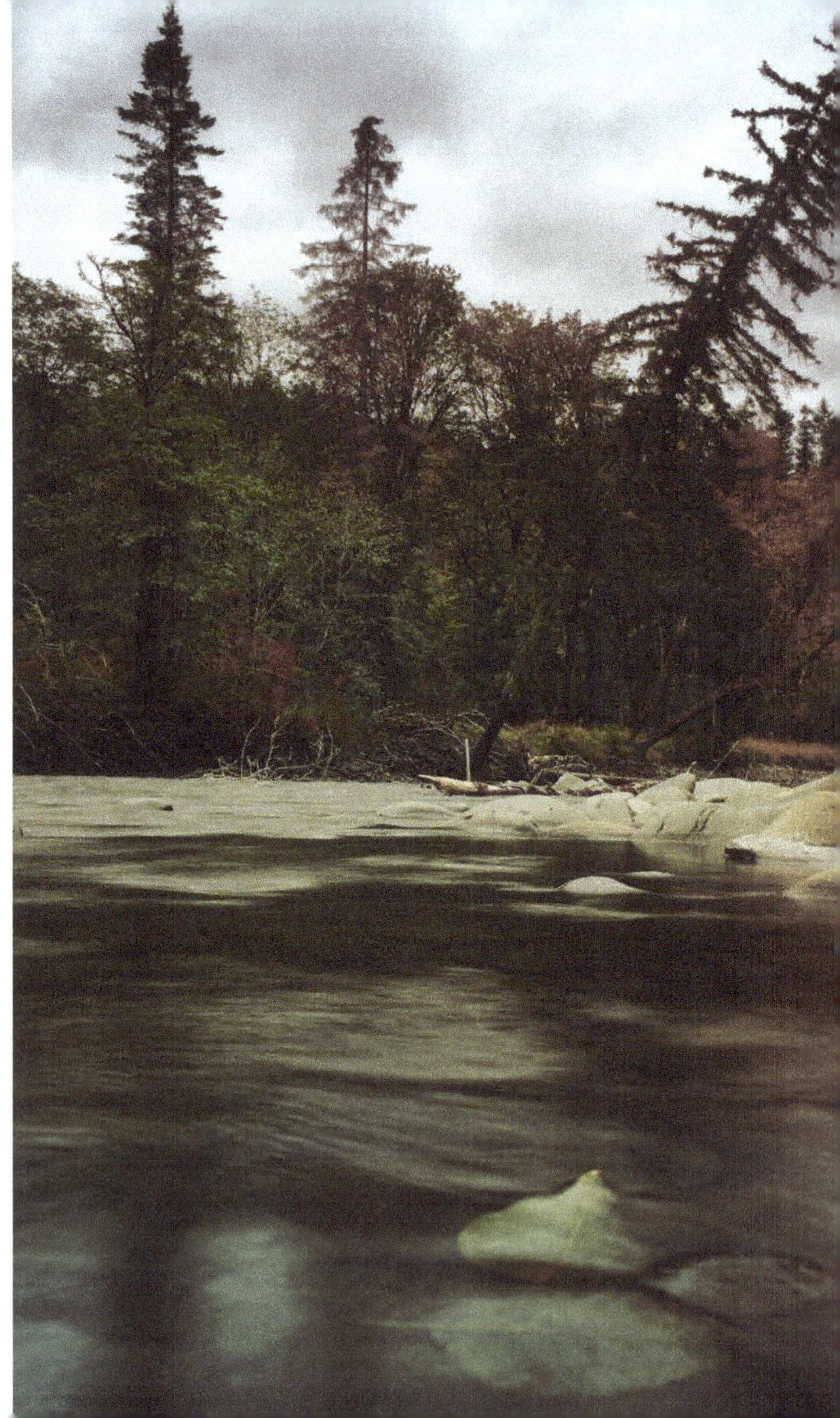

# A CLOSER LOOK
## *san juan islands*

Washington's San Juan Islands are situated in a group called an *archipelago*. They were named by Spanish explorer, Francisco de Eliza, who charted the islands in 1791.

Over 400 islands and large rocks remain at high tide, of which 128 are named. Added together, they make up 480 miles of coastline. No bridges to the islands exist so all travel is by water or air.

Horseshoe-shaped Orcas Island and San Juan Island are the most populous. San Juan's Friday Harbor is a lovely seaside town. Its Lime Kiln Point State Park serves as a popular whale lookout, while nearby Lucia Island is known as the 'Crown Jewel' of the state's marine park system.

*Elwha River*
*(Next page: The Narrows, Gig Harbor side)*

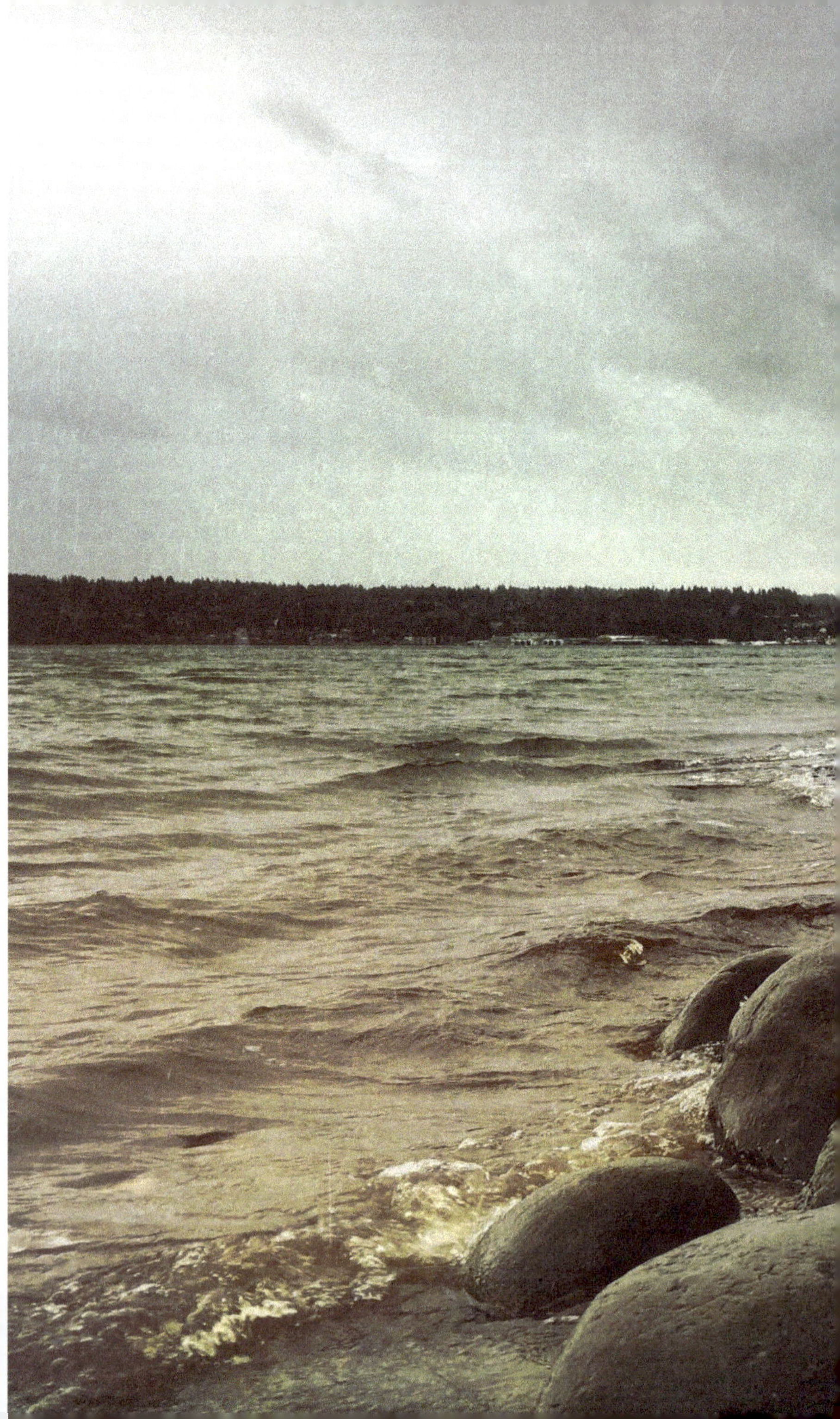

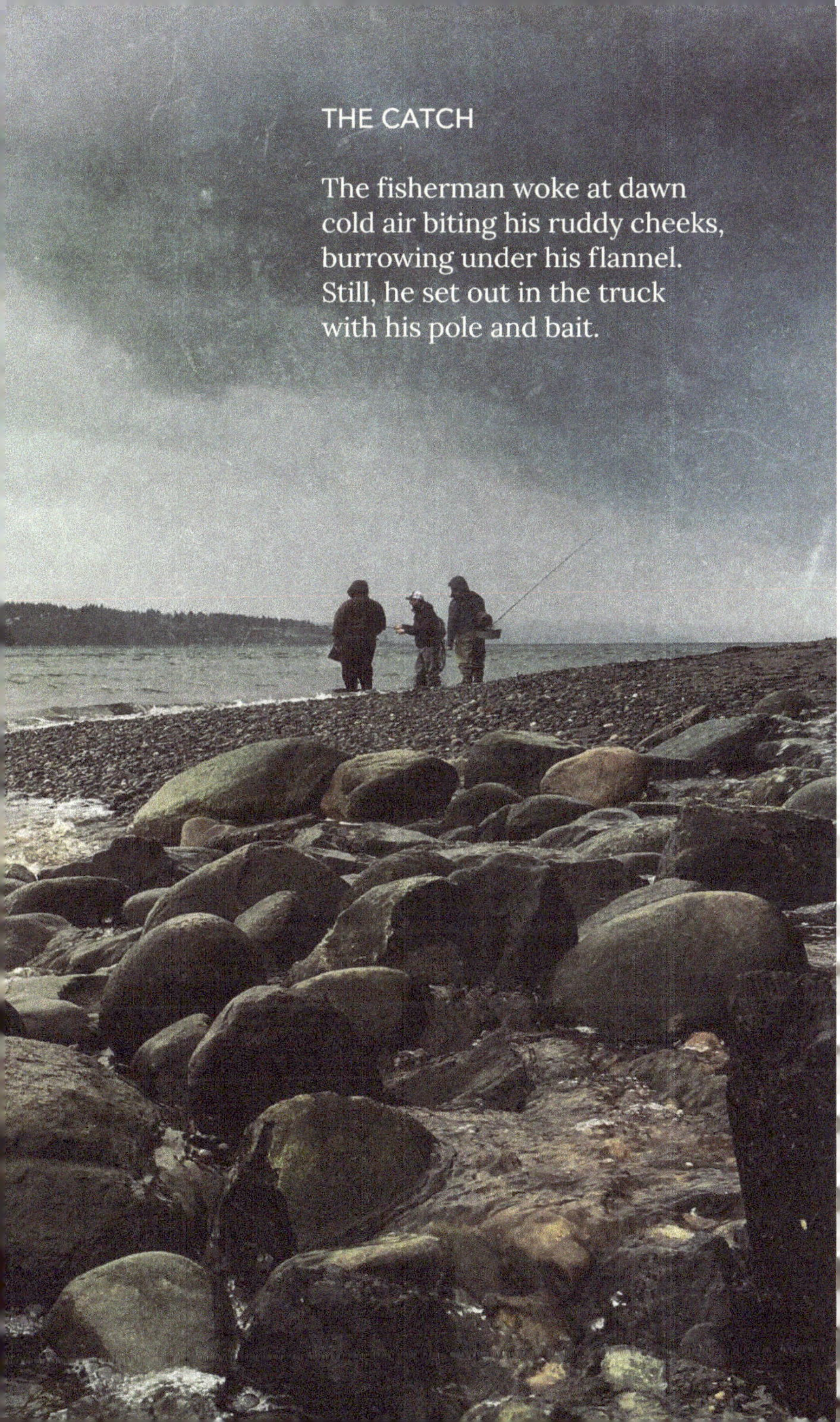

THE CATCH

The fisherman woke at dawn
cold air biting his ruddy cheeks,
burrowing under his flannel.
Still, he set out in the truck
with his pole and bait.

He cast out
into the fog,
into the murky blue.
The plunk of his line was the only sound
        the only sound.

That, and his breath, hot from his lungs
mingling with the ancient mists, which
settle on the bay each night,
as the sea's cool exhalations
touch land's warm body.

The fisherman's nose fills with damp air
and it is strange this morning.
There's something not quite right.

The pier, black with wet, stands quiet
underneath him
waiting for him to see
what it sees
what it feels.

His line goes taut,
something's tugging at the bait
something's caught on the hook.
He forgets what he was thinking
        there's catch to reel in!

Already, he's sizing up his fish.
He feels the sluggish way it pulls his pole
as if its vigor has gone out.
But it's large, he can feel it in his palms
the resistance
        the heft of the thing.

There's a small part of the man,
which he'll deny,
that doesn't want to see the creature
he's pulling back to shore.
He doesn't want it to emerge
from the black ice water.

For the first time,
he feels lonely,
not just alone
on the pier.

The catch is pulling near,
its strange outline pushing
 a v–shaped ripple.

The fisherman stops,
and lets the thing rest
to float on the surface.
There is no resistance,
no struggle to dive down deep.

The pier knows
the man has finally seen
the body brined in sea water.
He cuts his line, then instantly regrets it,
since now the thing is free.

They scrape the water.
The body dips and drowns again
wanting to be left alone,
but that's not how things are done.

*(Next page: Commencement Bay, Tacoma)*

Police in diving gear finally fish it out
from underneath the pier.

The man considers asking to retrieve his hook
for a sort of show and tell,
as all fisherman are drawn to.

Instead, he moves along
to find another fishing spot.

What a story this will be, he thinks,
about the one that got away
and he was glad.

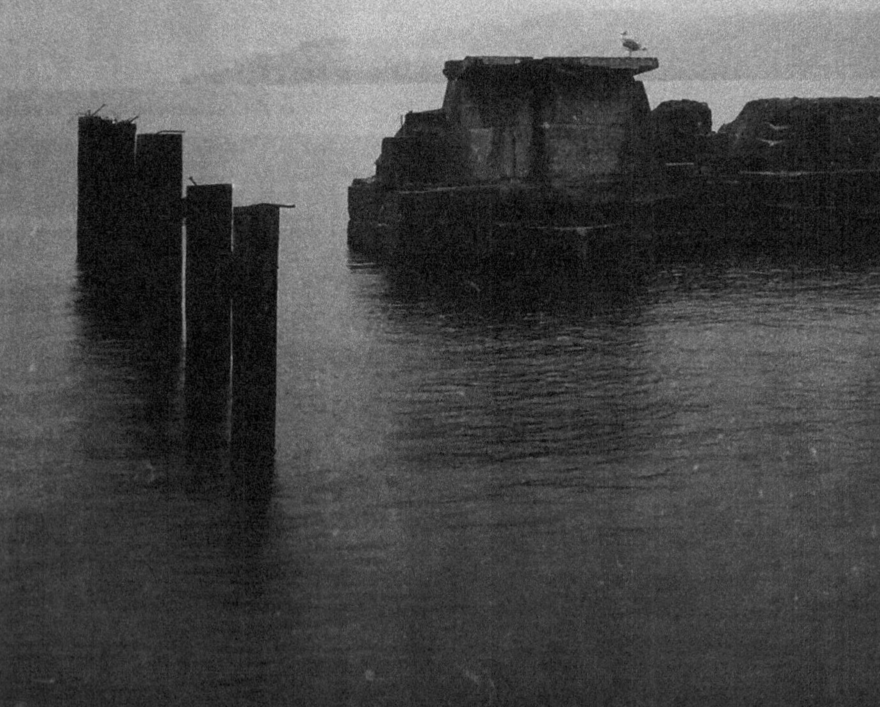

THE PILINGS

It's Friday night
and Katie Downs' heroic humming
rumbles over thick-planked floors
tumbling to the sea below
mixing with the ancient echos.

The sea remembers when
docks drape around the Bay
like a busy necklace, but now
scattered pilings lean
and kneel to fate,
sprouting weeds and Cormorants.

The wood has been retired,
bent from time and
berthing ships.
Briny hulls once chafed their hides,
engraving scars and raking splinters
as they delivered goods.

Still, the pilings stand,
as stubborn as Greek columns,
their prehistoric tar waking in the heat, oozing
sticky, iridescent blood
reminders of an early age and industry
when people coursed their docks,
beating busy rhythms
with their leather, hobnailed boots.

Here, Washington's wheat
was scattered to the world
in grain sacks slung in shoulders.

Asia's tea arrived in dark, carved chests.
Just to keep the pace, sawmills buzzed
throughout the night
peeling fresh-cut lumber.

Today, the river's mouth now opens
on a gallery of trade where
men hoist railcars with machines
from ship to road and rail.

In intermodal yards,
container cranes
lug 20 foot-long boxes
filled with Chinese goods.

Somewhere just below
whales in rubber-skins
still pursue the seals while
seals pursue the salmon:
Coho, Sockeye and Chinook.

Restaurants dotting Ruston Way
watch out their windows,
guarding tired timbers
as new ships cut the Bay
sending sheets of water
underneath their hungry hordes.

I'm thankful for their old and steady bones
as I take another bite.

*(Next page: Hawaiian Chieftain, Tall Ships Festival)*

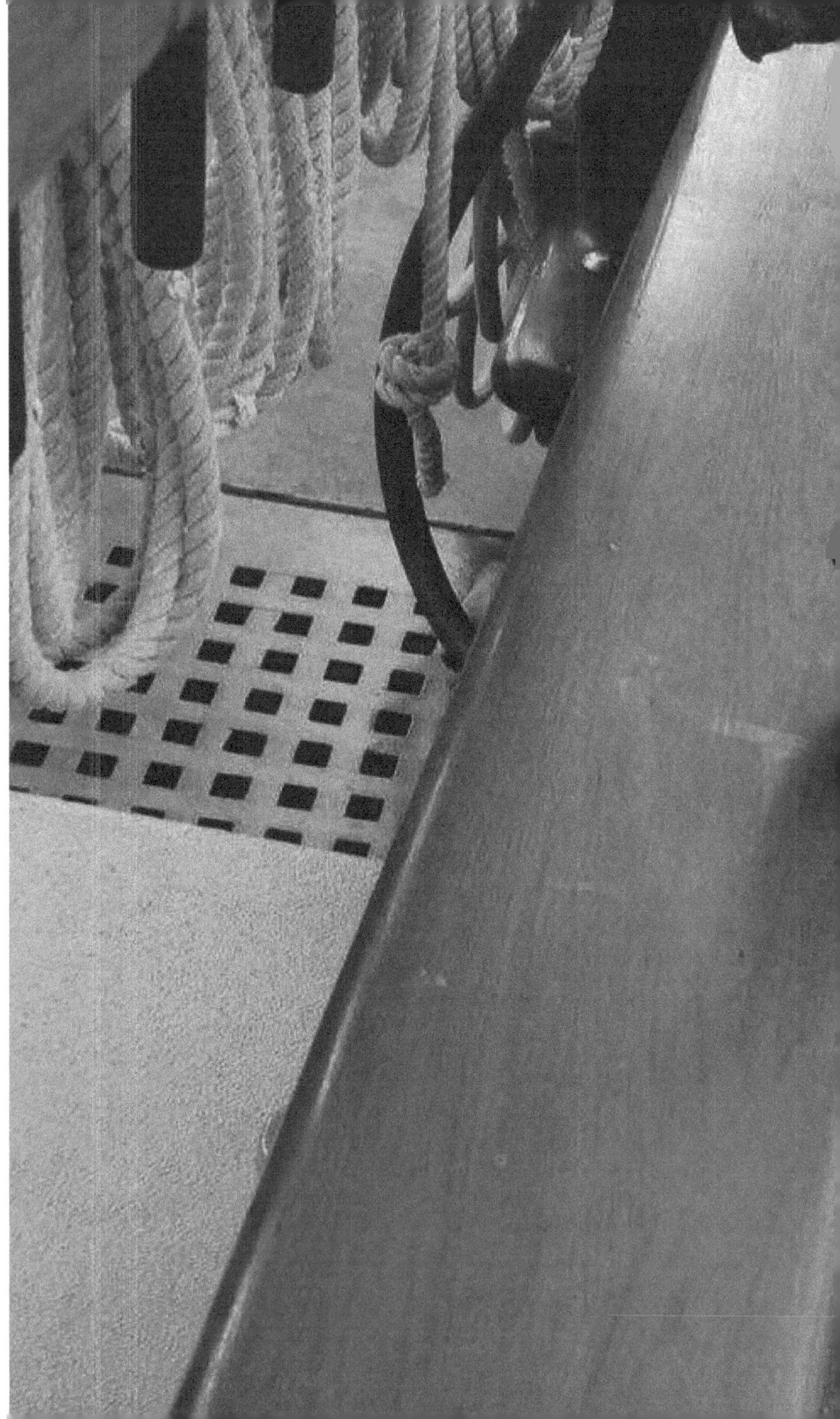

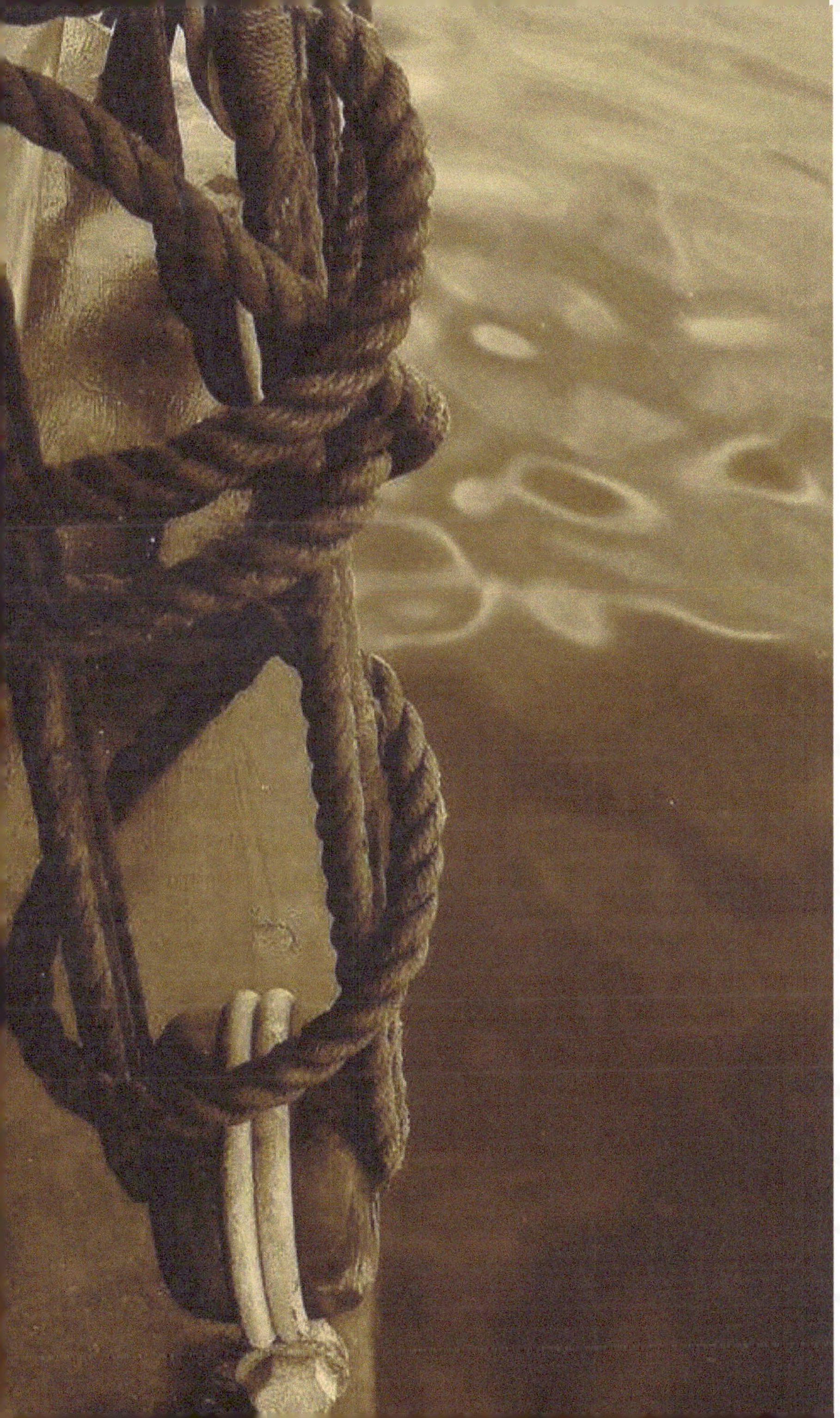

# WATER FEATURE

*Popular sport fish in Puget Sound include: salmon,*
*steelhead, trout, bass, perch, bluegill and sturgeon*

The raccoon celebrates
dinner, scattering fish scales
like confetti,
like iridescent cherry blossoms,
trailing up the stone steps.
A full belly.
An empty pond.



*Closeup of fish scales*

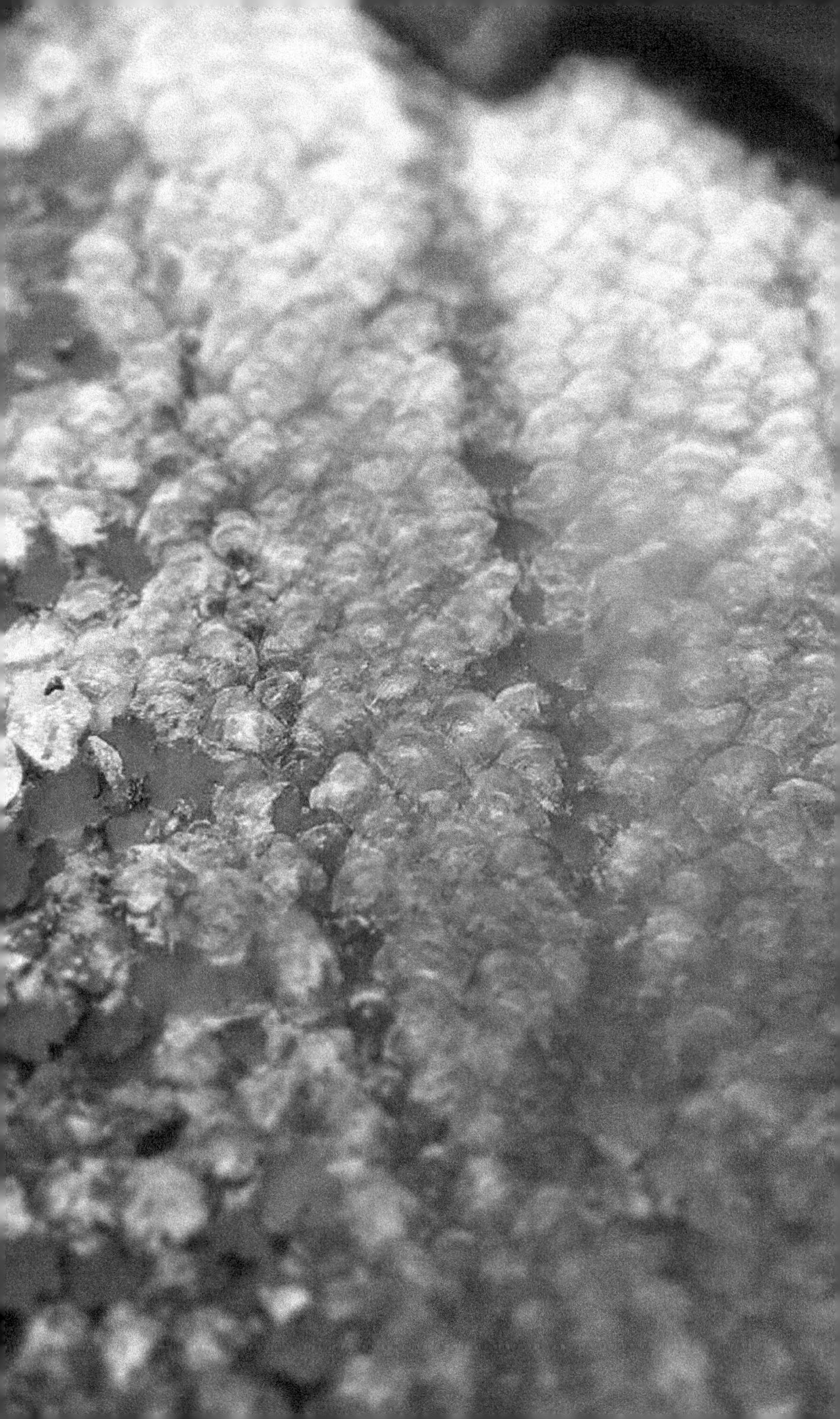

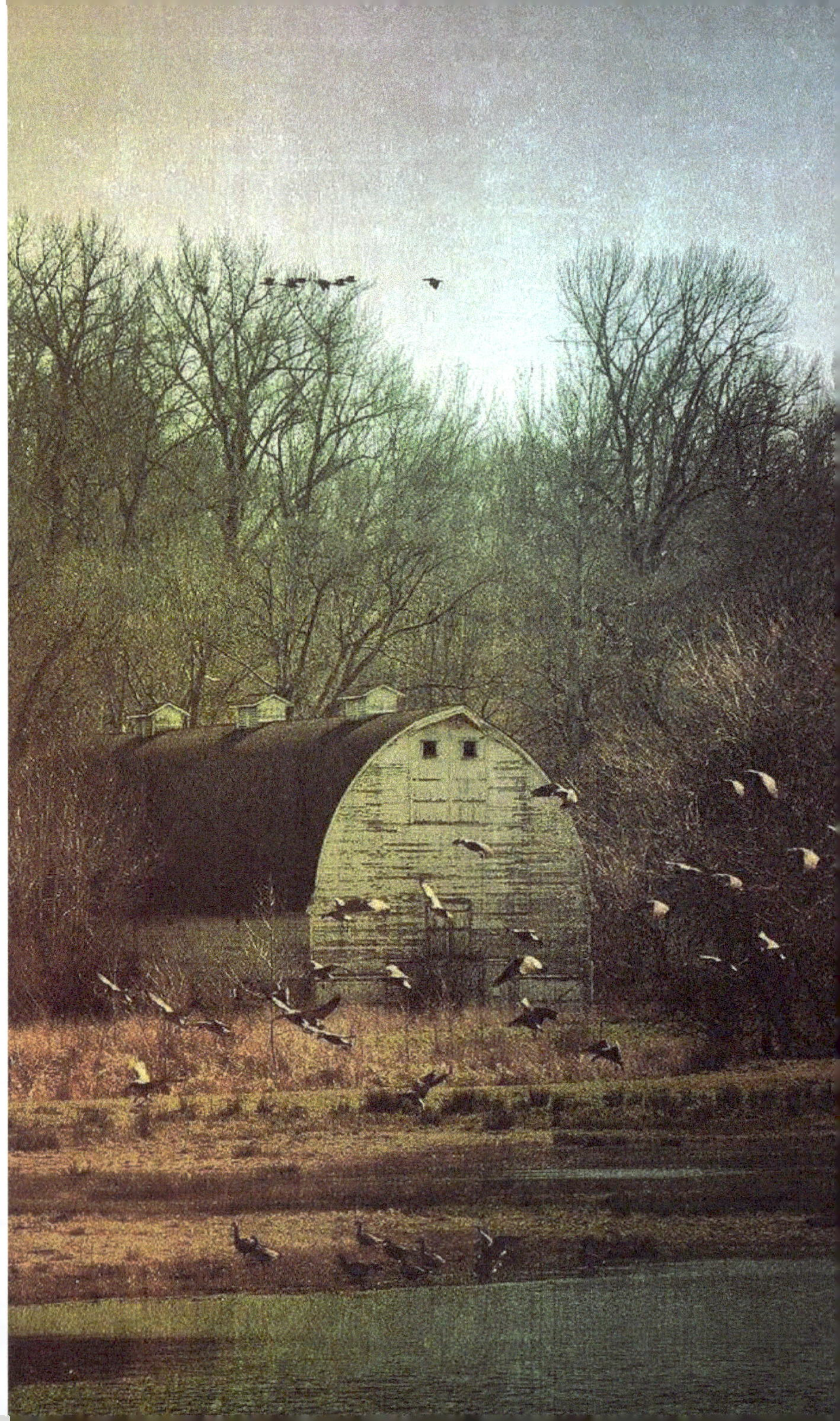

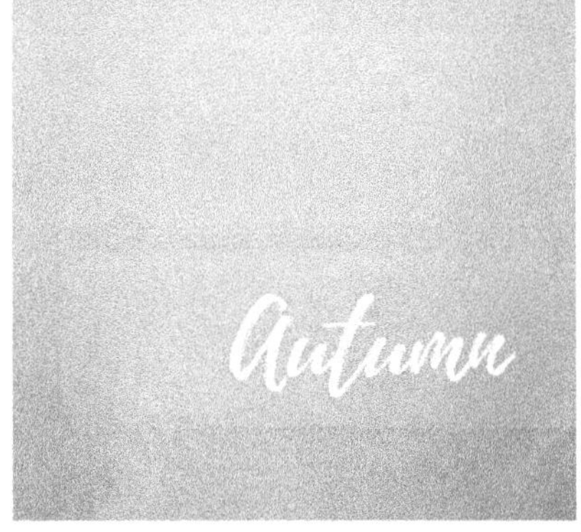


The fall is my favorite time of year. The cool air turns crisp and everything feels fresh. The fertile Puyallup and Orting valleys are filled with plump pumpkins and specialty squash ready for harvest.

Washington's coast gets busy in its cranberry bogs and Eastern Washington plunders its vineyards for wine grapes. Apples all over the state are plucked and squeezed into delicious cider. It truly is a 'second spring.'

Deciduous trees are dropping their leaves, but before they go dormant they develop rich hues like, burnished copper, fiery red and golden ocher. It's our last chance before winter arrives to visit the vegetable garden for cabbage, carrots, broccoli and brussel sprouts.

As we huddle close to the fireplace sipping hot cocoa, coffee or a cabernet from the Columbia Valley, the wind picks up outside and all those gorgeous leaves let go.

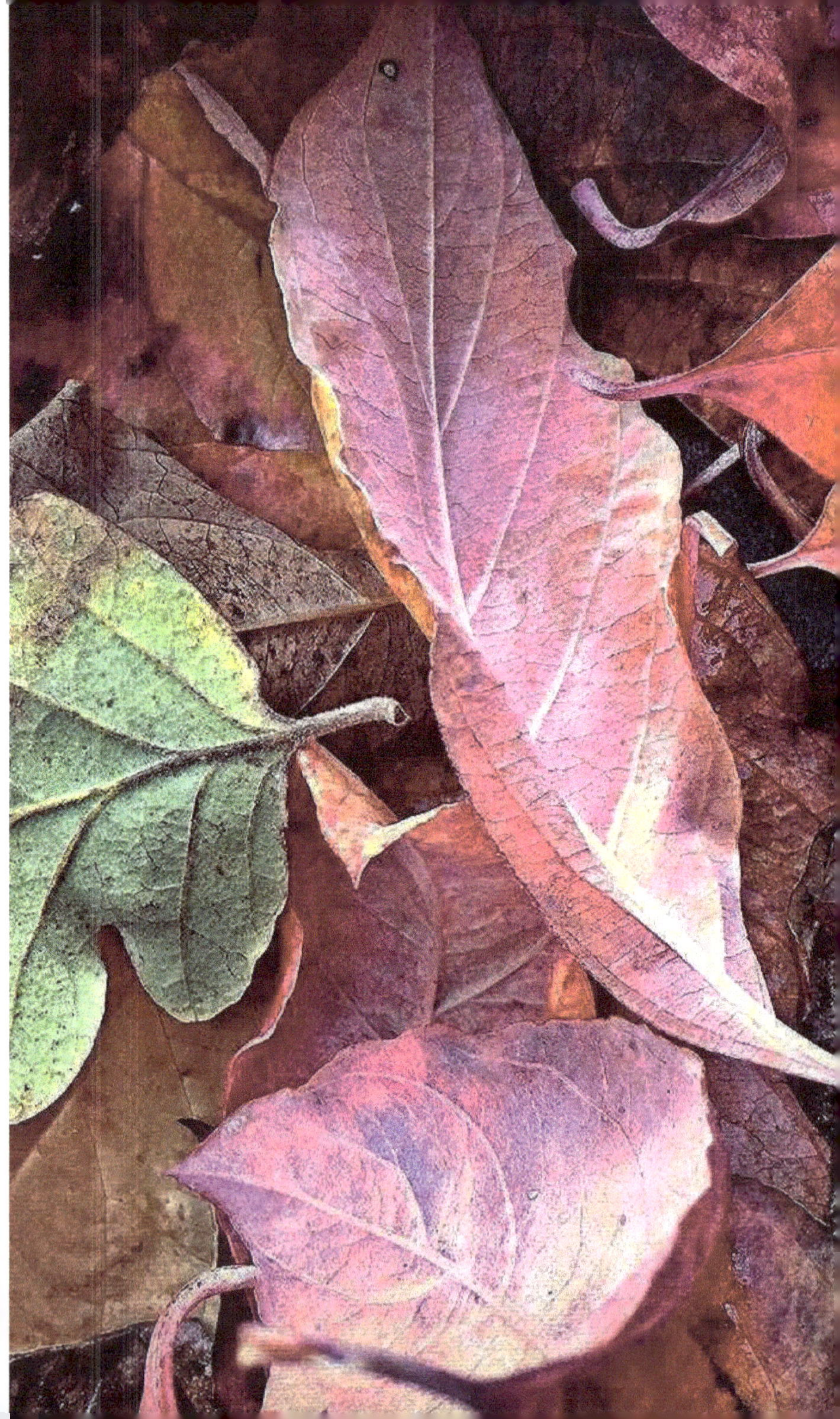

# A CLOSER LOOK
## *fall colors and moisture*

* As days get darker, trees prepare for winter and stop producing chlorophyll. Once the green color is no longer reflected red "anthocyanins" and yellow "carotenoids" are revealed.

* Leaf color intensity is controlled by weather. Moist soil leads to stunning displays, while droughts create less vibrant colors.

* Washington's amount of daylight undergoes dramatic seasonal shifts. Western Washington's shortest day is December 21st at 8:29 hours. June 20th is the longest day at 15:56 hours.

* Western WA gardeners depend on spring's cool, wet weather to water their gardens.

* Though the summer season is short, the sun lasts up to 16 hours a day because of the northern latitude. We have to wait until 10PM to start 4th of July fireworks! However, we pay for the long summer days in the fall and winter, when darkness descends as early as 3PM.

*Oak, cherry and dogwood leaves mingle.*

## PORTAL

Did you know
that circles can
look like lines?
Or that a ringed
rock is a wishing
stone?

Here is one for
you to hold.

Three wishes
wait
for your voice,
your dreams,
soft magic born
from rock and
water, rock and
        water,
restless rock
and
        water.



*Kalaloch Beach, Forks*

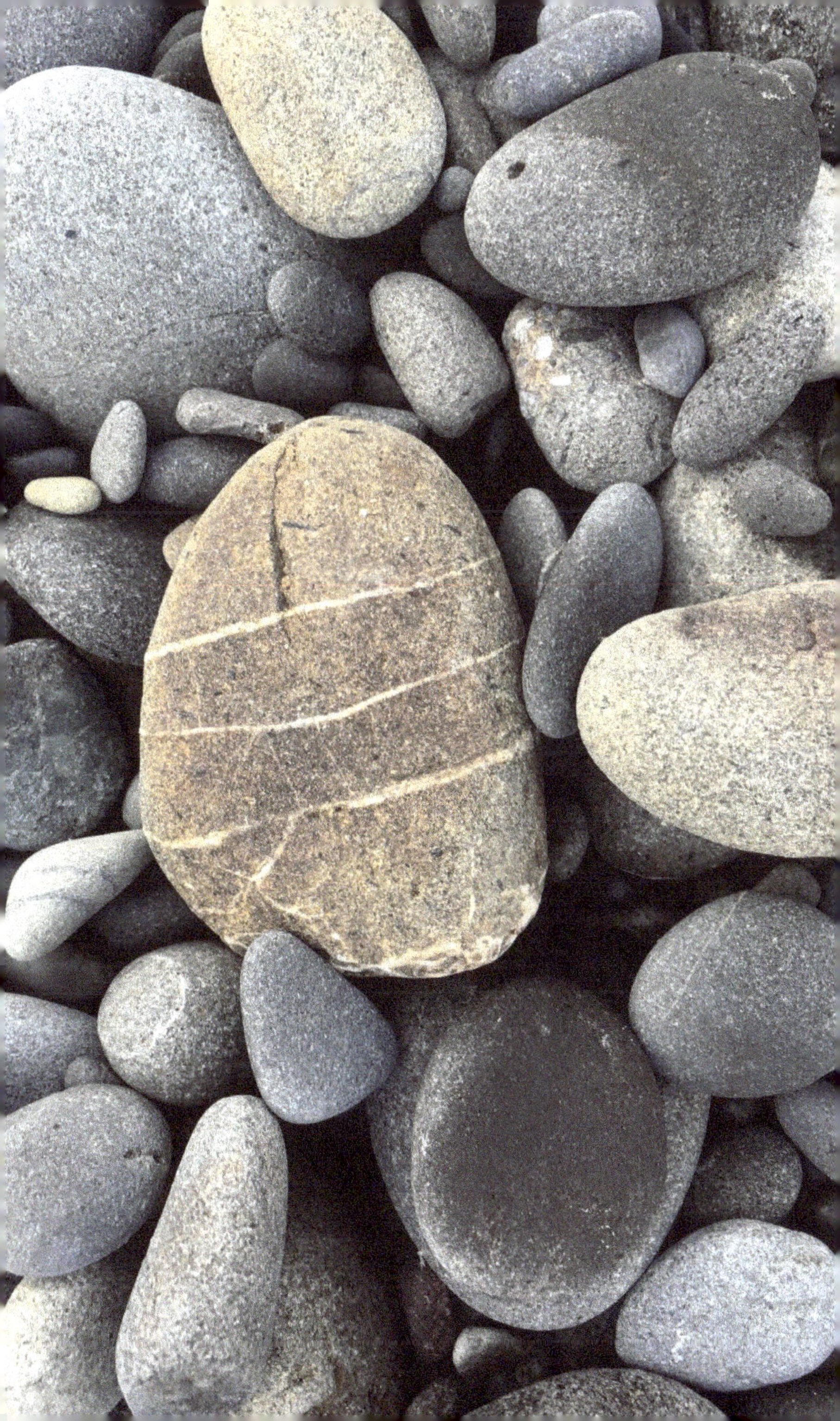

## alien landscapes

Eastern and Western Washington are complete opposites. Beyond feeling like different states, they feel like different planets. The first time I drove Snoqualmie Pass I was struck by the contrast. Fir trees gave way to pines, which gave way to scrub brush. Once over the mountain, the landscape became flat and brown.

It's also much warmer and drier with an average annual rainfall of 8". Compare that to Western Washington's 48". The dramatic difference is caused by the Cascade Mountain Range, which blocks the ocean's cool, moist air.

Another extraordinary feature are the Channeled Scablands. They are extremely unique; only the planet Mars has similar landforms. Early settlers called them 'scablands' because of their pockmarked appearance. Much of it is scoured bedrock covered with a thin layer of soil leaving the area unsuitable for farming. Numerous rock outcroppings also made settling the land difficult. Even today large swaths of the landscape are undeveloped and you can drive for miles without seeing signs of habitation.

The Scablands are scattered with geographical features that look like huge, water-filled potholes. These depressions are called, *kolks*, and were scoured out instantaneously by the incredible power of underwater tornados as the Missoula floods passed through. For an idea of how large the deluge was, water backed up behind a massive landform called the Wallula Gap, which has a 1.2 mile opening.

*The Columbia River, Vantage*
*(Next page: Dry Falls)*

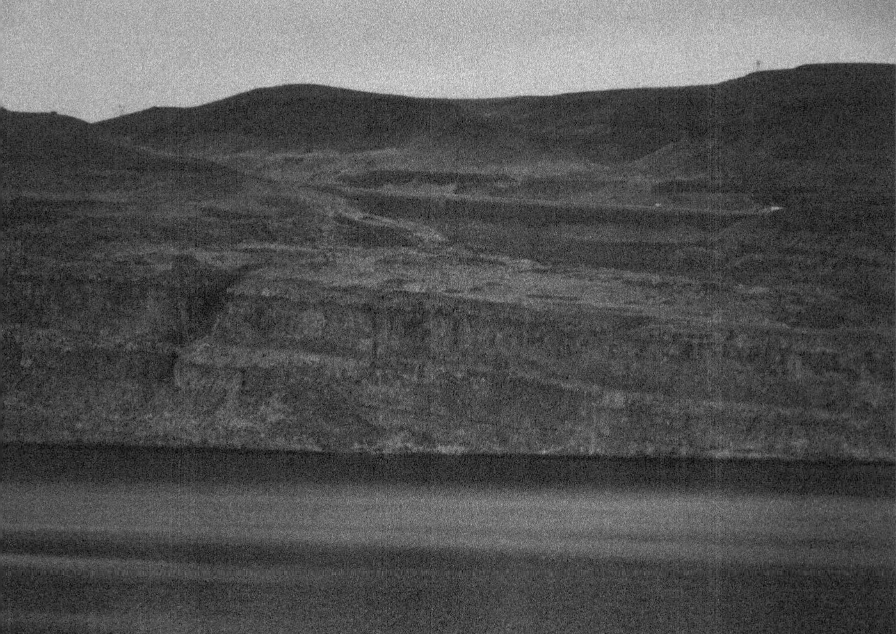

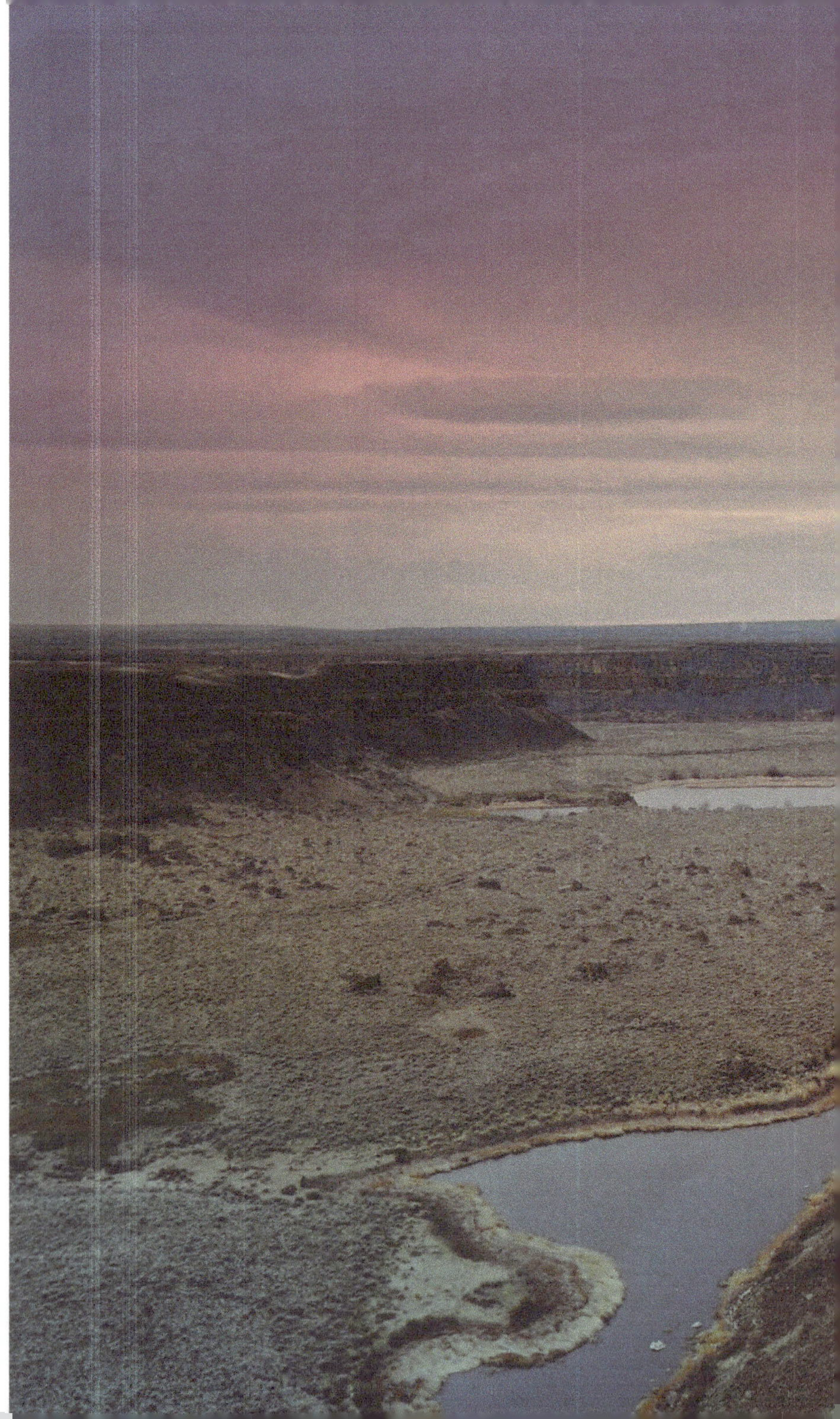

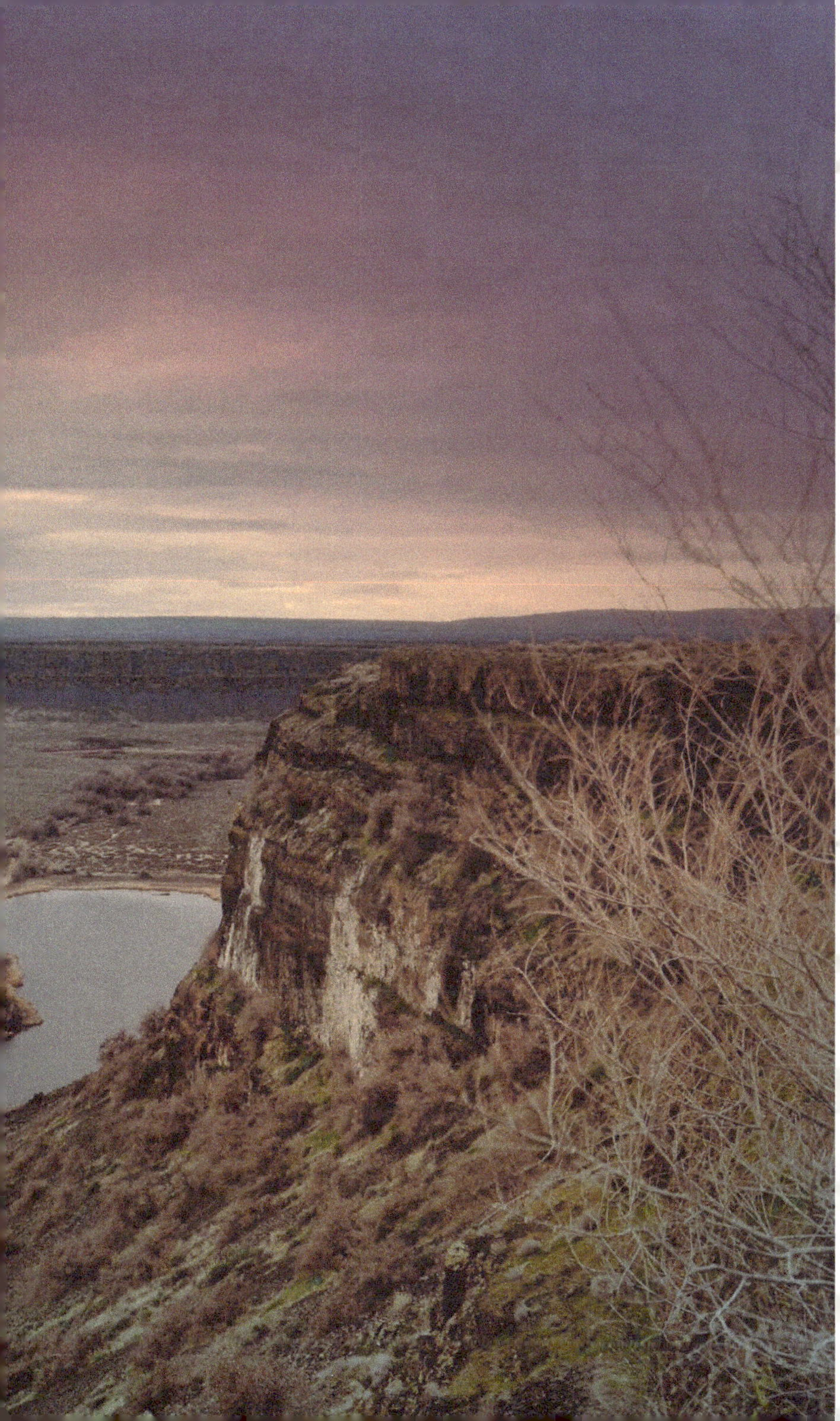

UNTIL THEN

When you're old
as the river
then you'll know,
when you're deep
as the ocean
then you'll believe,
when you're wild
as the fields
and vast as the mountains
then you'll see,
the beginning
was dark
and it is why all living things
stretch to the light.



*Closeup of dew on grass*
*(Next page: closeup of cranberry)*

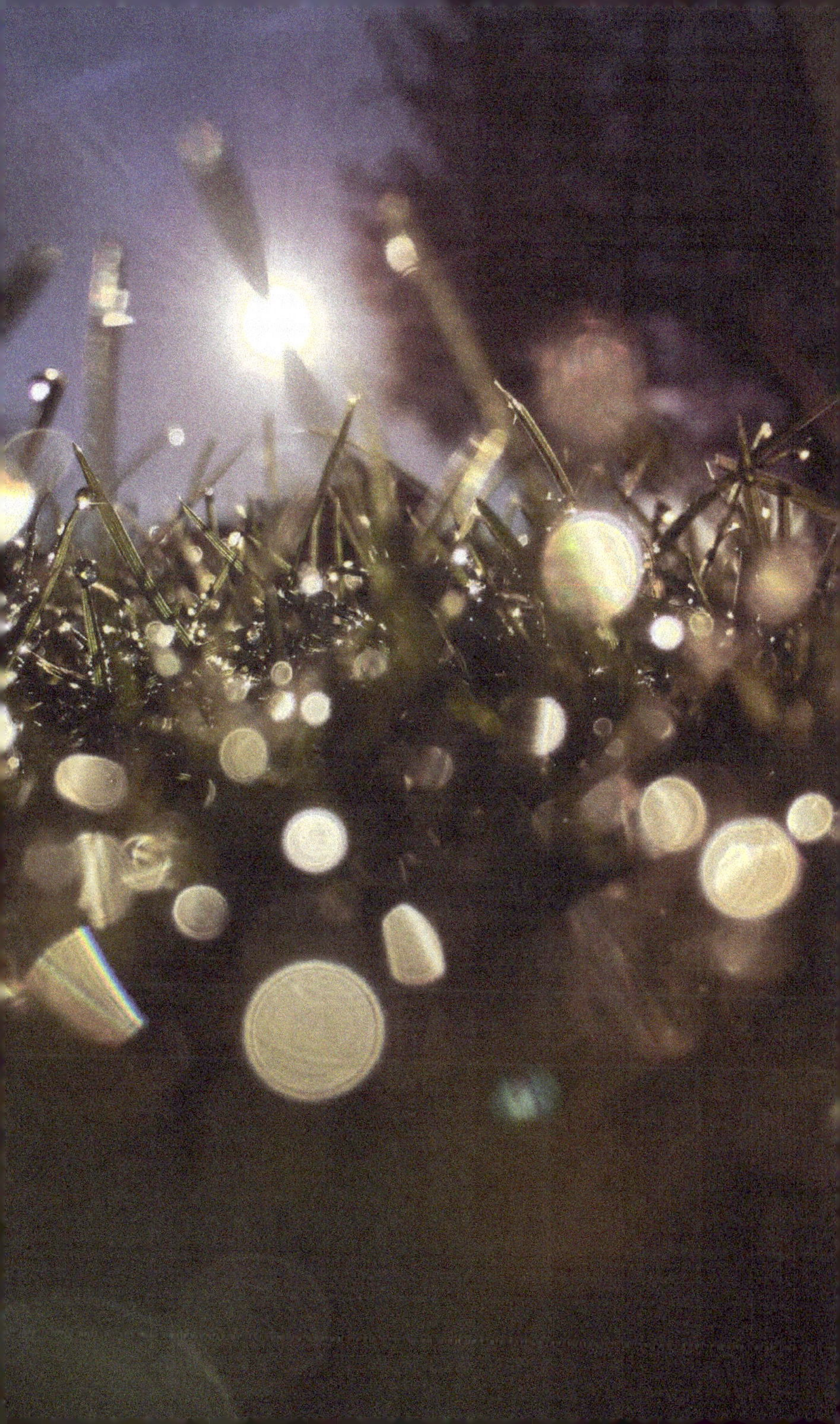

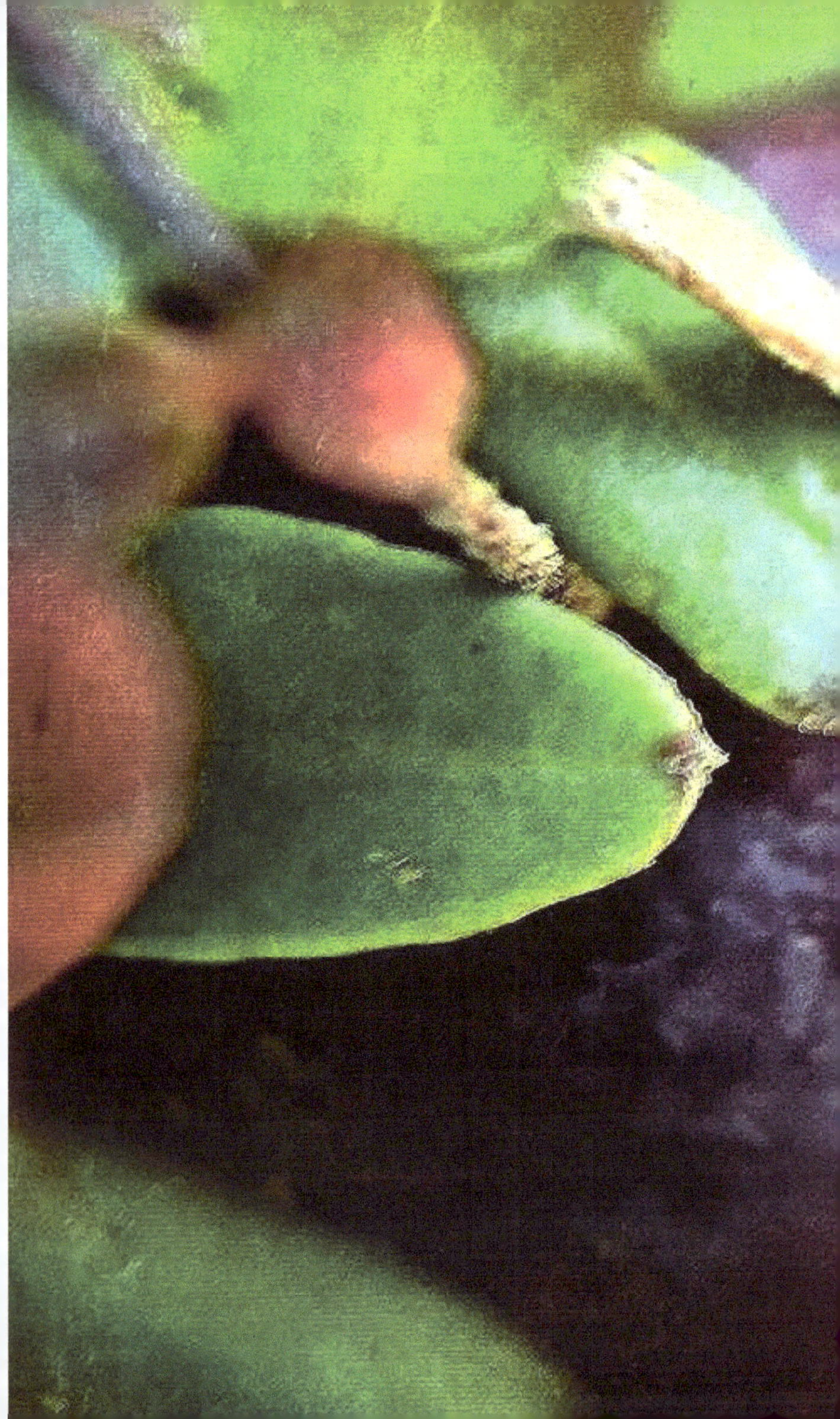

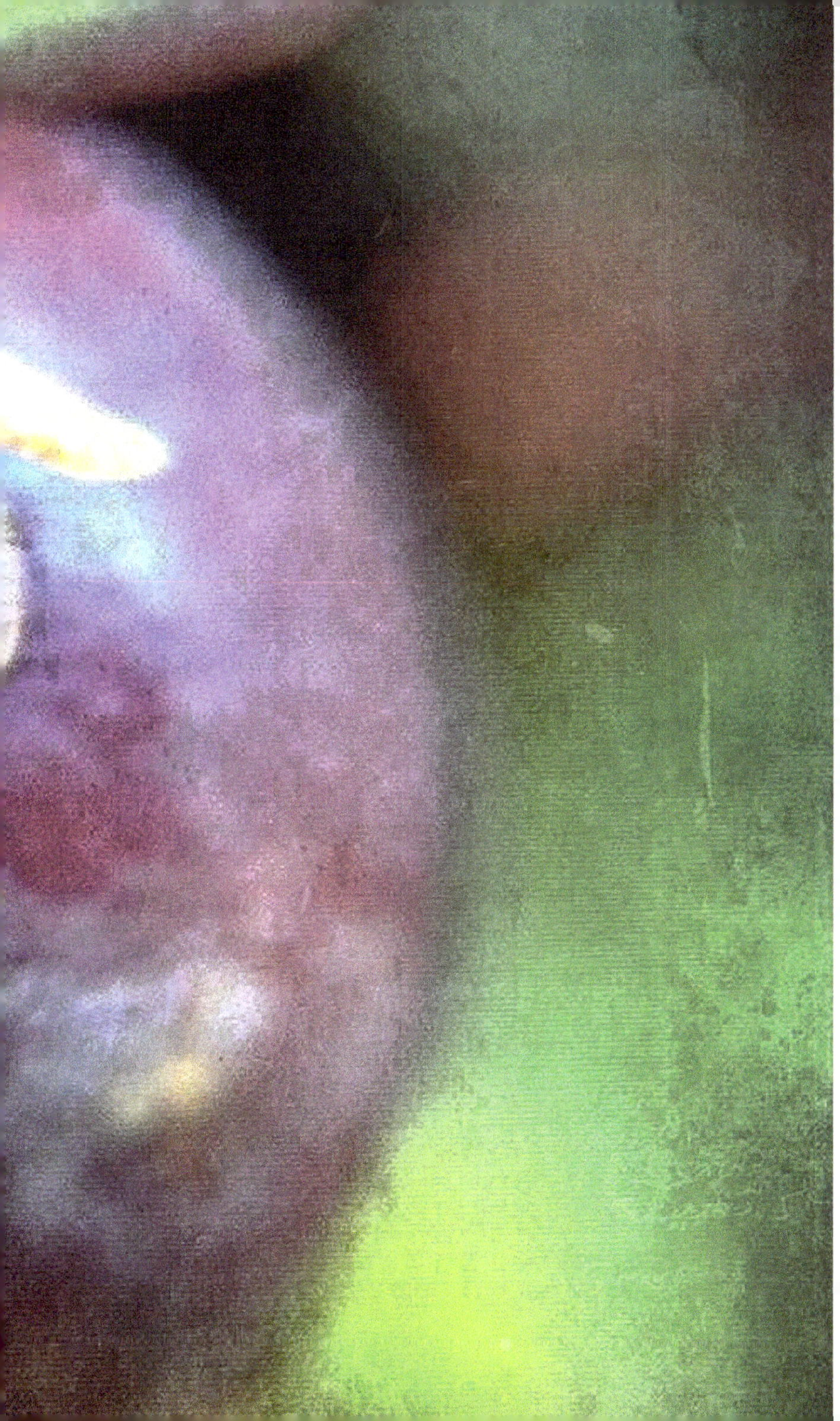

# A CLOSER LOOK
## cranberry bogs

Washington is one of the top producers of cranberries in the USA. They're native and grow on trailing vines in beds known as bogs or marshes. These peat bogs were created by glacial deposits thousands of years ago.

The tiny, tart berries were used by Native Americans as a medicine, dye and food. They were made into a poultice for wounds and mixed with cornmeal to cure blood poisoning. The juice was squeezed to color rugs and clothing. The berries were combined with dried deer meat and melted fat then pounded to a pulp and shaped into cakes, which were dried in the sun. It was called 'pemmican' and had the qualities of a modern energy bar.

Most Washington cranberry growers on the Long Beach peninsula use wet-pick methods for harvest. First, they flood the bogs with a nearby water source, like a pond, then use equipment to loosen the fruit from the vine.

The good berries float to the surface since each one has four air pockets. Afterwards, they're corralled with boom boards, skimmed off the surface with paddles and guided up a conveyor belt to a waiting truck.

In 2015, there was a drought and farmers were concerned about having enough water to flood the bogs. There was just enough, but some vines weren't as submerged, which made it harder to round up the berries.

Contemporary cultivation requires water-based landscapes that include, wetlands, flumes, ditches, ponds and lakes. These all provide a healthy, natural habitat for birds, insects and animals. Often the bogs' borders are planted with heather to attract bees for pollination.

A hard frost can kill the vines, so farmers must stay alert. They will flood the bogs to protect the crops if the temperature drops. There's a lot of work that goes into the beautiful, ruby-red cranberry sauce on your Thanksgiving table.

THE GATHERING

The heart of a cranberry
is in the bitter,
in the tart white
that wakes your tongue.

Its skin is the blood-red
of living memory,
a capsule of
sustenance,
a ruby reservoir.

The annual flood,
an autumn water birth,
floats it free from the peat bog
and the trailing vines
that tethered it
to earth.

That jubilant sea of
buoyant berries
reminds us of a perfect
peace,
and returns to us each year,
garnet spoonfuls of hope.

*Cran Mac Farm belongs to the Ocean Spray Cooperative.*
*Most of its cranberries become juice and Craisins.*

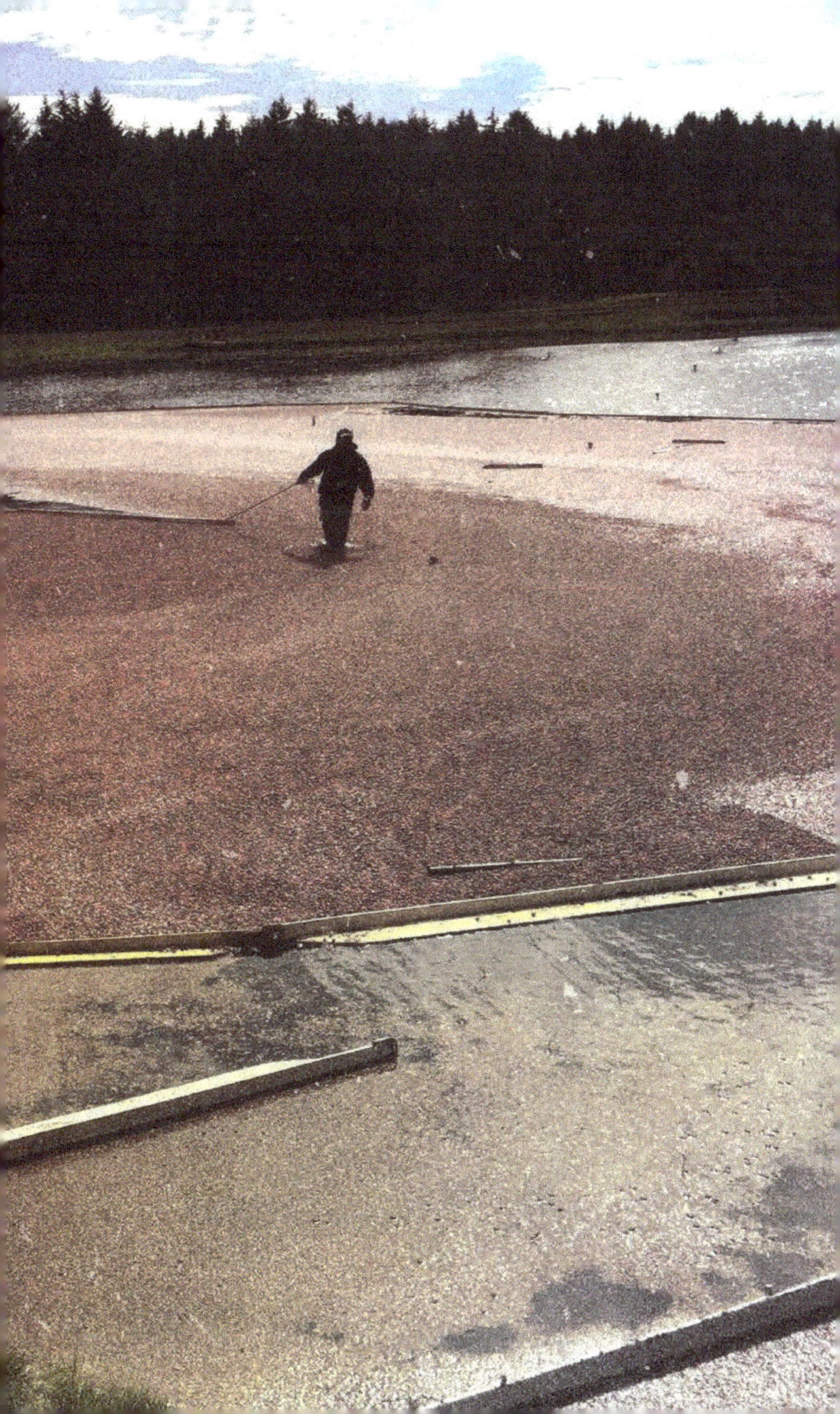

# A CLOSER LOOK
## the mosquito fleet

Between the 1850's-1930's, thousands of steamers traveled throughout Puget Sound. They transported people and goods over 40 different routes. The various boats were nicknamed the "Mosquito Fleet" because they were so numerous people said they looked like a "swarm of mosquitoes" on the water. Their numbers declined in the 1920's as cars rose in popularity.

There's a story by Newell and Williamson about the last voyage of the *Tacoma as* she made her final run under the only captain she ever knew, Captain Everett Coffin. It was 1930.

*"The Tacoma and the Indianapolis passed a little south of Three Tree Point. . . . Capt. Coffin pulled down a window and leaned out in the driving rain. The Indianapolis floated by, a dozen squares of light topped by a star. She spoke; three long, lingering blasts. . . . Capt. Coffin reached for his own whistle cord. Three long blasts. And he let the last blast die away slowly, until it was only a moan in the throat of the whistle. 'That's the last time we pass each other,' he said."*

When she arrived at the dock, every ship saluted her with three whistle blasts. Andrew Foss, the owner of Foss Tugs, sent a tug to help her dock, though it had been two years since Coffin could afford assistance.



*The Key Peninsula's Von Geldern Cove, Home*
*(Next page: Fisherman's Terminal, Seattle)*

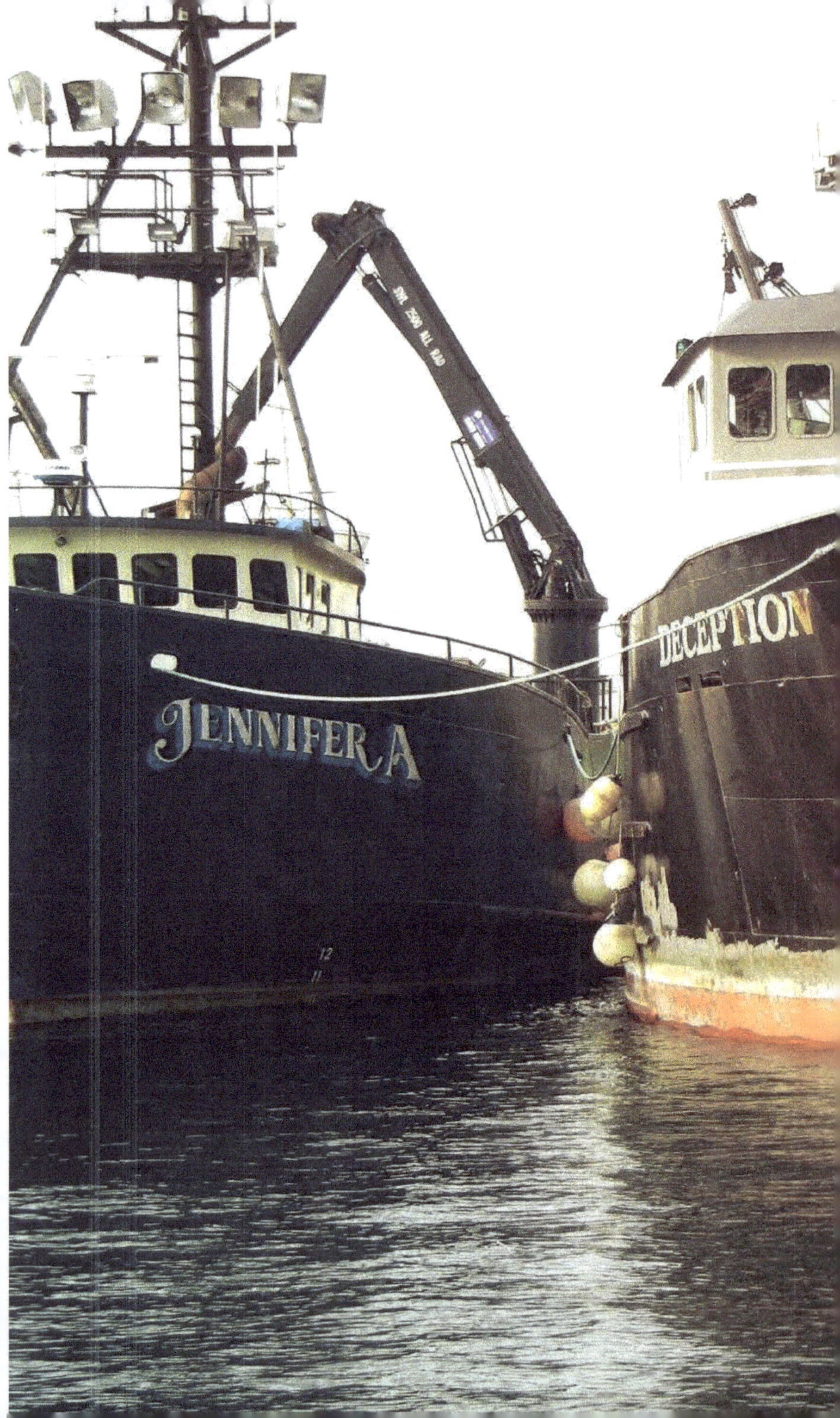
JENNIFER A
DECEPTION

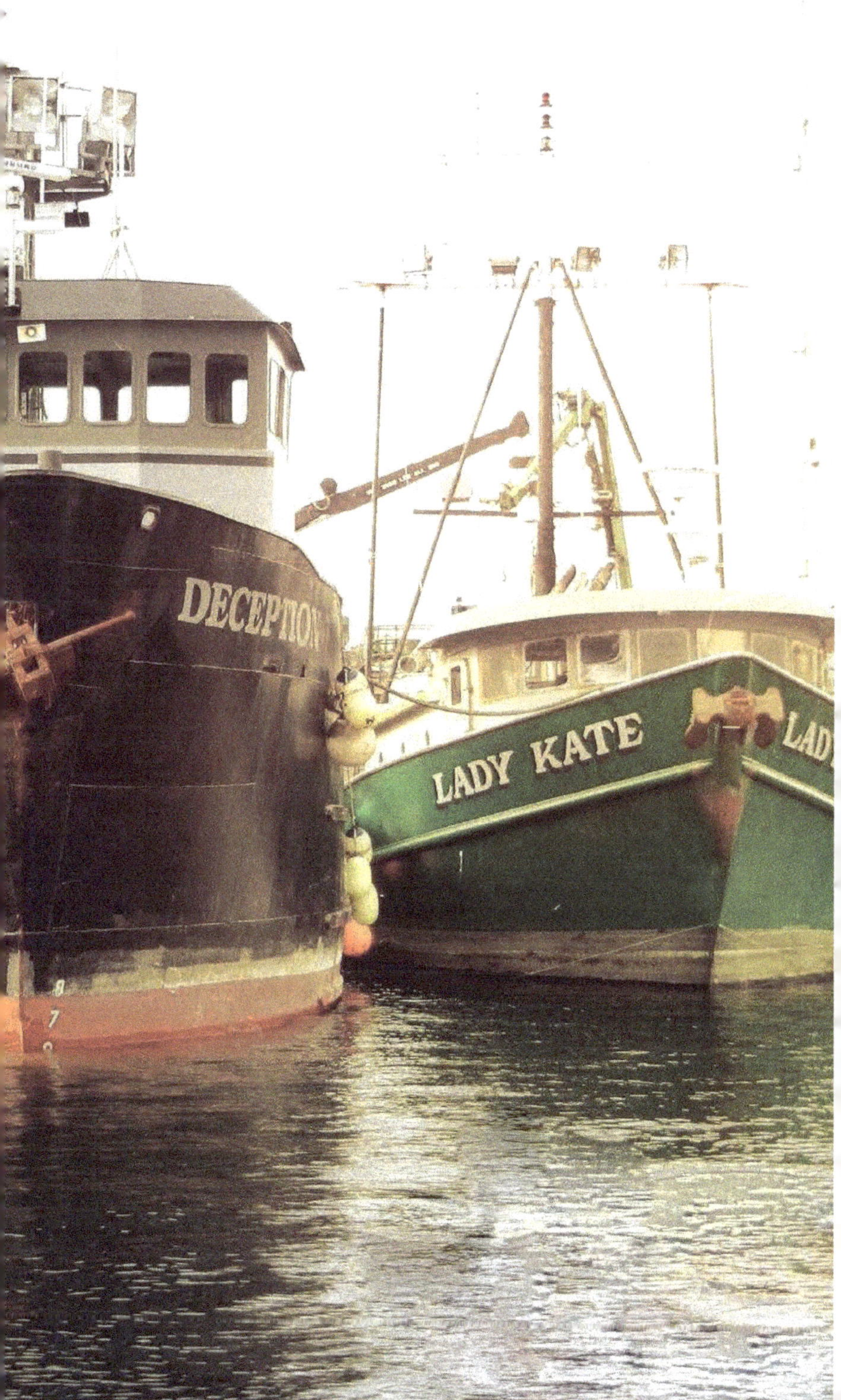

DECEPTION
LADY KATE
LAD

DROUGHT

There is a desert that
waits for water.

No. It doesn't wait.
It burns,
it falls in on itself
it shakes its brittle layers
into sheets of dry parchment
an ancient, lost lake bed
its back
sunburnt into split layers
of fractured skin
ruptured.

Now. Can you feel the need?
Can you sense this eager thirst?

"Before I leave.
Before I go away
for good,"
it seems to say,
"Know that I am here
underneath this stricken
pose. Know that I am here.

I am here
in this wasteland
where drought has
dried my bones.

And you are the answer
you are the
deluge, the cloudburst
you are the rainstorm
you are the fresh, green field
the cool hands of
quiet night.

You are the clean breeze
of late autumn afternoons.
Redemption is written on
your skin
your soft touch
something so simple,
so free to give."

The desert is growing.
The desert is gone.

*(Next page: salmon skeleton)*

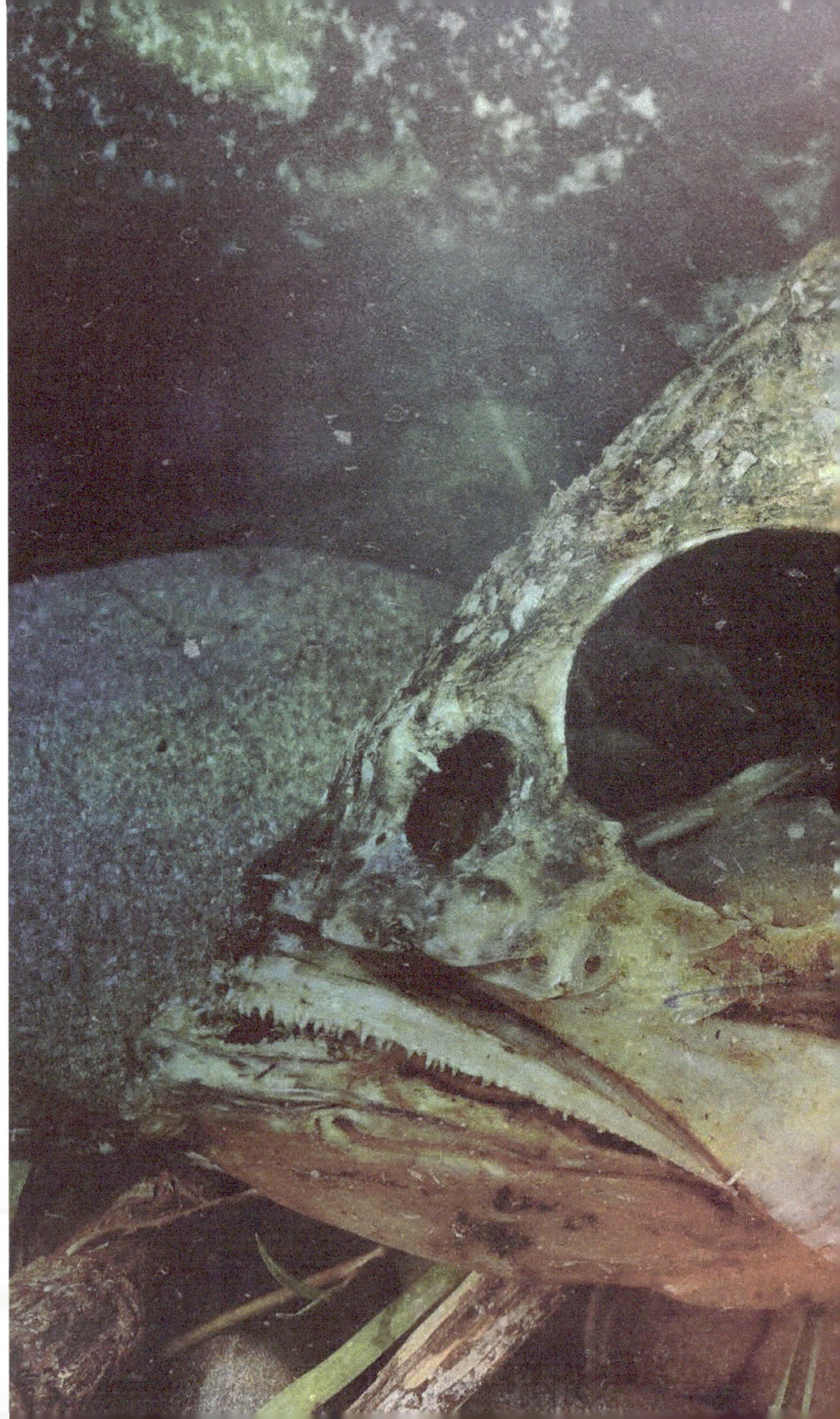

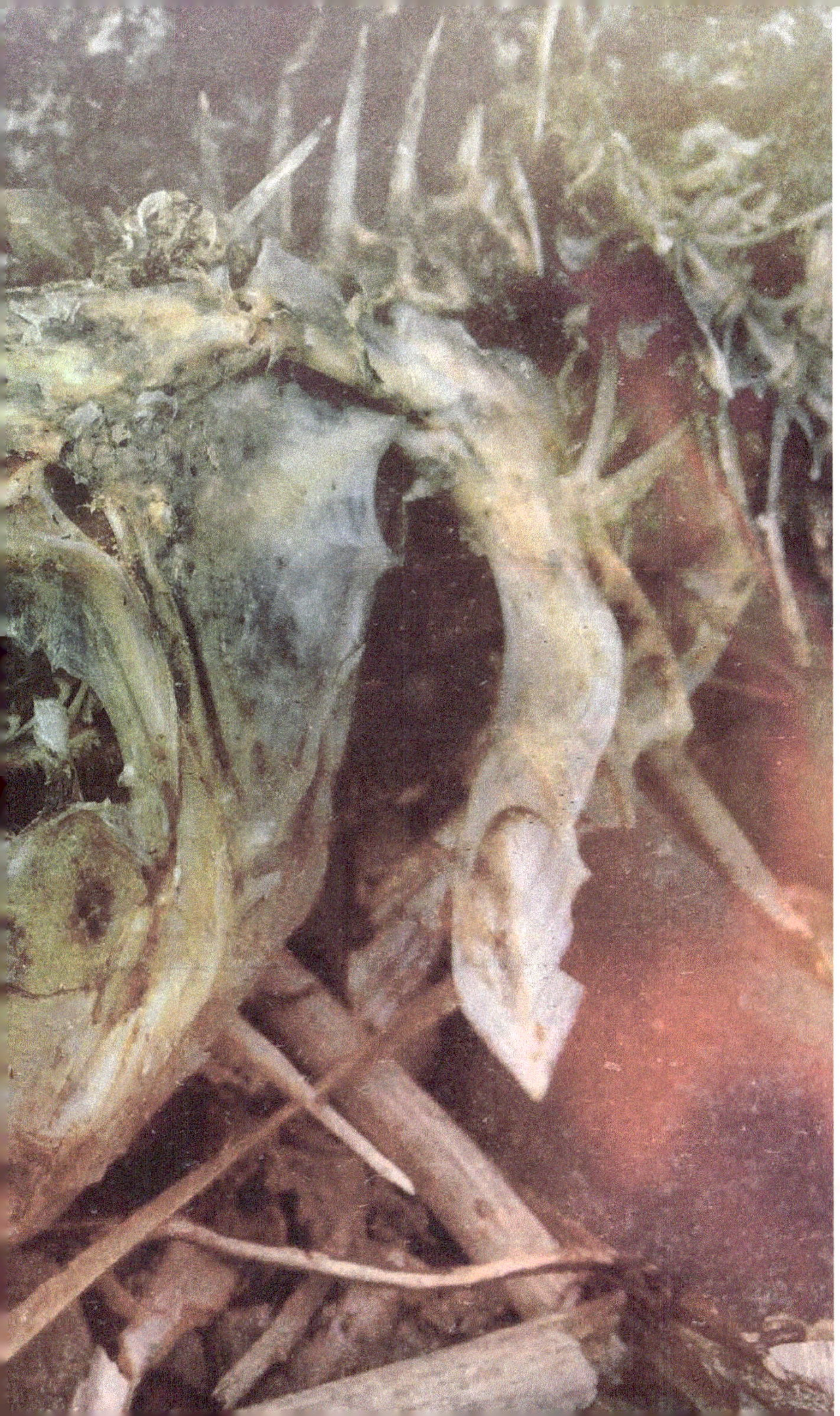

BAPTISM

This poem is no
apocalypse
nothing you haven't heard before
just this one
small revelation –
you fall in love too easily.

Too many
people, places, things,
they break your heart
and lift you up,
filling a reverential soul.

Every layer of your skin
hums with a vast array
of music in the veins,
the power of the image,
of words, a forgotten melody.

You gather sights and sounds
and embrace this broken world
to fill a sandy reservoir. And though
it's all been sifted, you still wait
for something more.

You allow the sun and rain to penetrate
and know the look in stranger's eyes,
because they feel it, too.

We ate the apple
and live our own obliteration.
We burrow into others and
excavate the soul,
but still, there's something
missing.

On the table, at the end,
in the cleansing fire
we're pale-boned brothers,
sisters dressed in stale gray ash,
burnt offerings,
echoes hoping memory
will keep our light alive.

Where do we pour our treasures
when all our lives we burn
to feel the familiar in each other?

Can this broken faith be mended
when we're made of glass,
kept in caves with such small hearts
and this half-blind sense of sight?

Perhaps, I feel too much,
this keen awareness
a compulsion
to kneel in muddy water and remember
the wet blessing that
will never wash away.

The Church was buried in my skin
while faithless preachers hurt the helpless.
These were not dull shepherds
abandoning their sheep.
They were the wolves
devouring God's children.

There is no greater sin.

We come of age each day,
on the eve of redemption,
to walk the path alone.
But in the distance, all our roads converge.
We must remember this.

There's music in our language,
to remind us,
every word a proper note,
a glimpse at elevation
to wash away the gilded
systems of belief.

Maybe these words will pluck
a long forgotten note,
a harmony of being buried deep inside.
The revelation will reveal
we're coming close
and not alone
in our undoing.

You see, I feel too much
and fall in love too easily.
And I am revealed
by you.

Ellensburg

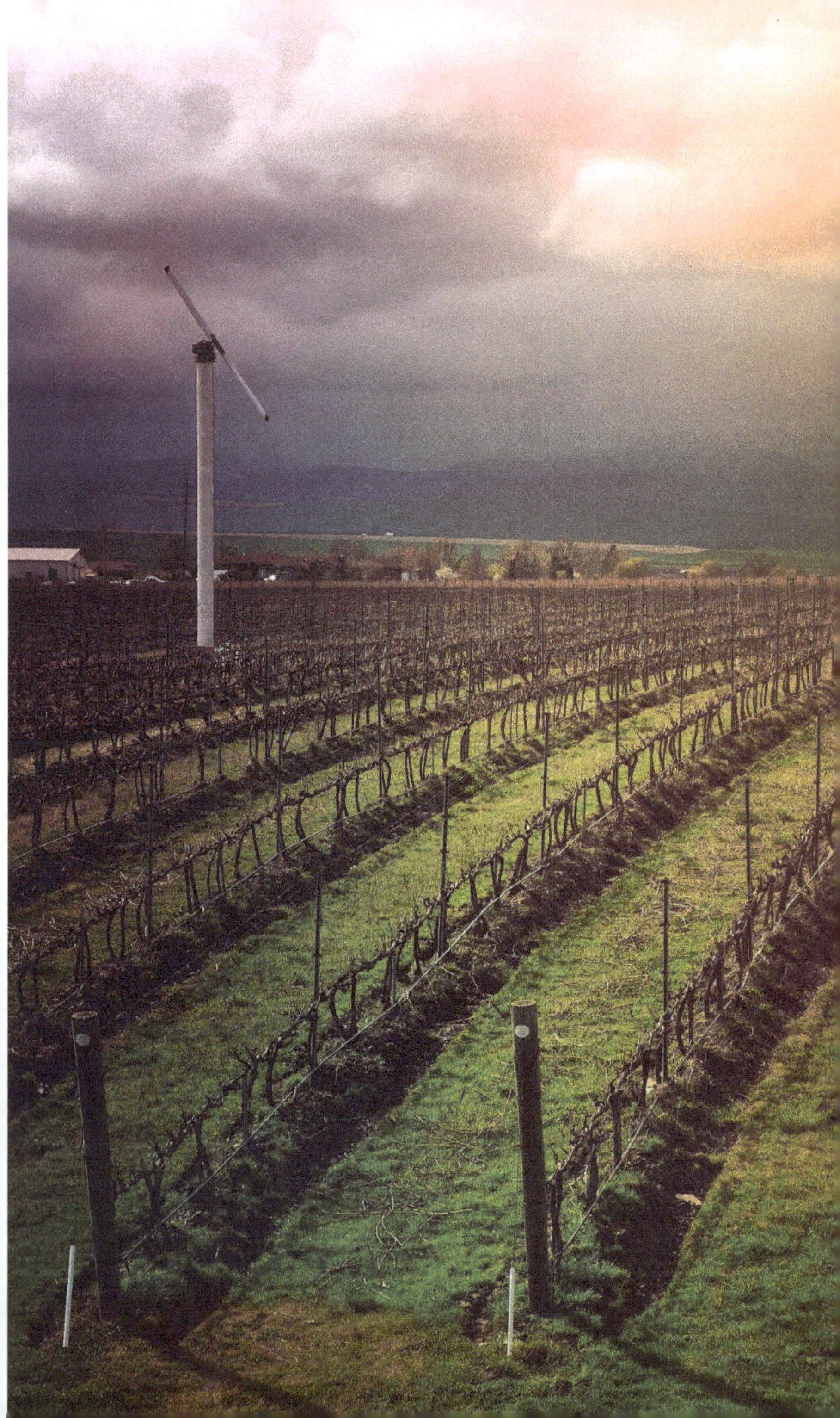

# A CLOSER LOOK
## viticulture

* Washington is the second largest premium wine producer in the nation with over 850 wineries and 13 *American Viticultural Areas* (AVAs), which are specific federal and geographical growing regions.

* *Terroir* is a combination of environmental factors like soil, climate and water that gives wine its unique flavors.

* Temperatures can swing up to 40 degrees between night and day. This is called *diurnal shift* and allows grapes to ripen and develop acidity.

* Washington averages 16 hours of sunlight a day, about 1 hour more than California's wine growing region.

* Cold night air will settle in the low areas of a vineyard, causing frost and endangering crops. Fans, or wind machines, are placed at key points to draw down warm air.

## WADE

Why does water move
the way it does
through us
in ebbs and
eddies
in drips and
dips
of turbulence,
a current in our veins?

We are merely the
wake
and the song at the
beginning of time
was a spoken word,
the word was
water,
and its melody
remains.



*Horsehead Bay, Gig Harbor*

SAMSARA

I walked a
well-worn
path between
salal, fir and
cedar,
a keyhole in the thick
woods that hug
the coast.

The prehistoric shore
had worn away,
its tide pool creatures
stranded in a liminal
existence.

The sky, the sea, something in between,
caught in an axial age.



*Ruby Beach, Olympic National Park*
*(Next page: Ruby Beach)*

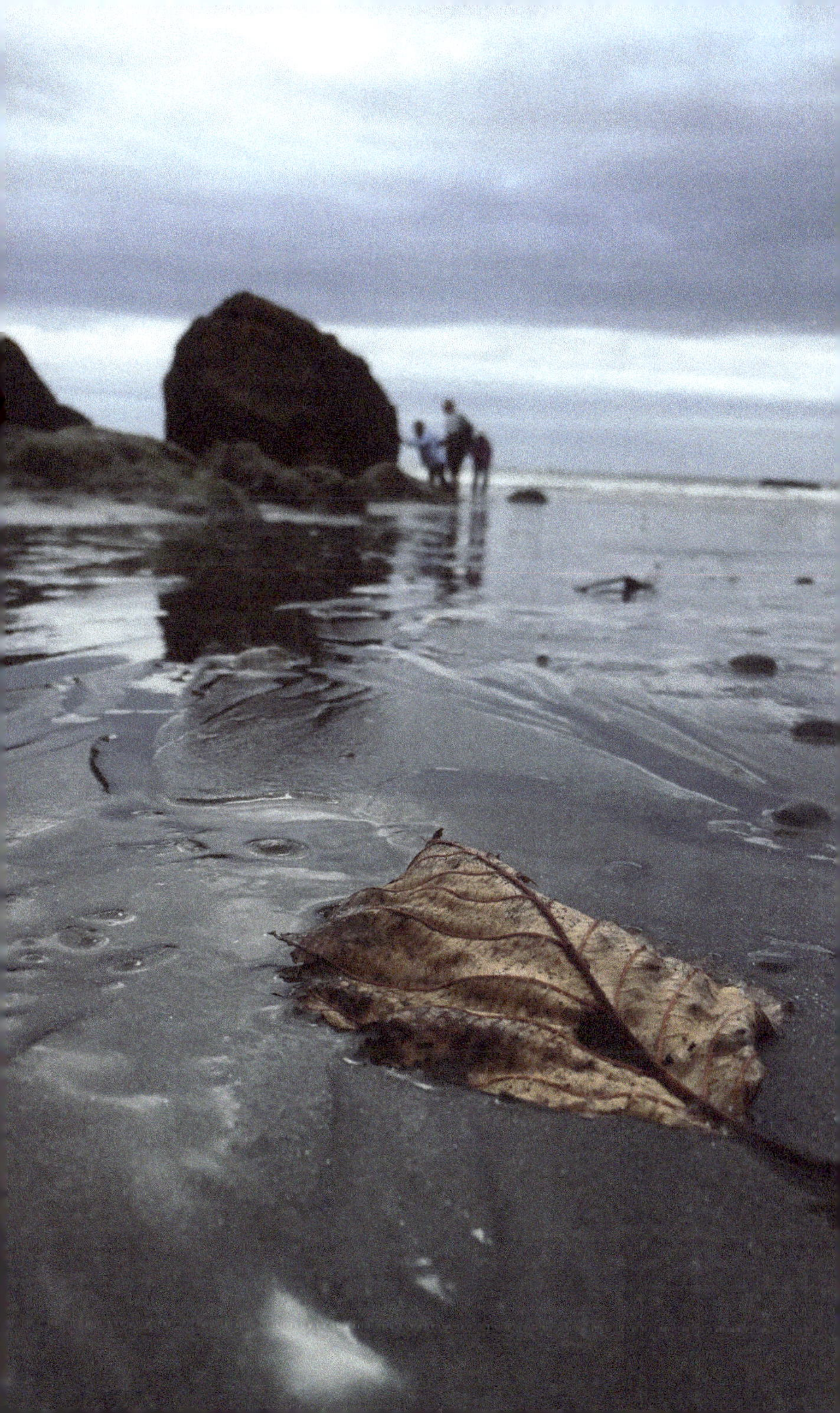

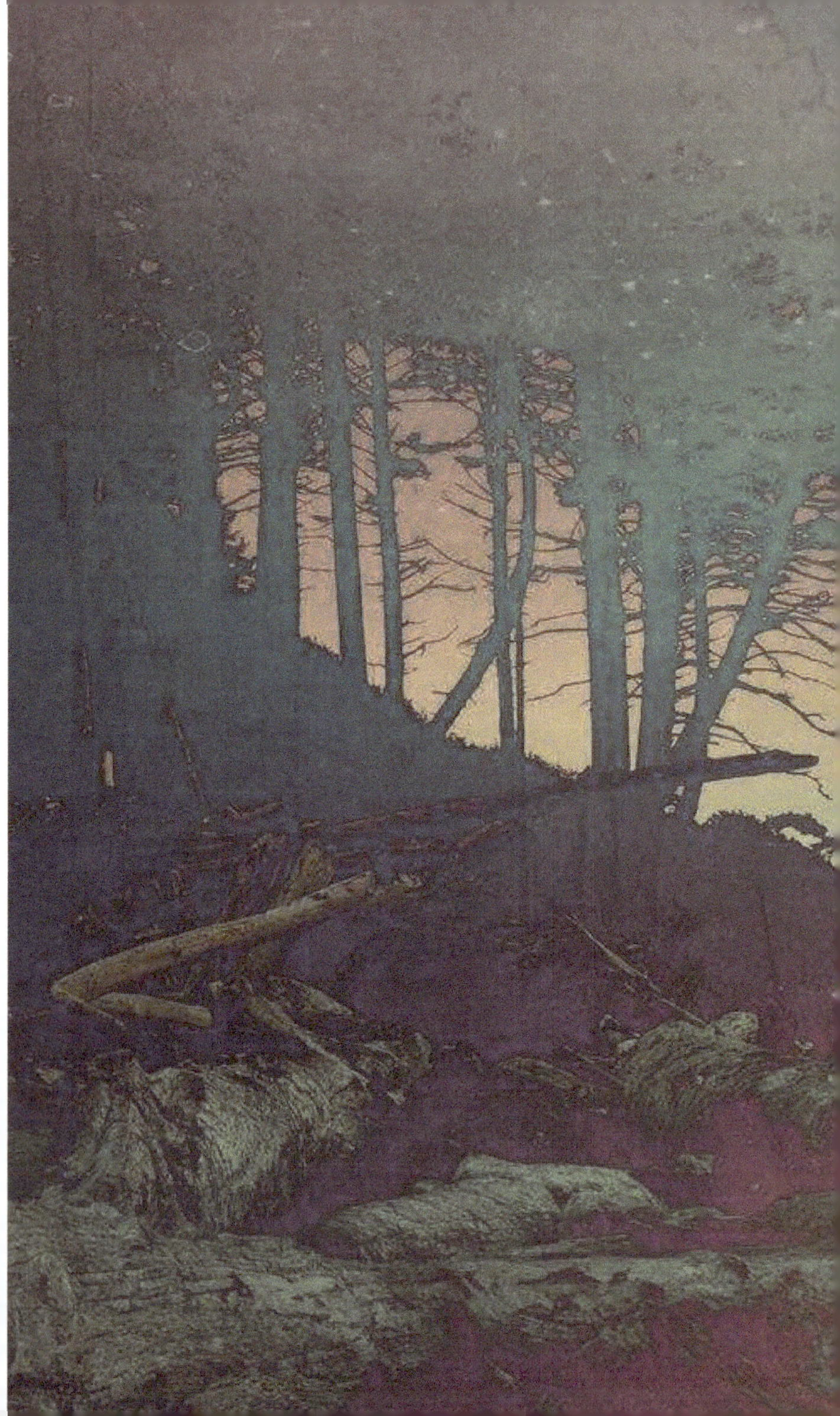

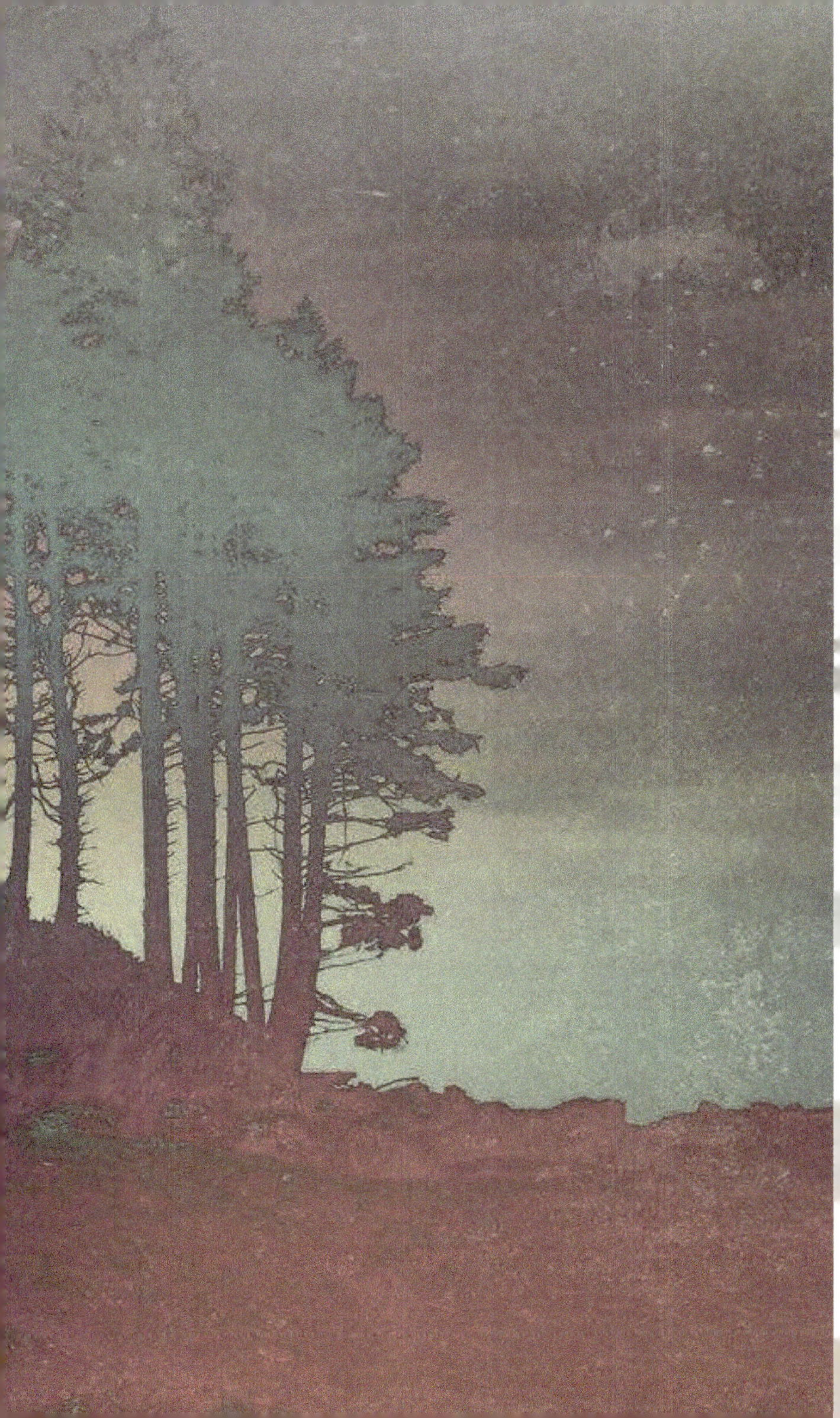

PROOF

Everything an
algorithm
tide pools full of
pentagons, a five-point
symmetry.

Arms and petals,
leaves unfurl,
bound by a geometric
blueprint.

The architect has left
a mark,
signed every living
thing in phi and
Fibonacci.



*Nautilus shell*
*(Next page: closeup of nautilus shell)*

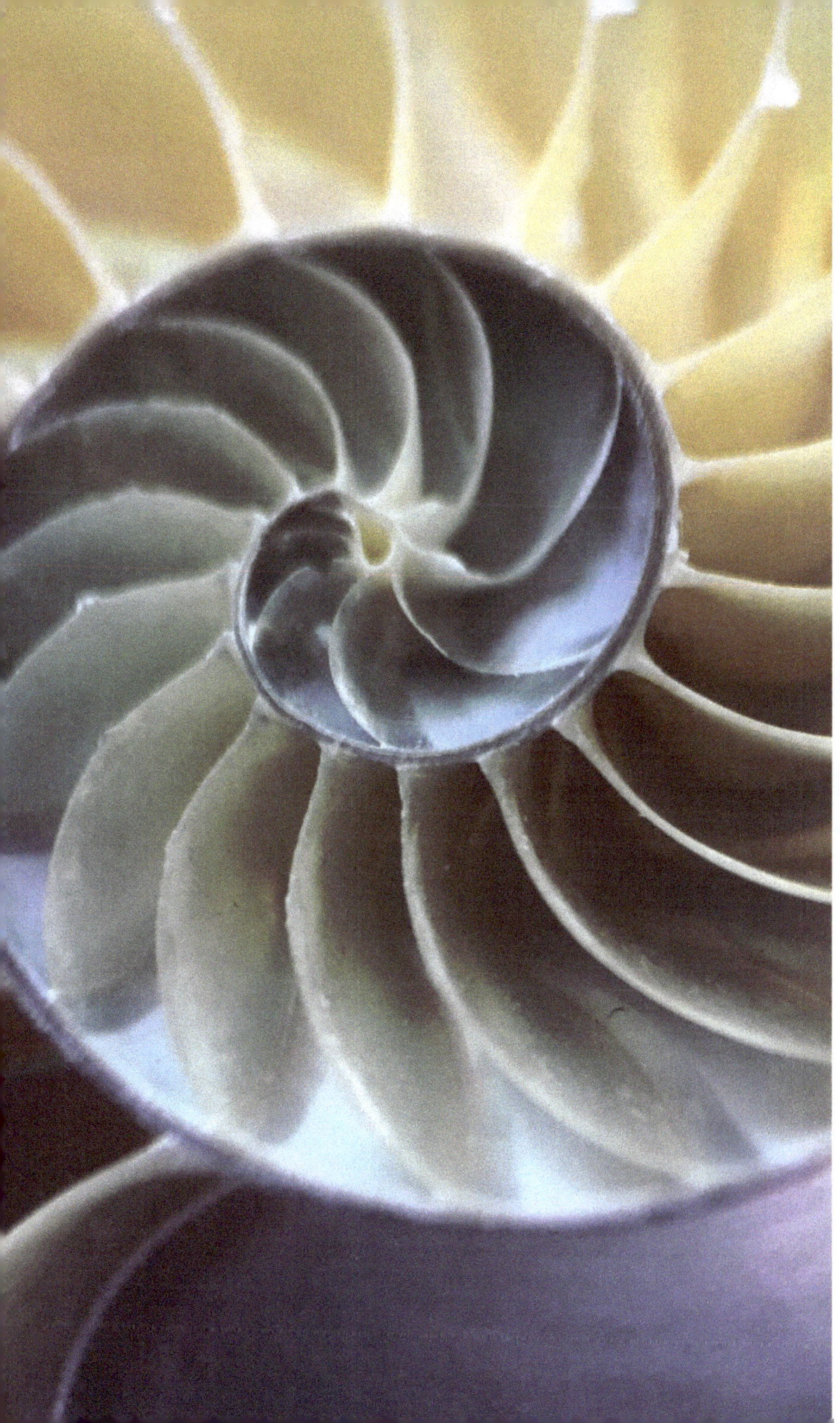

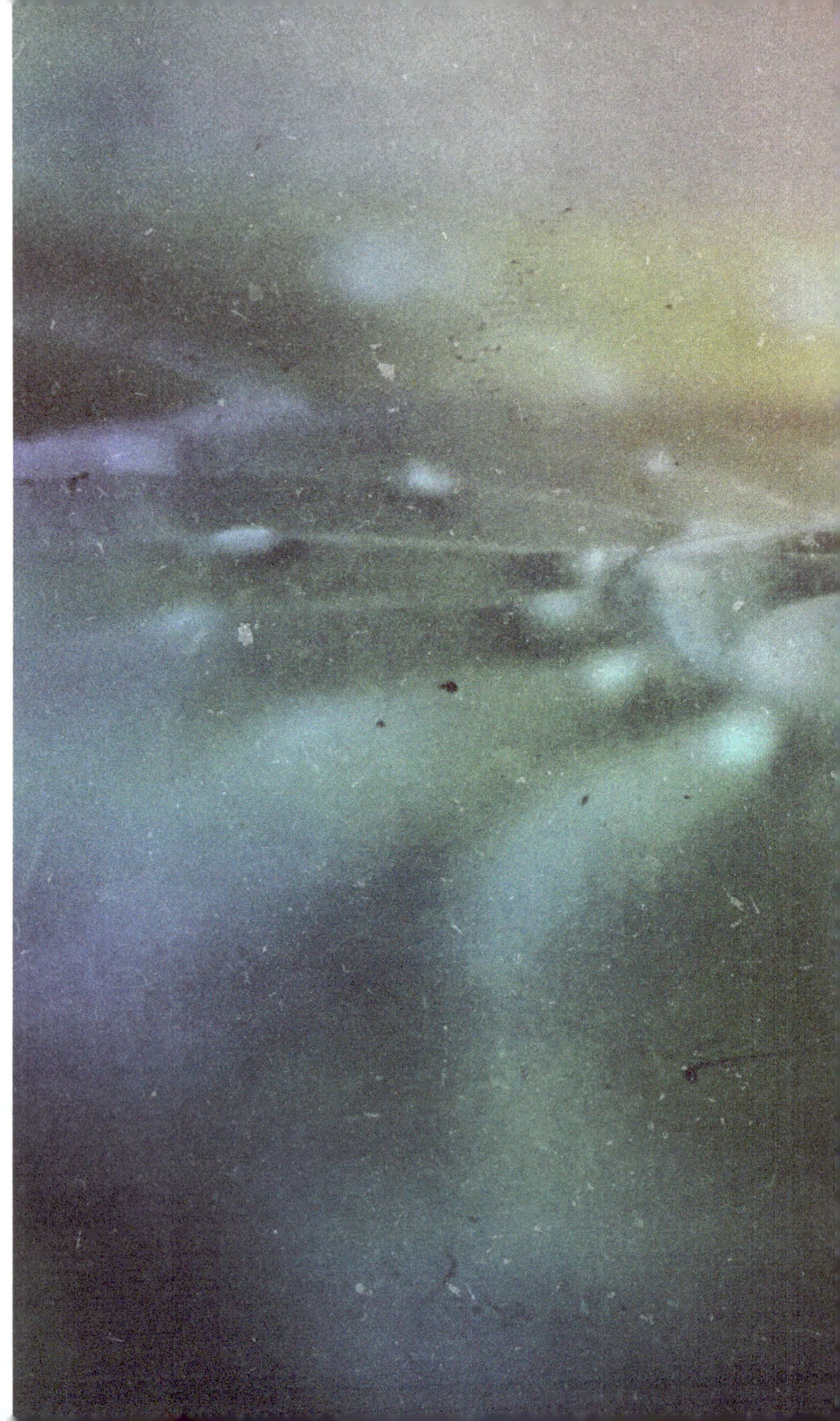

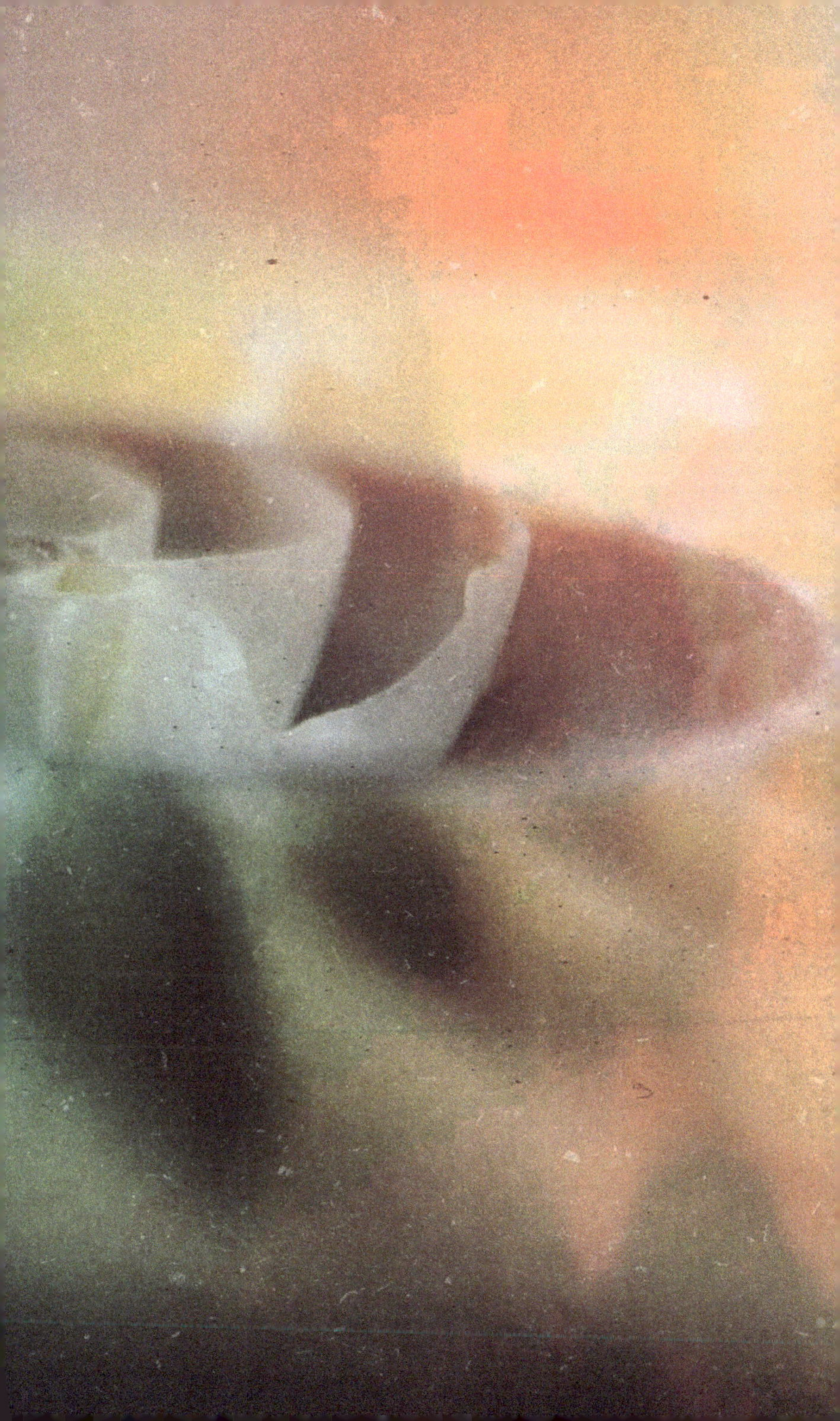

## UNCLAIMED

*Sea burials have occurred since the ancient Greek era. Locally, unclaimed remains are given a dignified ceremony aboard a sheriff's boat and scattered into the Puget Sound.*


It is the time of day
when salt-brined air
fills your lungs, collects on
your lips.

We are out on the water, opening
boxes.

Ross. Swanson. Porter.

The chaplain's prayers
hang in the air
as contents slip into
silent gray storm clouds
under water.

We remember, even if
others have forgotten
and the sea accepts
the offering.

                    *Commencement Bay, Tacoma*

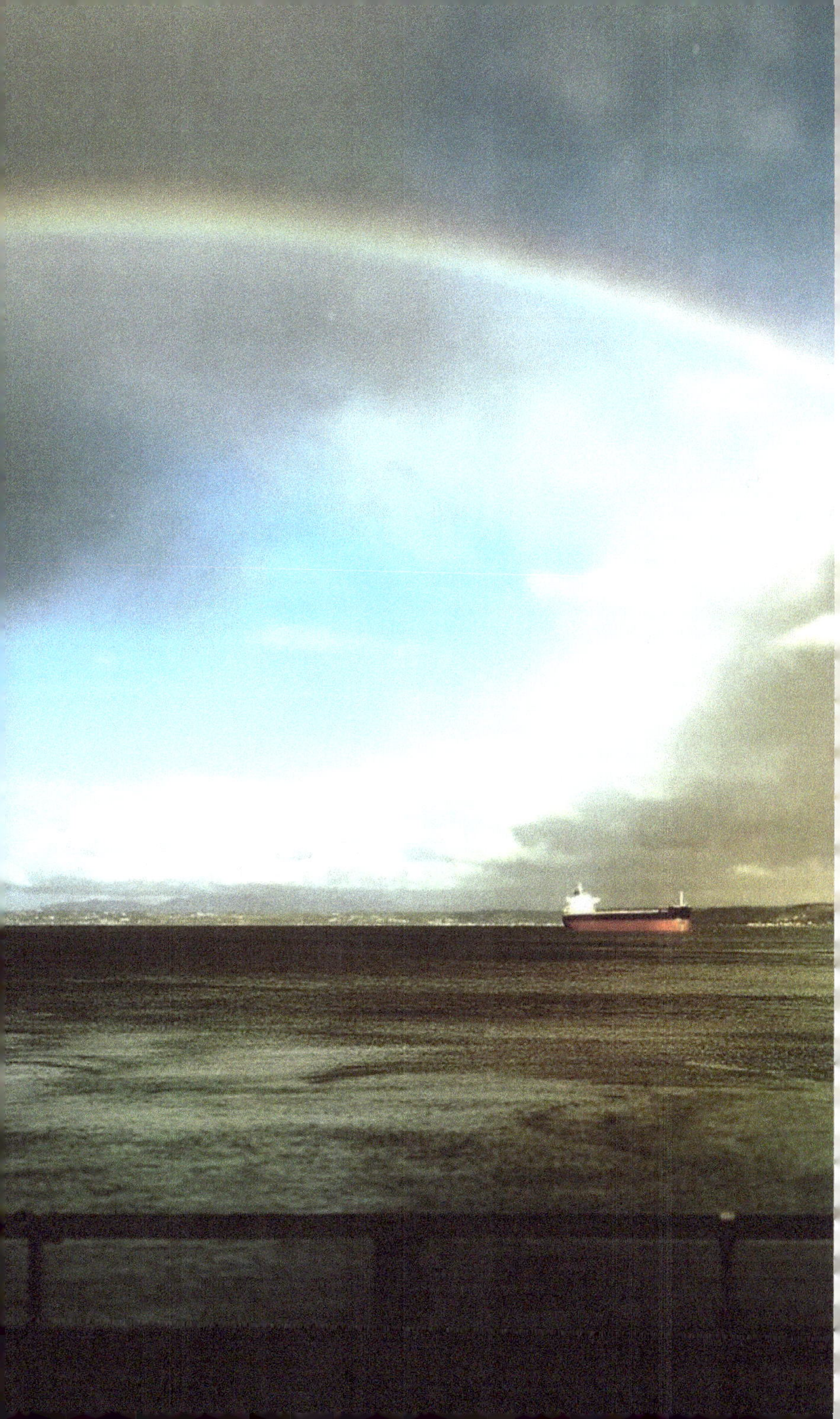

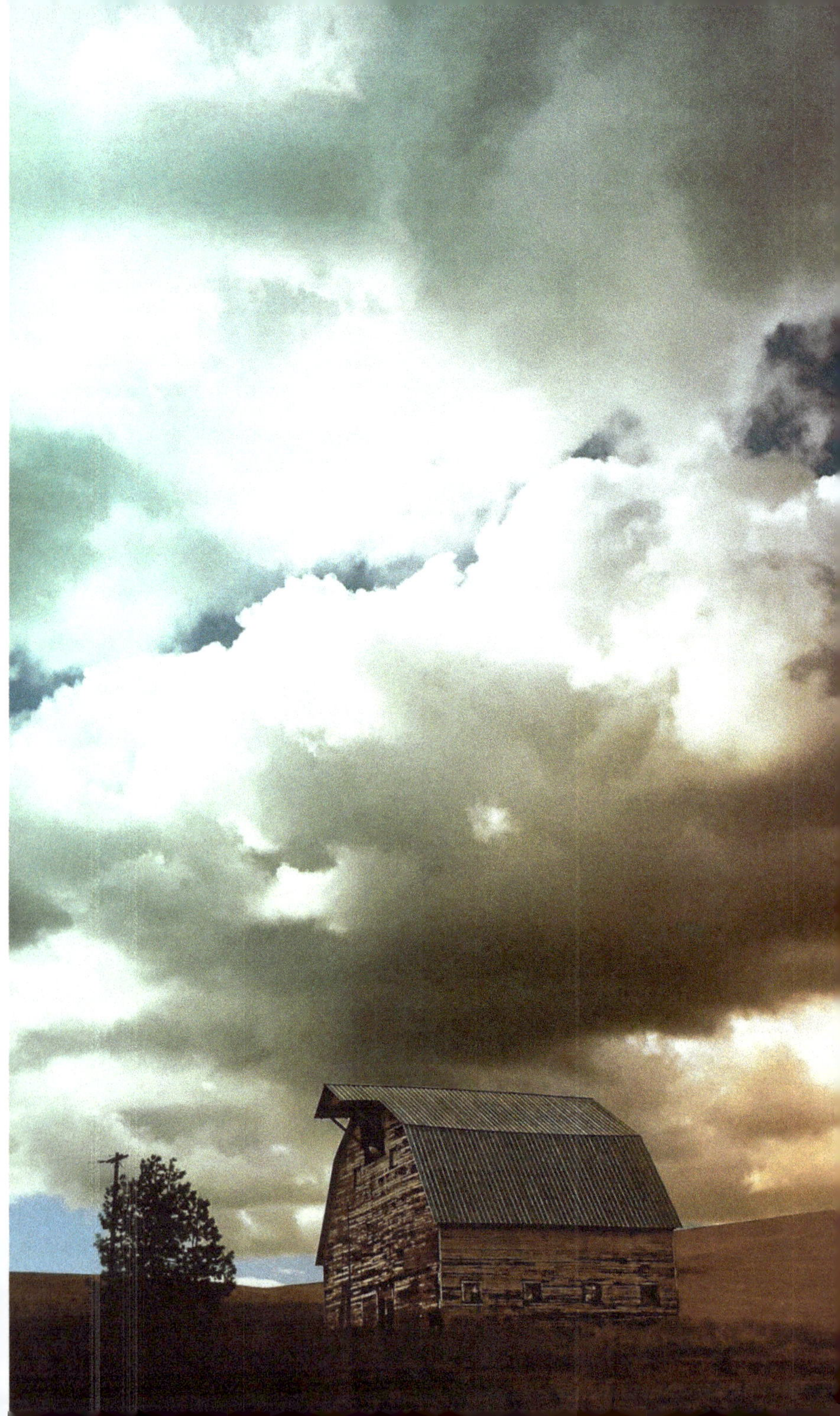

# A CLOSER LOOK
## *the palouse*

The 2 million serene, rolling acres known as the Palouse are located in southeastern Washington, on the dry side of the Cascades. The area was named after the native Palouse Indians and it is a landscape unlike anything in the world with coulees, plunge pools and buttes.

It formed after the massive Missoula floods rushed over it to the Columbia River. The muddy water carried a tremendous amount of rich sediment. Over time, southwesterly winds blew fine silt over the undulating landscape and created dunes hundreds of feet thick. The wind-blown dirt is called, *loess*. Its perfectly-sized particle retains the exact amount of water required to support life.

Wheat is grown on the dunes, along with barley, onions and 30% of the world's lentils. More recently, the area has become famous for its wine production, which happens to be the same latitude as France's Bordeaux region.

With few trees and homes, some see the Palouse as barren and lonely. Others see an ancient land full of mystery and life.

*Abundoned barn in Pullman*

# THE PALOUSE

Soft white
winter wheat
sprouts in the
humps and the
hallows.

We're lost in a sea of
capsized boats,
their full-belly
hulls bloat in the
sun.

Wind, the patient,
invisible architect,
whispers the
golden grained
dunes into
existence.



*Palouse Scenic Byway, Colfax*

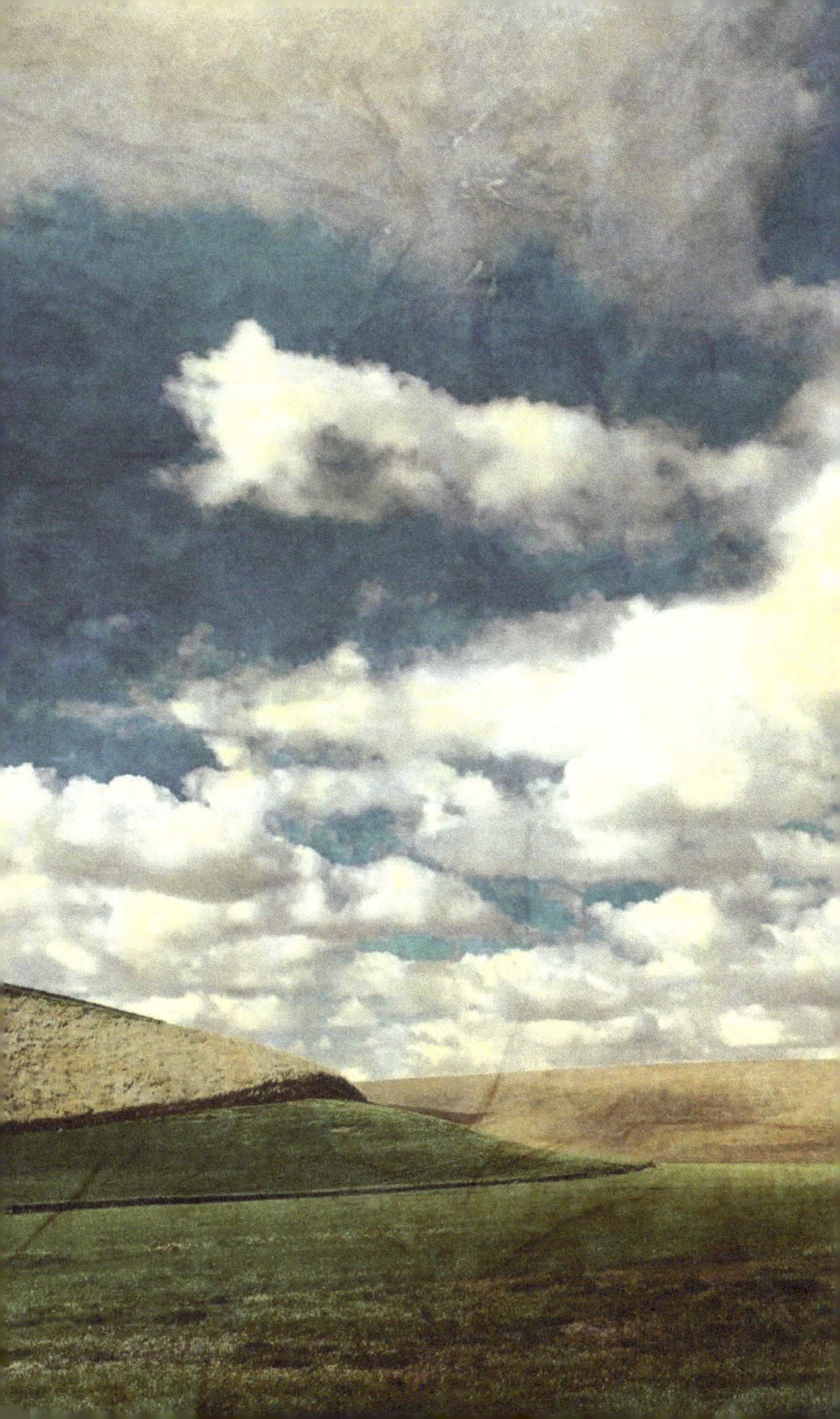

BUBBLES

I've let all
my air out.

I've emptied
my lungs in
        bubbles

        to sink to the
        bottom

                the world on mute
                in slow-motion drifts

                                maybe down
        here
                        the Miseries
                        will pass me by?

                                    *Wollochet Bay, Gig Harbor*

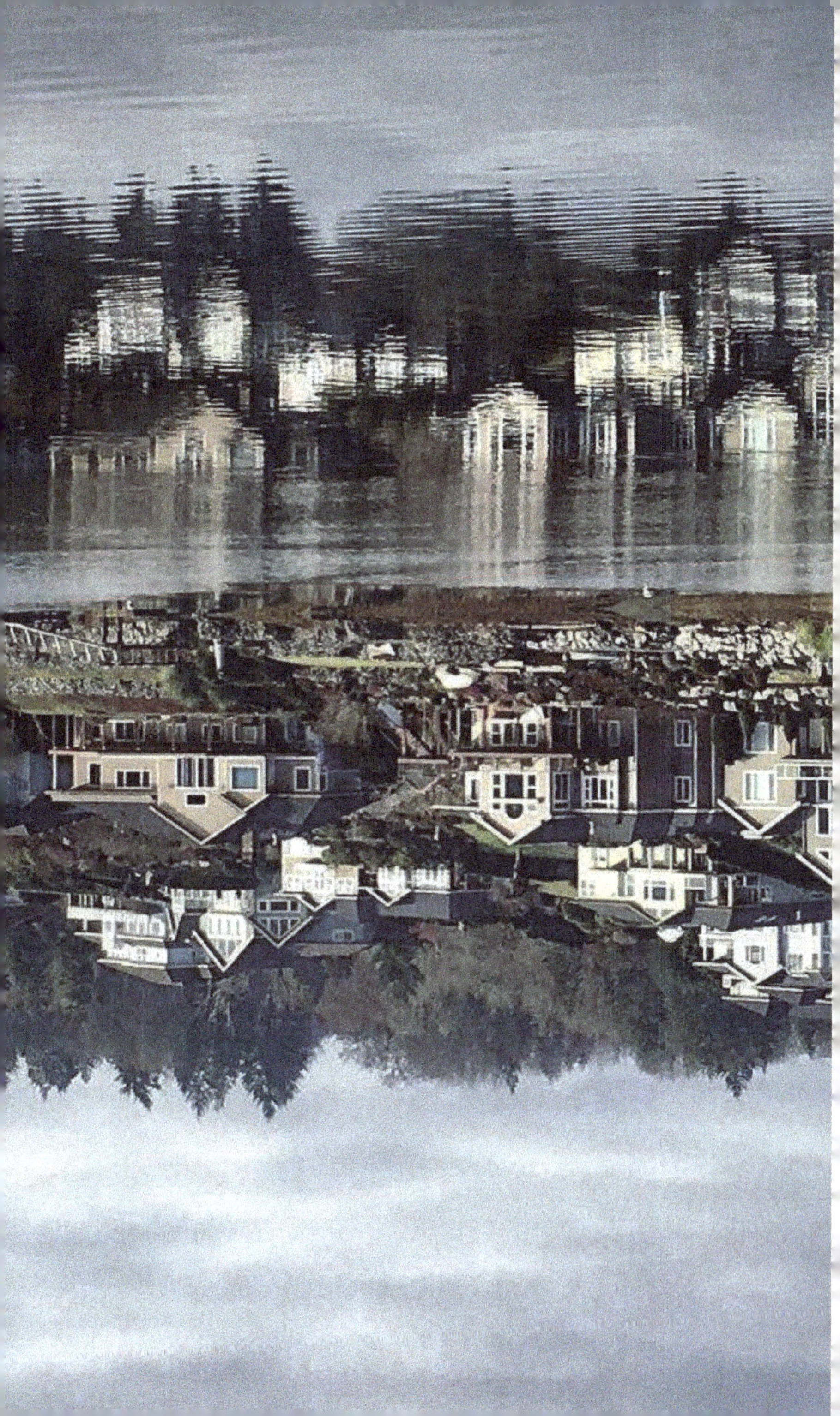

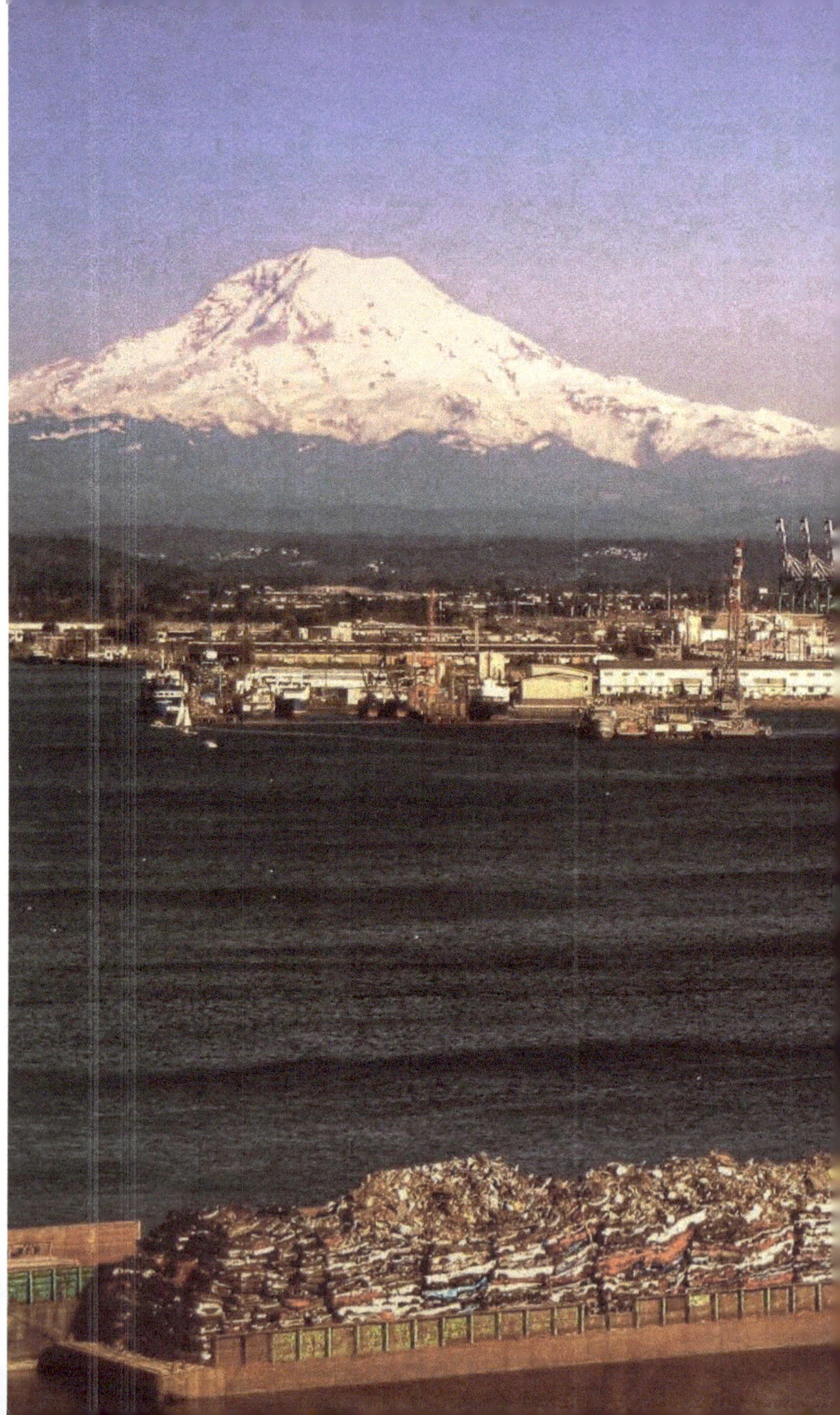

# A CLOSER LOOK
## *washington's fire mountains*

Four Washington volcanoes are classified "Very High Threat" by the US Geological Survey: Glacier Peak, Mount Baker, Mount St. Helens and Mount Rainier. Mount Rainier is also on the *Decade Volcano* list, which lists the 16 most dangerous volcanoes.

Mount Rainier is located in the Cascade Mountain Range and has 26 major glaciers. It is one of the  largest active volcanoes in the entire world. Since it has a tremendous amount of ice along its flanks, its considered a deadly threat to the population living below it. An explosion would create *lahars*, which are gigantic mud flows full of debris with the consistency of wet concrete. Lahars rapidly flow down the sides of a volcano, following rivers and destroying everything in their path.

The massive mountain (14,411 feet summit) lies completely in Pierce County, which runs all the way to the Puget Sound. This is the widest range in elevation of any county in the United States.

*Mount Rainier looms over the Tacoma Tideflats*

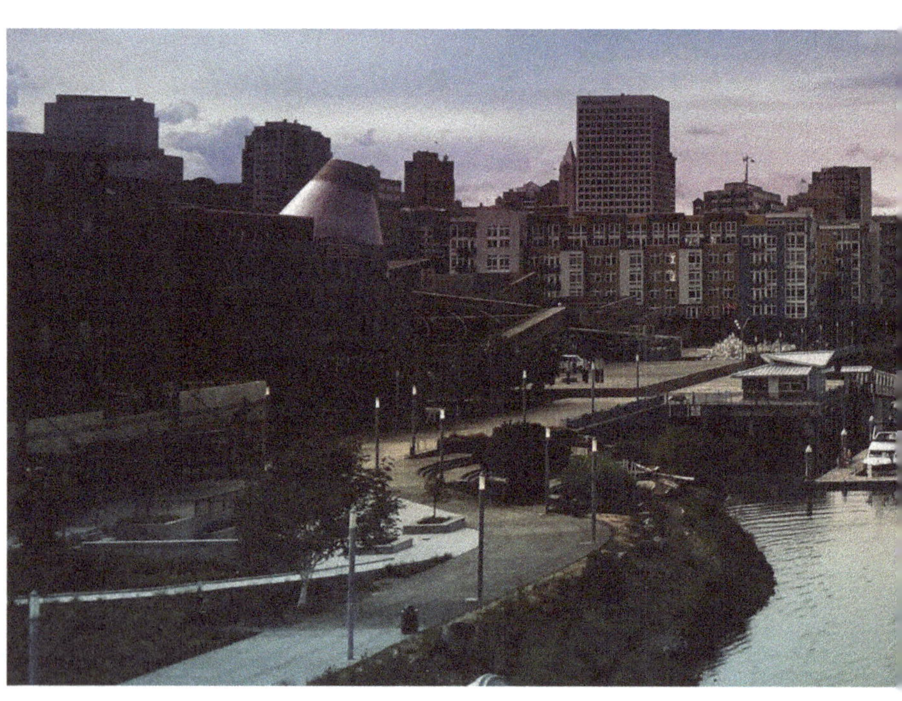

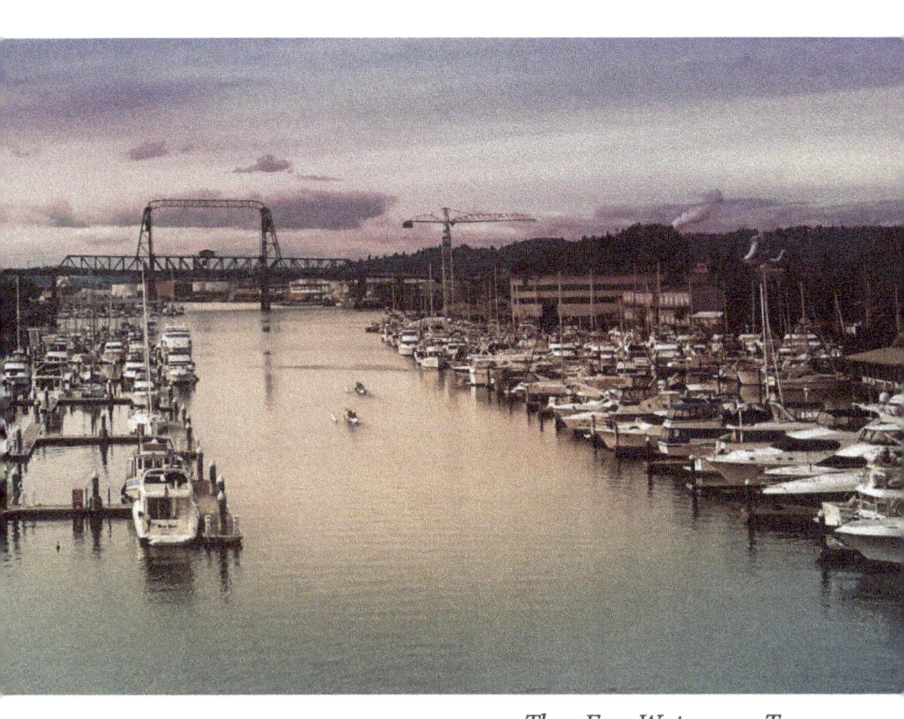

*Thea Foss Waterway, Tacoma*

## THE LANGUAGE OF WATER

The language of water
is languid, easy,
slow
until the hillsides
hug in close and pinch
it back.

It runs in
mad rushes, tumbles,
froths, a mindless
frenzy forward until
it falls, a reckless
plunge into soundless
green depths.

It churns beneath its
cool exterior, stretched
between extremes,
until it bobs back up,
languid, easy,
slow.



*Beebe Bridge Park, Orondo*

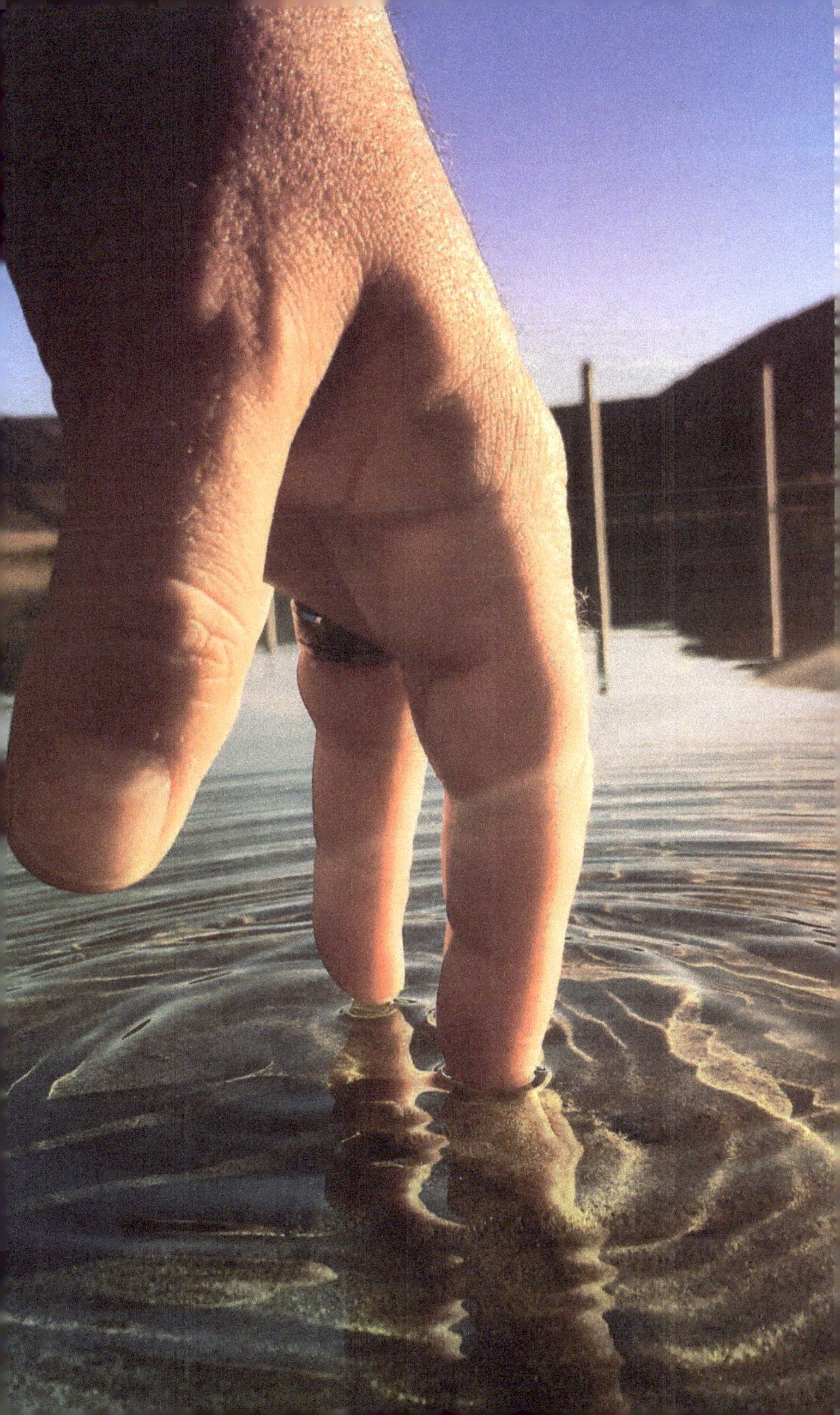

## WET

Wet sand accommodates
my toes, my feet,
and now my ankles
are sucked down
into this deliciously
smooth sludge.

My ankles are mere
memories.

My legs, two stalks
sprouting from
dark soup.

It won't take long
before the sea
reclaims its own.



*Columbia River, Stevenson*

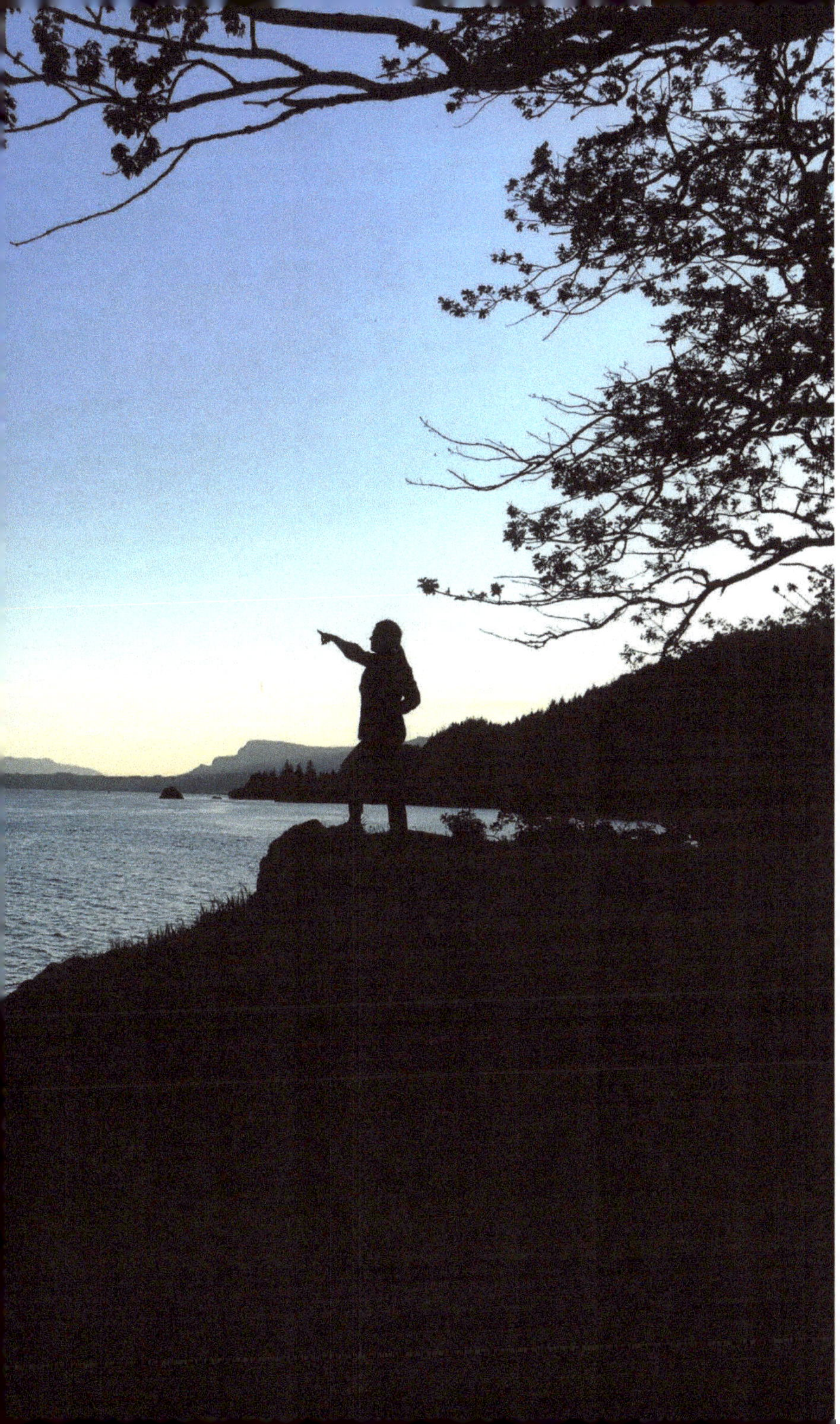

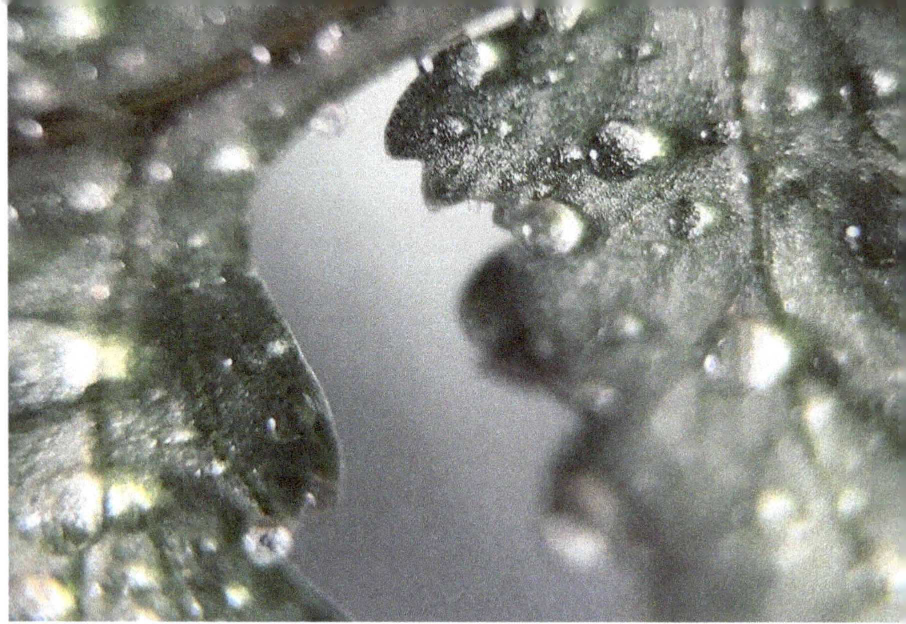

# NAME THE RAIN

## Dictionary

**Bombardment:** Rain that comes from all angles.

**Bumbershoot Wreck:** Heavy wind and rain; no matter which way you move, your umbrella turns inside out and you walk home soaked. Denise Steuer

**Comfort Day:** When you are having a bad day, but the rain makes you feel better.  Kawanis Washington, Lincoln High School

**Dry Rain:** You walk through the rain, impervious. You're rain proof. Elizabeth Beck

**Doom Drop:** That first single raindrop that falls on the top of your head. You'd better get inside. Now!

**Dupe Drops:** You won't need an umbrella; you can make it inside before it rains. Wait. No. You can't.  Elizabeth Beck

**Frizzle Drizzle:** Just enough moisture in the air to ruin your hair. Wendy Stephens Firth

**Feather Falls:** Soft, slow rain falling like feathers.
Elizabeth Beck

**Frog Strangler:** Heavy, persistent downpours.
(see: Gully Washer) Sam Hranac

**Gully Washer:** Heavy, persistent downpours.
(see: Frog Strangler) Sam Hranac

**Hydro-ovation:** Rain on a metal roof. Kevin Groeneveld

**Irish Spring:** A light spring shower during a sunny day; just enough to create a rainbow or two.  Sam Hranac

**Lifesaver:** Rain that makes an appearance in the middle of a heatwave. Also, rain that falls on a life raft adrift in the ocean.

**Liquid Sunshine:** When it rains while the sun is out, so both rain and sunshine appear at the same time.  Aaron Curtis

**Micromist:** The nearly invisible droplets of water that form gentle waves of wet air.  Pat Foran

**Mizzle:** A cross between a mist and a drizzle that creeps into your jacket until you're damp all over, AKA, a misery drizzle. Bethany Maines

**Night Patrol:** Rain that falls at night and keeps miscreants off the streets because they don't like being cold and wet.
Sam Hranac

**Plant Mister:** A light misting of droplets barely more than humidity turned solid. Cool and tends to collect on glasses.
Sam Hranac

**Proto Sludge:** Heavy rainfall into rural livestock corrals; a common ingredient of slurry.  Cameron Kobes

**Sauna Scorch:** When it's hot outside and it starts raining. Courtney McCauley, Lincoln High School

**Shy Showers:** These stall offshore or over islands, building pressure without the appearance of rain for several hours inland, if at all. Sam Hranac

**Slobber-Clobber:** Sudden downpour of big drops on a warm day because the departed Pavlov rings a bell and all the dogs in Heaven start drooling. Sandy King

**Snappers:** Rain is falling down so hard it hits the ground and makes a snapping sound. Luvander Faatiti, Lincoln High School

**Snoop Drop:** Evidence that it rained while you were inside, like wet sidewalks and windshields.

**Sucker Hole:** A brief sun gap between clouds that tricks you into taking off your raincoat. Elise Koncsek

**The Drop:** The giant drop of rain that hits your head and soaks you. Anthony Tran, Lincoln High School

**Waterfall:** When it's pouring down really hard. Karina Soltero-Torres, Lincoln High School

**Weekend Visitor:** Rain that ruins the weekend while leaving Monday through Friday sunny and pleasant. Sam Hranac


Thank you to everyone that participated!

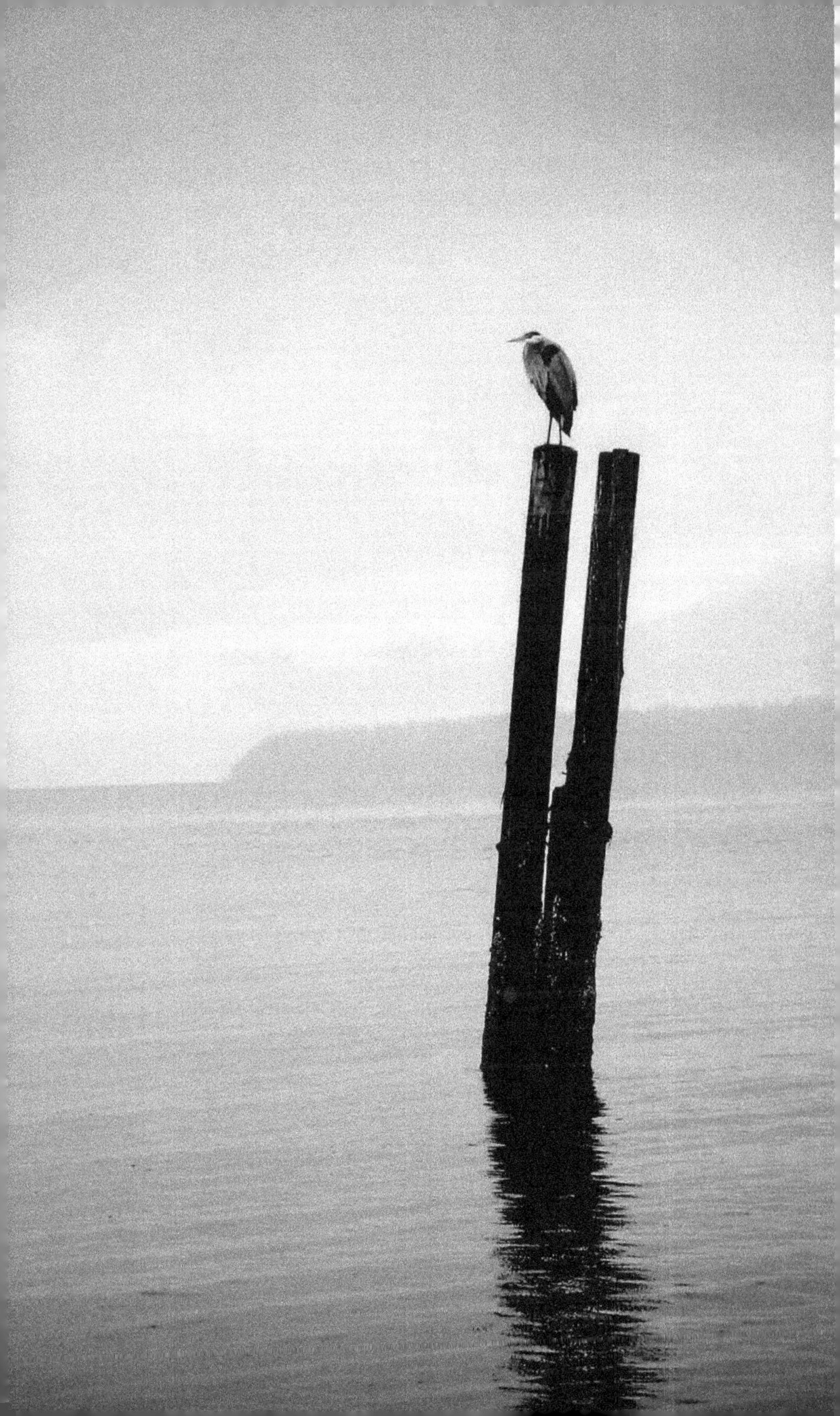

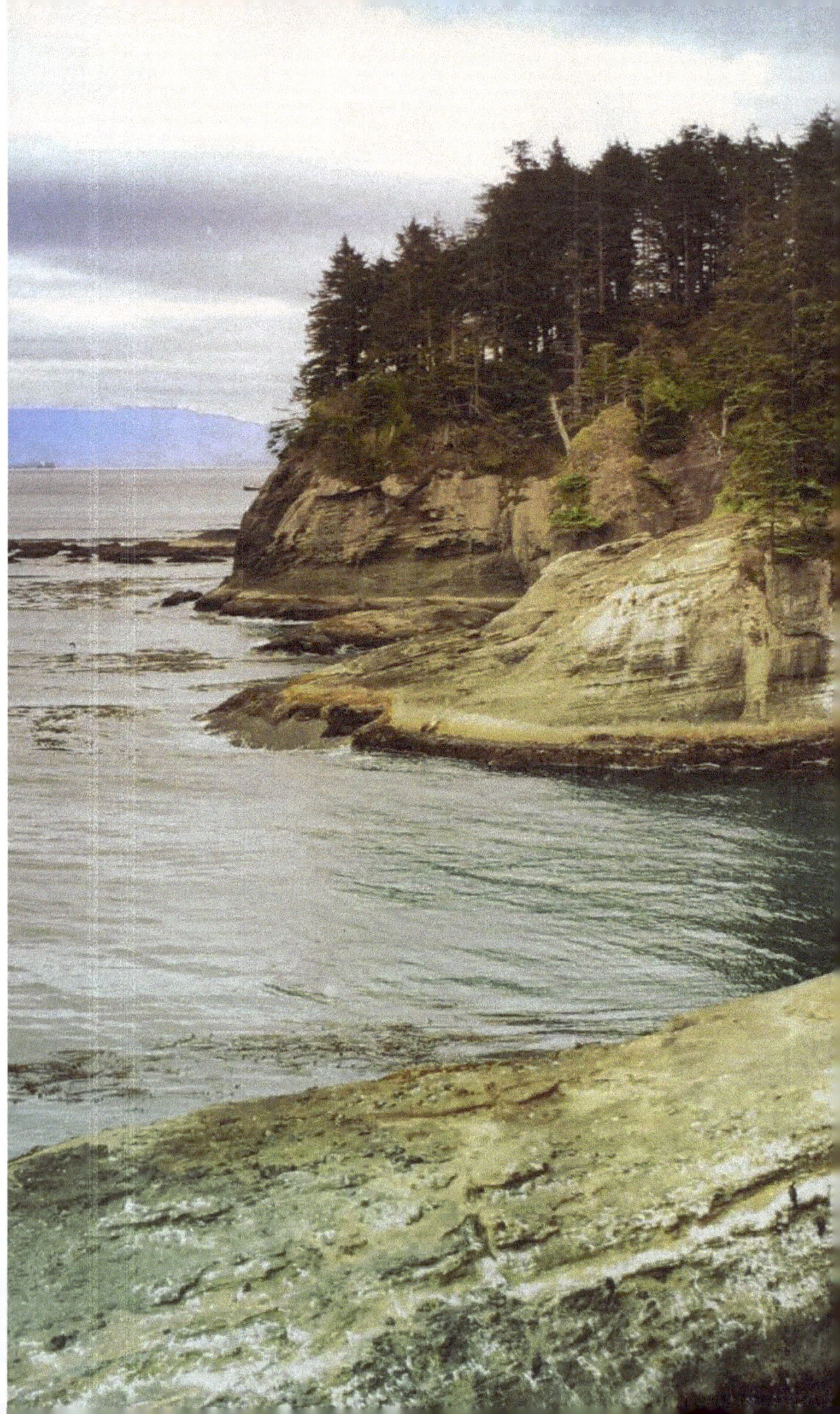

# GLOSSARY

**Advection frost** (also called **wind frost**): Tiny ice spikes that form when cold wind blows over branches of trees, poles and other surfaces. It looks like sugar crystals.

**Aquifer:** Pockets of water below the water table.

**Artesian Well:** Naturally filtered water that comes from a higher source and collects underground.

**Archipelago:** A group of islands.

**American Viticultural Areas (AVAs):** Specific federal and geographical growing regions for wine.

**Anadromous:** Ascending rivers from the sea for breeding. These fish are born in freshwater, spend their life at sea and return to their natal waters to spawn and die.

**Bisphenol A (BPA):** A component of most plastics including water bottles, baby bottles and dental work. It is endocrine-disrupting, acting like a synthetic hormone and exposure increase risks for breast cancer, prostate cancer, infertility, early puberty, metabolic disorders and type-2 diabetes. Significant levels have been found in air and water, as well as human blood, urine and fat.

**Epiphyte:** A plant that grows on another plant without harm and derives its nutrients and moisture from the air or rain.

**Estuary:** Area where saltwater and freshwater mix, such as the mouth of a river.

**Coulee:** Abandoned river valley.

**Ground Water:** Water beneath Earth's surface that collects between soil particles and rock. It originates from rain and melting snow, and is the source of water for aquifers, springs and wells.

*Looking across to Vancouver Island, British Columbia from Cape Flattery where the Strait of Juan de Fuca joins the Pacific.*

**Guttation:** When drops of moisture are extruded through a plant's leaves because there's too much water in the soil.

**Hoarfrost:** White ice crystals that form on exposed objects during a cold, clear night. It appears in two forms: *columnar*, which is needle-shaped, and *tabular*, which has a flat, hexagonal shape. Different temperatures determine the form, but the mechanism is unknown. The word 'hoar' is an old term meaning white or gray-haired.

**Intermodal Yard:** An area where freight transportation occurs using multiple transport modes: ship, rail, truck.

**Kolk:** Rock basins that were formed by underwater tornados brought on by the rushing water of the Missoula floods.

**Loess:** Fine, mineral-rich windblown silt.

**PCB and PBDE:** Polychlorinated biphenyls and polybrominated diphenyl ethers are major environmental pollutants. PCBs were used in electrical components and banned in 1979. PBDEs are used as flame-retardants in electrical equipment, construction materials and textiles. Both chemicals accumulate in the fat and breast milk of humans and animals.

**Reservoir:** A natural or artificial lake used as a source of water supply; a place where fluid collects, like within rock strata.

**Rime:** White ice that forms when the water droplets in fog freeze to the outer surfaces of objects. Basically, frozen fog.

**Surface Water:** Water on the surface of the Earth like oceans, rivers, streams, lakes and reservoirs.

**Slough:** (slou) 1. Swamp, an inlet on a river, creek, marsh or tideflat. 2. A state of moral degradation or spiritual dejection.

**Terroir:** A combination of environmental factors like, soil, climate and water that gives a crop, like wine, its unique flavor.

**Water Table:** The boundary between water-saturated ground and unsaturated ground. It often follows the upward and downward slope of the land above.

loroethylene, brom
ea, Bisphenol A, butylated
e, perchloroethlene, et
an salts, aluminum et
ethylene glycol ethers, alu
radichloro ene, b
ethyl acetate, benz
orethylene chloride, Me

# CONTRIBUTORS

The following businesses, organizations and people helped this book come about by providing research and resource materials, acting as fact checkers, hosts, contributors or by sharing their inspirational videos, artwork and photos. With sincere gratitude for your time and talent - thank you!

Bryan Chushcoff (p. 217 and author photo)
B Sharp Coffee House
Cheryl Burlingame, Mimi's Teas
Mark Burlingame, Steilacoom Public Works Director
Norma Jean Byrkett
Jackie Casella
Heather Conklin
Cranberry Museum; Pacific Coast Cranberry Research Foundation
Cran Mac Farm
Chris McMeen, Tacoma Deputy Water Superintendent
DamNation documentary
Dennis Ellis
Estes Fruit Stand and Lady Bugs Hanging Flowers
Explore Hood Canal
Ginkgo Petrified Forest State Park
Green River Coalition
Haiga Adventure Study Group
Heritage Distillery Co.
Mark Hester

Fumiko Kimura
Gregory Knight Miskin
Marilyn Lepape
Kenneth Libbrecht
Lincoln High School Art Students
Ardell and Malcolm McPhail
Marcus Whitman Hotel
Cliff Mass
Blake Merwin, Gig Harbor Fly Fishing Shop
Mount Rainier National Park
Peter Munro
Nikon
NOAA
Olloclip
Olympic National Forest
Olympic National Park
The Orca Network
The Tacoma News Tribune
Traci Kelly
Trudy Orzio
Carl "Papa" Palmer
Pepper Bridge Winery
Point Defiance Park
Rosemary Ponnekanti
Sun Lakes-Dry Falls State Park
Patricia Rasmussen
Katie Regnier
Steven Sauke
William Turbyfill
U.S. Fish and Wildlife Service
Washington State Dept of Agriculture
Washington State Dept of Ecology
Wild Reverence documentary

# PRONUNCIATION GUIDE

**Chinook** shin-NOOK

**Coho** COE-hoe

**Coulee** COO-lee

**Deschutes** dez-SHOOTS

**Duwamish** doo-WAH-mish

**Enumclaw** EE-num-claw

**Geoduck** GOO-ee-duck

**Ilwaco** il-WAH-co

**Juan de Fuca** wahn de FYOO-ca

**Kalakala** ka-LOCK-a-la

**Makah** ma-KAW

**Methow** MET-how

**Mount Rainier** ray-NEER

**Mukilteo** muck-il-TEE-o

**Naches** NAT-cheese

**Naselle** nay-SELL

**Neah Bay** NEE-a bay

**Nisqually** nis-KWAHL-le

**Ohanapecosh** oh-HAN-uh-puh-cosh

**Okanogan** O-ka-NOG-gan

**Palouse** pa-LOOSE

**Puget** (Sound) PYOO-jit

**Puyallup** pyoo-AL-up

**Quilcene** KWILL-seen

**Quileute** KWILL-ee-oot

**Quillayute** KWILL-a-yoot

**Quinault** kwin-ALT

**Salish** SAY-lish

**Sammamish** sa-MAM-ish

**Sekiu** SEE-kyoo

**Selah** SEE-la

**Sequim** skwim

**Skagit** (County) SKAD-jit

**Skamokawa** ska-MOCK-a-wa

**Skykomish** sky-KOE-mish

**Snohomish** sno-HOE-mish

**Snoqualmie** sno-KWAHL-mee

**Suquamish** soo-KWAH-mish

**Swinomish** SWINN-oh-mish

**Tlingit** KLING-kit

**Tonasket** ta-NAS-kit

**Tukwila** tuck-WILL-a

**Tulalip** too-LAY-lip

**Wenatchee** wen-NAT-chee

**Willapa** WILL-uh-puh

**Yacolt** YACK-olt

**Yakama** (Tribe) YACK-uh-mah

**Yakima** (City) YACK-uh-mah

*A Northwest Pronunciation Guide
by Steven M Sauke*

# HOW TO HELP

## Ways to Clean and Conserve Water

* Use drought tolerant, native plants in your landscape.

* Consider going lawn-less. Lawns are high maintenance, requiring a lot of fertilizer and weedkiller. When it rains, these chemicals enter storm drains, which empty directly into the Puget Sound.

* Replace your sprinklers with a drip irrigation system. If I can do it, you can do it.

* Use a car wash that recycles its water.

* Do not flush expired or unused prescriptions into the toilet. Check the internet to find your drop off location. Many pharmacies will dispose of them properly for you. Prescriptions, plastics and flame retardants have entered our water system. Chemicals that were banned decades ago continue to pollute. These same chemicals are found in the fatty tissues of sea creatures and in our own bodies. Many have been shown to effect hormones and cause cancer.

* I can't recommend a low-flow showerhead since I have to stay under them twice as long to get all of the shampoo out!

* Never pour or dump anything into storm drains.

*If you have tips to share, post them on the WA is Water Facebook Page, www.Facebook.com/WAisWater.*

# FURTHER READING

ELWHA: A River Reborn by Lynda V Mapes and Steve Ringman

EXPLORING WASHINGTON'S BACKROADS: Highways and Hometowns of the Evergreen State by John Deviny

THE SNOWFLAKE: Winter's Frozen Artistry by Kenneth Libbrecht and Rachel Wing

THE SNOWFLAKE: Winter's Secret Beauty by Kenneth Libbrecht and Patricia Rasmussen

THE WEATHER OF THE PACIFIC NORTHWEST by Cliff Mass

THE LAND THAT SLEPT LATE : The Olympic Mountains in Legend and History by Robert L Wood

THE SEVEN WONDERS OF WASHINGTON STATE
by Howard Frisk

WASHINGTON'S CHANNELED SCABLANDS GUIDE
by John Soennichsen

WASHINGTON ROCKS: A Guide to the Geologic Sites in the Evergreen State, by Eugene Kiver, Chad Pritchard and Richard Orndorff

# ACKNOWLEDGMENTS

Many had a hand in creating this book. I am full of gratitude for the Tacoma Arts Commission and the Tacoma Artists Initiative Program, which helped bring about this project. Because of the grant, I was able to purchase photography equipment, research books and attend writing conferences.

Thank you to my family and friends who gave me the courage to set sail on this grand adventure.

Thank you to my early readers and editors, especially my sister, Elizabeth. Your keen eyes and encouragement kept me going.

And of course, thank you to my parents, Susan and Robert. Without you, I'd be nothing. Literally.

Finally, thank you to my husband, Bryan, my traveling companion in life and on the open road. You've given me the greatest gift, after life, the gift of time.

Thank you all for your love and support along the way.

*~ Jennifer*

*What would the world be, once bereft*
*Of wet and wildness? Let them be left,*
*O let them be left, wildness and wet;*
*Long live the weeds and the wilderness yet.*

Gerard Manley Hopkins